D0837263

2ND EDITION

From Script to Screen

THE COLLABORATIVE ART OF FILMMAKING

Linda Seger and
Edward J. Whetmore

lone eagle

From Script to Screen
The Collaborative Art of Filmmaking, 2nd Edition
Copyright © 2004 Linda Seger and Edward J. Whetmore

LONE EAGLE PUBLISHING COMPANY
1024 N. Orange Dr.
Hollywood, CA 90038
Phone 323.308.3400 or 800.815.0503
A division of IFILM® Corporation, www.hcdonline.com

Printed in the United States of America
10 9 8 7 6 5 4 3 2 1

Cover design by Sean Locke
Book design by Carla Green
Storyboards from *A Beautiful Mind*, courtesy Ron Howard
A Beautiful Mind still photo, courtesy of Universal Studios Licensings, LLP © Universal Pictures and DreamWorks Pictures

Library of Congress Cataloging-in-Publication Data

Seger, Linda
    From script to screen : the collaborative art of filmmaking / Linda Seger, Edward Jay Whetmore — 2nd ed.
       p. cm.
    ISBN 1-58065-054-6
    1. Motion pictures—Production and direction. I. Whetmore, Edward Jay.
II. Title.

    PN1995.9.P7S38 2003
    791.43'028—dc22   2003054672

Books may be purchased in bulk at special discounts for promotional or educational purposes. Special editions can be created to specifications. Inquiries for sales and distribution, textbook adoption, foreign language translation, editorial, and rights and permissions inquiries should be addressed to: Jeff Black, Lone Eagle Publishing, 1024 N. Orange Drive, Hollywood, CA 90038 or send e-mail to info@ifilm.com.

Distributed to the trade by National Book Network, 800-462-6420.
IFILM® and Lone Eagle Publishing Company™ are registered trademarks.

Contents

Acknowledgments

My special thanks to the people who helped make *From Script to Screen* possible: Lee and Jan Batchler; Hindi Brooks; Mimi Cozzens; Linda B. Elstad; Leonard Felder; Colin Greene; Linda Griffiths; Greg Henry; Chris Jorie; Kevin Klinger; Barbara Lawrence; Jan Lewis; Lisa Lieberman; Cindy Margolis; Carolyn Miller; Jim Pasternak; Ralph Phillips; Don Ray; Steve Rekas; Ron Richards; Tom Shoebridge; Dov Simmons; Treva Silverman; Sandi Steinberg; David Summerville; Howard Wexler; Judity Weston; and Marsha Williams.

To my readers: Cathleen Loeser; Dara Marks; Anne Cooper Ready; Madeleine Rose; Lynn Brown Rosenberg; and Helene Wong.

To all our interviewees and their assistants and secretaries who took my phone calls and helped make the interviews happen.

And a special thank you to Ron Howard for the storyboards and for his help on our case study of *A Beautiful Mind*.

—L. S.

Special thanks to all my readers: Shari Beauchamp; Kar Davis; Vincent Fratello; Christa Taylor; Chris Kawamura; Jennifer Miles; and Rachelle Whetmore.

And to two special filmmakers for their inspiration: Lawrence Kasdan and Oliver Stone.

—E. J. W.

Special Acknowledgment

To our editor, Cynthia Vartan, and our agent, Martha Casselman. Thank you both for your patience and support. And particularly to Tom Schulman, who helped us all the way "from script to screen!"

Sneak Preview:
The Magnificent Risk-Takers

"That's the fun part about movie collaboration," Director Oliver Stone explains with a sly smile. "You work intensely with a lot of people who are different from you and you learn a lot from them. People you don't always like. But you learn to live with them. It teaches you tolerance."

This was one of the first lessons Hollywood's most gifted and successful filmmakers provided as they tolerated our questions, responding with remarkable and precise insight into the collaborative art of filmmaking. While conducting some seventy interviews in busy offices, editing rooms, wardrobe trailers and sound stages, we were continuously astonished by their willingness to share what they have learned.

Those of us "in the dark" are generally satisfied with paying admission, munching our popcorn and losing ourselves for a while in the mysterious worlds filmmakers create. But if you have ever wondered what they do, how they do it and *why* they do it, then this book is for you.

Countless books have been devoted to the creation of the story and the writing of the script. Many others define precisely what an assistant director or key grip does during production. *From Script to Screen* does neither of these. Instead, we follow the path of the script as it passes through the hands of all the collaborators. In their own words, they share with us the secrets of the alchemy they use to bring a story to life. It begins as they sit alone, reading the script. But the real magic is glimpsed most often in the ways they work with one another.

In today's Hollywood the production of a major motion picture is not the work of one "auteur" director. Nor is it the result of the latest whim of a box office superstar who helps draw the audience to the theater. These perceptions are quite popular in the press and in certain film schools.

They are wrong.

The truth is that by the time the script appears on the screen, it is a product of the collective effort of writers, producers, directors, actors, cinematographers, editors, composers and others who have labored for years to bring it to life.

Feature filmmaking has become a *collaborative art,* a unique synthesis of artistic vision married to an unwieldy commercial marketplace populated by a volatile and fickle audience. To make a studio film you need a willingness to write checks every day for more money than most folks spend on a house. Lace it with cost overruns and sprinkle with unpredictable weather and you've got the recipe for a major motion picture. Amazingly enough, about 500 of them find their way into our theaters each year.

Of these, only a handful will be considered for the major awards and only a few of those will go on to be remembered as "classics," films that somehow profoundly move or affect the audience. Wherever possible, we focused our investigation on these extraordinary films and on the artists responsible for transforming them from script to screen.

Over the past two decades, these are the people who, have created Academy Award-winning pictures such as *A Beautiful Mind, American Beauty, Dead Poets Society, Driving Miss Daisy, Rain Man, Thelma & Louise* and *Witness.* As we began to seek out those who always seem to be associated with the best the medium has to offer, the same names surfaced again and again. In these pages you'll meet them and share their personal insights into the collaborative art of filmmaking.

In her book *Uncommon Genius,* Denise Shekerjian interviewed forty recipients of the MacArthur Prize, which is also known as the "genius award". As she combed through the transcripts, she discovered something quite interesting:

> *In the end the common themes linking these creative people separated and floated to the surface like cream.... They were all driven, remark-*

ably resilient, adept at creating an environment that suited their needs, skilled at honoring their own peculiar talents...capable of knowing when to follow their instincts and above all, magnificent risk-takers, unafraid to run ahead of the great popular tide.

We found all of these characteristics among our interviewees, but the one that surfaced most often was "magnificent risk-taking."

These are the writers, producers, directors and others who are willing to gamble their careers on projects of several years duration, even though the material often seems completely contrary to the prevailing wisdom about what the audience wants to see.

After all, who wants to spend two hours in a theater watching a film about an aloof, delusional mathematical genius? Yet it is *precisely* this magnificent risk-taking that produces classic films like *A Beautiful Mind* and *American Beauty*. Even when the subject matter is more familiar to the audience, there are large hills to climb. Oliver Stone told us that when he first proposed *JFK*, "they" told him as politely as possible:

"Who wants to watch a three-hour JFK murder?" They said, "Who the hell even remembers JFK?" It was unbelievable. Certainly Vietnam was a turn-off when I started. Everyone told me Wall Street *would never play...there are no history of business movies that are successful.*

It only goes to show you—stick to your guns if you think you're right. What was it Archimedes said? "Give me a place to stand and I'll give you the world." Now, that's leverage.

Writer Akiva Goldsman spent a decade of his life working with mentally ill patients. He was determined to bring their story to the screen somehow. In the end he found a book about John Nash and "completely fabricated" Nash's inner life to create *A Beautiful Mind*.

Producer Steven Haft remembers optioning *Dead Poets Society* after every major studio had passed on it—many of them more than once. He was hoping to find an independent company that would do it on a shoestring but wasn't having much luck. Then a call came from Disney head Jeff Katzenberg....

Tom Schulman, who won an Academy Award for the script, fondly remembers that when the Disney people started trying to market the film, industry buzz had it that the only title with less audience appeal would have been *Dead Poets Society in Winter.*

Again and again our interviewees treated us to variations on this story. It is precisely the film that goes "against the grain" and runs counter to the prevailing wisdom that provides collaborators with their greatest challenges and affords the audience its most memorable celluloid moments.

Our quest was to start with those magic moments and uncover the methods that were used to create them. Having completed the interviews, we began by identifying the steps in the process that tended to surface as the artists discussed their work.

Once an idea has been turned into a screenplay, the pages serve as a blueprint for all that is to come. Common wisdom has it that movies would be much better if producers and directors shot them as they were originally written. While the urge to order endless rewrites can and does get out of control, the truth is it is a rare screenplay that cannot be improved upon as it makes its way to the screen.

The very essence of collaborative filmmaking requires that each person who works with the script be able to contribute something to the process. It's not so much about leaving a mark but rather contributing to the realization of the script's most powerful potential.

Perhaps the single most important thing any director does is impart a sense of collective vision to all of the other collaborators. Everyone needs to be able to "see" the same movie if what is in the script is to find its way to the theater. Again and again we were told of projects that failed because the script's original vision got lost on its long, laborious journey to the screen.

Producer Richard Zanuck (*Jaws, Driving Miss Daisy, Road to Perdition*) told us that the first decision any producer makes is the most important— the commitment to make the movie. This is not an undertaking begun lightly, for each project takes on a life of its own and most often it's a very long life. By no means does the commitment guarantee that the script will eventually find its way to the screen. More often than not it won't.

Again and again we were told that the films that got made, especially the great ones, were the products of a tenacious persistence of vision. Sometimes it comes from the writer, sometimes from the director or producer—all are early collaborators involved in the development process.

Once production actually begins, there are a thousand ways for the original vision to go awry. So many people become involved at this point that problems are inevitable. Hollywood lore is replete with such stories. Suffice to say that the pure adrenal rush of the production process takes an incredible toll on all involved. Often it takes a toll on the script as well.

In spite of everything, every so often the talent and skills of the collaborators win out and their persistence of vision prevails. In that rarified moment new "classics" are born. Another film can be added to the small list of movies that truly make a difference.

In a speech at the Women in Film Crystal Awards, Barbra Streisand echoed the words of many of the filmmakers we spoke with: "I am committed to making films about positive transformations and unlimited growth. I want uplifting, life-affirming films, films not only about life as it is, but life as it can be."

Director Ron Howard (*A Beautiful Mind*) puts it this way:

I'm most concerned about characters and their evolution, their growth as human beings as they try to cope. Sometimes these moments of triumph are very small, sometimes they're bittersweet. I guess I'm an optimist. The mere fact that most people are struggling to do the right thing, to be happy, makes me feel optimistic.

This is not to say that all classic movies should have a "feel-good" quality or share the same philosophies or politics. Far from it. Yet in every extraordinary film, there is always a concerted effort by the collaborators to express a vision that will provide audiences with something that will help them find their own "moments of triumph." Actor Edward James Olmos (*Stand and Deliver*) puts it most succinctly. "Intent is content," he explains; such an approach, "may not always make dollars, but it does make sense."

So many films seem bent only on pummeling our emotions or providing a series of guffaws. That's not nearly good enough. Our interviewees were more than willing to take responsibility for the content of their films and discuss what they hope will be their long-term impact on the audience.

Yes, there are many things that can go *wrong* in the making of a film. Scripts get trampled, visions are shattered, egos career out of control. We hear about it all the time. We'd be the last to deny that the vast majority of well-intended films do not succeed commercially *or* artistically. Our mission was simply to seek out those few that succeeded in both arenas and see if we could discover how and why they did.

What follows are some of the secrets of the best screenwriters and the methods of Hollywood's most effective and respected producers and directors.

You'll hear about their struggles, their decisions and the visions that keep them going through the many years it takes to move a story from script to screen. You'll learn about the performance techniques of accomplished actors and meet the cinematographers, editors, composers and others who are literally "behind the scenes" of the movies you love. Whether you currently work in the industry or simply love great films, we promise that you will never see movies in quite the same way again.

*Audiences don't know
somebody sits down
and writes a picture.
They think the actors
make it up as they
go along.*

—*Billy Wilder*

Doing the Write Thing

Screenwriter Akiva Goldsman had everything going for him. The success of *Batman Forever* and *A Time to Kill* had guaranteed him fame and fortune—at least as much fame and fortune as is ever bequeathed to a Hollywood screenwriter. But something was wrong. Goldsman remembers thinking, "If I don't write something that is very particular to me, I will have squandered this enormous opportunity."

Long before he wound up in Hollywood, Goldsman spent ten years of his life working with his parents at the Blueberry Treatment Centers. There, he encountered the unique and often frightening world of autistic and schizophrenic children. It was a world where children ran terrified from hidden men in coat-racks, where they brushed imaginary fires off their shoulders. And he never forgot it.

Years later he found himself impressed with Sylvia Nasar's biography of the brilliant but troubled mathematics genius John Nash, Jr. It was then that he discovered that "something particular." He would find a way to transform Nasar's *A Beautiful Mind* into a feature film. Surprisingly, he did it with "blatant disregard for fact...I made the delusions up. I had to, John Nash doesn't remember his delusions."

The result was an Oscar for Best Adapted Screenplay—and congratulations from the Nash family, who told him it was true to the spirit of the journey. "I think it's true. It is not their journey, but it is true to the spirit of it."

Some years earlier a similar story unfolded. Screenwriter Tom Schulman (*What About Bob?*; *Honey, I Shrunk the Kids*) began *Dead Poets Society* with a threadbare premise, a few personal experiences and a desire to write something "about pursuing your dream, no matter what."

"I was frustrated with trying to write scripts I had no real emotional connection with. I was writing action pictures, horror films, *Kentucky Fried Movie*-type comedies. Things I had very little aptitude for—they simply weren't special enough. They were like other movies I had seen versus something I really believed in. I never thought of *Dead Poets Society* as a commercial script. I figured it wouldn't sell, but as I got into it, I thought it felt awfully good."

When Schulman finished the first draft of the script, he was one of twenty five thousand writers annually who register their projects with the Writer's Guild. By the time it was all over, Schulman was living the dream of every screenwriter: he was standing on the stage of the Shrine Auditorium accepting his Oscar for Best Original Screenplay.

Footprints in the Dark

Unless writers are fortunate enough to win one of two Academy writing awards handed out each year (Best Original Screenplay and Best Adapted Screenplay), no one outside the industry will ever have the faintest idea who they are. Paid far less than the star or director, their names will appear "up there" for all of a second or so. And then the name is gone and the audience forgets.

Now as ever, screenwriters labor in anonymity. As the late William Kelley once observed, "It's a monastic existence." Nevertheless it was Kelley who collaborated with Earl Wallace to create *Witness* and who received an Academy Award for his efforts.

You have heard of Harrison Ford? He starred in *Witness*. You may even be familiar with director Peter Weir. But unless you are a writer, chances are you are unfamiliar with names like Kelley or Wallace, Frank Pierson, or Alan Ball, Babaloo Mandel and Lowell Ganz, or any of the other top screenwriters whose words and ideas, characters and conflicts have produced so many of Hollywood's recent classic films.

The best screenwriters may labor in anonymity, but what they leave behind is a future all their own, the unmistakable "footprints in the dark" that illuminate the way for all who follow.

The writer begins with a blank page and must create the story, imagine the characters and start the long visualization process that will eventually yield a motion picture. Everyone who follows will be interpreting—for better or for worse—this original blueprint.

The journey from script to screen will be long and arduous, and, it is hoped, afford a good collaboration. When it does, everyone along the way—producers, directors, actors, production designers, composers and many others—will embellish and hone the ideas, adding layers to the characters and the story. Yet all will be interpreting and enhancing the original screenplay.

In order for a writer to function creatively under these conditions, a certain mindset is required, a firm belief that what you are doing can make a difference.

If you were casting the part of a veteran sixtysomething screenwriter, you'd probably want Frank Pierson. Though you may recall having seen his face briefly on Oscar night in his "other role" as the president of the Academy of Motion Picture Arts and Sciences, he is also the man who gave us *Presumed Innocent, Cool Hand Luke, Dog Day Afternoon* and *Soldier's Girl*. He explains that the idiosyncratic nature of the screenplay all but guarantees writer anonymity as it makes its way from script to screen.

"A screenplay is a very strange form of creative writing. Structured like a play, flowing like music, consisting of 120 pages or so of dialogue and a few sparse stage directions that will act as the creative impetus for *everything that is to come*."

And stay tuned, there's a lot more to come. Since the making of a studio film is a collaborative art, whatever immortality screenwriters achieve comes not from name recognition but from the work they leave behind. Pierson explains:

The fact is that a successful film, one that works on the level it was conceived and finds an audience, carries one's feelings and ideas about the life we share to literally hundreds of millions of people all over this fragile planet. I hope for some kind of future for the human race and I'd like to illuminate that in some way.

William Kelley once recalled that the need to express oneself has to be guarded and nurtured. "The writer is given a little bit of madness and we must take very good care of it, preserve it and let the world think that we're nuts. And we are, to the degree that we're willing to isolate ourselves for weeks at a time and not go anywhere." Out of the writer's isolation comes ideas and for Kelley, an accountability to the audience, the "final collaborators" who will eventually watch the film.

> *We see darkness and we try to light a candle. We try to be proper citizens of what we occupy. We are allied in a specific time with an audience of contemporaries and we owe them the best of our talent that we can give them.*

Like many creative endeavors, a script begins in darkness. But if the writer is to leave those footprints in the dark, a candle must be lit. It begins with an idea, a creative spark. But where does that spark come from?

What If...

Despite his Oscar-nominated credit as the co-writer of *Tootsie*, Larry Gelbart is perhaps best known for his four years as a writer-producer on TV's M*A*S*H*. Where do his ideas come from?

> *Ideas come from within and without. They spring from your own observations or your need to say something, not necessarily a message, but the need to tell a story. It's partly a need to communicate something about the human condition, to communicate to people who might have the same experiences, feel the same emotions, be influenced and impacted by the same stories.*

Tom Schulman remembers long ago when the first small portion of an idea for what was to become an Oscar-winning screenplay began to grow:

> *I first got the idea that became* Dead Poets Society *when I was in acting school. We had an incredibly volcanic teacher who would talk about theater, acting and movies and how relevant those things were to our lives. Every night after he'd speak we'd all go out for drinks and we'd*

say, "We've got to do that, we've got to form a theater that means something about life and happiness and love and politics." We were all imbued with this sense of purpose.

Much later, that experience would lead to a failed attempt.

I thought it would be exciting to write a script about a theater school and about a teacher or director. But it just didn't work. There was no text to it. Acting can be a very self-involved profession and I couldn't say what I wanted to say that way. So I started thinking back on my dad and an English teacher I had in high school who taught poetry and who had the same kind of passion for it my father had.

My father loved poetry. He was a big fan of Tennyson and The Rubaiyat of Omar Khayyam—*things he had learned in his school days. So I was aware that poetry had wisdom and that a poet could be accessible.*

I went to a high school that was modeled on a British academy so I knew what the school should be like. It would be set in the late 1950s and there would be this atmosphere of repression where the parents would try to get their children to become businessmen, doctors and professionals. Part of the idea would be about pursuing your dream, no matter what.

And pursuing that dream is something that every aspiring screenwriter knows something about. Screenwriter Gelbart has also written a highly acclaimed TV movie (*Barbarians at the Gate*) and is an accomplished playwright. His multimedia credits afford a unique perspective. "It's not the size of the idea, but the temperature of it," he explains. "Ideally it's something you shouldn't merely want to do, but something you absolutely have to do."

Computers, Cards and Boxes

The process may begin with many ideas that must be winnowed down to one story, or a small spark that lights a fire that spreads rapidly and eventually takes over. For Writer-Director Lawrence Kasdan the ideas that "bubble up to the surface" tend to be very personal. "I work out of my own interests, enthusiasm, obsessions and neuroses." The man responsible for

Grand Canyon and *Dreamcatcher* admits that for him, even one movie idea is hard to come by.

> *I don't have a lot of ideas floating around. I wish I did. I tend to have a few things that interest me and one tends to bubble up to the surface more strongly than the others and demand my attention. Then I start to let my mind play with that. Of course, once you start writing, almost anything else seems more appealing, but I don't desert what I'm working on for the most part.*

Though he employs a different system now, most of Lawrence Kasdan's early scripts *(The Big Chill, Body Heat)* were done utilizing a card system. He describes it as a three-step process:

> *I would begin to make cards—they were just total free association—any thought that crossed my mind. It could be an image of someone on a stairwell or a bit of conversation that I overheard. It could be a joke. And I would just create a stack—no editing. Then I would go to the second stage—which was an outline for the movie. That would be a different kind of card. Those would be scene cards. And to each of those scene cards, certain of the idea cards would apply. I would literally take those ideas and put them with the appropriate scene cards. Some of the idea cards never found a use—some were stuck on scenes but not used. I just couldn't make them work.*
>
> *Then I would work my way through the script in my mind—making a final card for each scene or sequence. Eventually I would wind up with a set of cards, which would take me through the movie.*

At the ripe old age of twenty-four, Writer-Director John Singleton *(Boyz N the Hood, Shaft)* had already been nominated for two Academy Awards. He uses a similar system.

> *I keep a journal and write in it about what's going on right now and how it pertains to the film. Eventually I transfer it to three-by-five cards. Every scene has a card. Each time I write about it or talk about it, it changes. It really has a life of its own.*

I come up with new ideas for dialogue and dialects. I write ideas for the style of the film, or the style of the scene. Timewise I may write three hours one day and ten minutes the next. It all depends. If I'm bored with what I'm writing I won't write. I try to keep rewrites to a minimum. I want every word that's there to have passion behind it. I can't write just for the sake of doing it.

Interestingly, it is the right title that acts as Singleton's primary catalyst. During the late 1980s he was a screenwriting student at the University of Southern California during a period in Hollywood when high-concept films such as *Twins* and *The Terminator* were all the rage. Though his films are decidedly different from those projects, he did learn what he calls, "an accepted show business notion, a Barnum and Bailey thing," about immediate and direct movie titles.

"*Jaws*, for example, you know what it's about. I think of a title first and then what goes with it. Like *Poetic Justice*. A woman named Justice who writes poetry. *Boyz N the Hood*. It says what it is."

While writers often begin with their own ideas, many of the industry's most successful screenwriters are hired guns, brought in to create a hundred pages or more from a single concept. For Babaloo Mandel and Lowell Ganz, "almost nothing is ever completely generated by the two of us. Generally somebody drops a what-if on us. A lot of them come from Imagine Films."

Ganz explains, "We run with about 5 percent of the ideas. We have a drawer full of about seven or eight scripts that we've been paid for that haven't been produced." Despite the frustration that goes along with the job, it's a record most screenwriters would envy. Mandel and Ganz tend to speak as one voice:

Usually the idea starts with a sentence. With City Slickers *it was, "What if three yuppie-type guys who have wives and families in New York go on one of those fantasy cattle drives?" Or Ron Howard might say, "I'd like to do a movie about being a dad," and that became* Parenthood. *For* Splash *Brian Grazer's idea was simply, "What if a guy falls in love with a mermaid?"*

Research: It's All in the Details

Whether the story is about a modern-day mermaid or the merry men of Olde England, the process usually incorporates research. And there always seem to be a few unexpected twists and turns along the way. Pen Densham's take on Robin Hood's adventures (*Robin Hood: Prince of Thieves*) is illustrative of how the writer's mind combines the story ideas and research that result in a completed script. "I started off with one line, which was 'Robin Hood á la *Raiders [of the Lost Ark]*' and that sat in my computer bank for five years."

Then one day I said, "Maybe I should start in an Arab prison, which would be a big twist because you wouldn't know where you were, you might think you're in Iran today." And then we suddenly go back and realize it's a thousand years ago. I always wanted to do something which would make a statement about the problems of the Protestants and Catholics in Ireland, it's like the problems of Arabs and the Jews, which is how to try and put two religions together in a cooperative way.

It was at this point that Densham began to research the cultural and political milieu that eventually found its way to the screen.

I read about the Arabs in Timetables of History *and found that there were Arab doctors at the Court of Germany. Arabs were doing brain surgery, they understood astrological navigation, so I kept making these notes, I started to get these little islands of what I wanted to do.*
I wanted the forces of religion and ethics to go up against black magic. I wanted Robin to be a sensible hero looking for spiritual development and the sheriff was his doppelganger trying to get spiritual development in sensual terms, carnality, ritual.

Any story set in a world unfamiliar to the writer presents special research challenges. Mandel/Ganz found themselves in no-man's land after being assigned to do the story of the reunion of a women's baseball team that became the hit film *A League of Their Own.*

We read articles from Life *and other sources. A woman had done a thesis on the women who had played in the league. We went to the reunion in Cooperstown of the original women players and interviewed them for a couple of days.*

What they encountered was a problem that has plagued all interviewers who must reconstruct history from the experiences of their interviewees.

It was very difficult because the women only wanted to answer questions or reminisce from the perspective that they had already done it. But we were trying to find the transformation. We had to get these women to go back forty-five years, to when they were really very different people, because the league had changed them in very fundamental ways and we wanted to know where they had begun.

We asked a lot of questions—basically feeling questions. "You're this terrific ballplayer and how did you view yourself? How did other people view you? Did you feel acceptance? Did they make you feel odd? Did you feel fine? Freaky? How frightening was it? Was it what you expected?"

Every project presents its own unique research problems. It's hard to imagine a more difficult research process than that required by Oliver Stone's *JFK*. Ideally, research springs from a passion for telling a story that the writer feels must be told. "The grist is in real life. To take from real life," Stone explains.

The umbilical cord is to other people. For JFK I spent a lot of time with Jim Garrison. Jim talks in a certain way and he gets your juices flowing. I try not to impose my own view from the outside. I really like to take it from the inside. With JFK I was very attached. I work as a profession-al—but I feel it.

Structure: Building the Perfect Beast

Once the concept is clear and research under way, most writers turn their attention to structuring the story—seeking out a natural beginning, middle and end. All mention three-act structure as their basic building block, though the degree of emphasis and use of other nuances varies from writer to writer.

"Story is structure" is one of screenwriting's most enduring clichés and not without reason. Many of the most successful writers say that story structure is the single most important function of the writing process, one that will ultimately determine the success or failure of the script and of the film itself.

Whether the project is a fantasy such as *Splash* or a historical drama such as *A League of Their Own*, Ganz and Mandel explain that the structure must be in place early on in the process.

> *We have a plan before we start writing. It goes from premise (idea), to character arc (change and growth), to story arc—the beginning, middle and end. We always think in terms of the three-act structure. Act breaks to us are thrusts.*
>
> *We do spend a lot of time on introductions. We're very patient with them. Our first acts might be long, maybe thirty to thirty-five minutes, but hopefully it's been fun along the way. For us, the second act takes up about 50 percent of the movie. The third acts are short, ideally about twenty minutes long.*

For Frank Pierson, one key to story structure can be found at the end of the first act. "In building the structure of the story, the first-act climax is usually an intense scene in which the nature of the main character is fully revealed, either to the audience or himself or both. It's a scene that changes the direction of the story and sets up the nature of the conflict." Pierson reveals how this theory applies to one of his most ambitious and successful projects.

> *In Cool Hand Luke, Luke is on a collision course with Dragline, the convict leader. The first-act climax is a fight scene in which Dragline, who is infinitely stronger, beats Luke to pulp. Luke will not stay down; he keeps getting up to face more blows. Finally Dragline quits, thus forfeiting the fight. In the end, Luke's will is stronger. Though beaten to a pulp he is a grinning winner.... This is the turning point at which Luke changes from an unknown and disturbing element to a man with a name and an unwanted position of leadership and the story changes direction.*

Bill Kelley's *Witness* provided another oft-cited model of screenplay structure. In this case the first and second acts have individual rhythms that are devoted to distinctly different purposes.

I have my three-act structure. I write a little description, two or three sentences. Then I envision the script as a series of sequences. The direc-tor doesn't think in terms of scene but sequence. Each scene has to carry the story forward and proceed from the scenes before it and then lead into the scenes following it. So I anticipate the director's use of sequence.

Usually the first act will fall rather nicely into three sequences. In Witness the first sequence is everything leading up to the arrival in Philadelphia. The second sequence starts with Samuel seeing the murder and goes through the shooting of John Book. The third sequence is the escape and drive back to the farm and includes the scenes up to John's ability to start walking around. Then you go into the second act, the idyll in the middle at the Amish farm. We see them falling in love, heavy on subtext. It gives you a chance to relish what you've learned and let it sink in. This idyll includes the barn raising, which I see as the fulcrum of the story and ends with their kiss, followed by the arrival of the bad cops.

In fact, the deliberate pace of the second act contributed so significant-ly to the success of the film that Kelley tended to use it in most of his proj-ects. "I see a screenplay now with the beginning of the second act of the movie slowing down after three fast-paced sequences. I'm going to slow it down and really get to know the characters and really define motivation."

At the same time Kelley always stressed the structure of each individ-ual scene. "The scene still must be beautifully done, it must rise and have its own three parts, just like an act." Story structure remains a vital issue at every stage of a screenplay's evolution.

Comedy Structure: A Funny Thing Happened...

Comedy can present special structural problems. David Zucker learned this the hard way after producing *Airplane!* with his brother Jerry Zucker (*Rat Race*) and Jim Abrahams. It's a movie that still makes many all-time funni-est film lists.

After Airplane! *came out, we took the wrong lessons from it because everybody thought it was so funny. So when we did* Top Secret, *which combined two genres, World War II spy movies and Elvis movies, we satirized them—but without a cohesive plot and without characters who had motivations and clear intentions. We didn't pay any attention to character arcs.*

Looking back on the box office failure of *Top Secret*, Zucker contends that its problems stemmed from the methods he and his partners used while constructing the story.

We focused too much on the jokes. We'd make notes on all the scenes and write down all the jokes and sometimes we'd put them on cards so that we could apportion them; this is a love-story joke, or a second-act joke. The pitfall of doing it that way is that you start falling in love with certain jokes and you start to shoehorn the plot so that it can encompass the joke.

The Naked Gun series of films certainly attested to the team's knack for delivering a box office winner. Today Zucker begins each new project with an initial emphasis on story and character. Yet there is always an elusive balance to be achieved between the jokes and the story.

The plot and structure are the most important parts of our films, not the jokes. We start by asking "Who's the villain?" That's what the plot is riding on. At the same time, there's a certain pace to these satires and you don't want to go too long without a joke. We figure about three jokes a page because it's satire. It's much easier to keep an audience laughing once they've started than to start them laughing all over again. There's a certain grace period at the beginning of the movie. People are eager to laugh, but if you let them down, the audience kind of settles back and you've lost their trust.

Ruthless People is one of those rare scripts that is as admired for its story structure as for its comedic elements. Zucker says it provided a working laboratory where he and his collaborators were able to combine comedy with what they were learning about plot and character.

Dale Launer wrote the script and it was almost there. We did know that there were going to be three acts in this—there would be a beginning, middle and an end. Every character was going to have an arc and a pay-off. Everybody was going to have a definite want at the beginning. Everything was somehow going to get resolved or satisfied at the end.

But even after doing the movie, we still ended up cutting one whole fifteen-minute sequence that was superfluous to the main plot. So we never stopped learning.

When writing comedy, Ganz and Mandel also tend to start with the needs of the characters and the actors who play them.

We look at character motivation, what will make the character do the next thing, not the joke. Our attitude is, they're just jokes, we'll write another one. If it doesn't help the scene, we cut the joke. I've seen writers fight for a joke, even when the actor isn't comfortable with the joke. In that case, throw it out and write another joke!

Whether comedy or drama, the primary task of the screenwriter tends to be the structuring of the story. Once the structure, or "spine," of the story emerges, it's time to focus on the characters who will inhabit that story and to structure the transformation they go through along the way.

The Driver's Seat: Character Versus Story

If you were to spend an average day inside the development offices of a major Hollywood studio, the two terms you might hear most often are "story-driven" and "character-driven." This unique shorthand signals a perceived dichotomy in feature films.

A script is said to be story-driven if it relies primarily on a high-concept plot, one that implies action and conflict and can be readily gleaned from a brief synopsis, such as: "A rich girl and a poor boy fall in love against the backdrop of the worst shipwreck in American history." (*Titanic*)

On the other hand, a script is said to be character-driven if its appeal relies primarily on the development of the characters and the changes that their personalities undergo during the film. For example: "A brilliant mathematician loses his sanity and then must fight to regain it." (*A Beautiful Mind*)

Character-driven stories are generally perceived to be "softer" and less marketable than more action-oriented story-driven projects. Yet a careful examination of the very best Hollywood films defies this type of categorization. Are films like *The Sixth Sense* and *American Beauty* about the characters or the story? *Witness* and *Thelma & Louise* include some memorable action sequences, yet clearly they are mostly about what the main characters learn along the way.

The point is that classic Hollywood films defy categorization because they combine story and character elements into a single, seamless and memorable theatrical experience.

Creating Unforgettable Characters

Bill Kelley always demanded that character and story elements work together and offered his own method for getting in touch with one's fictional progeny.

Every scene must reveal character and push the story forward. You know the heart of your story and you've already decided who your characters are. When you come down the stairs the next morning, you empty your mind and listen to your silence and those characters will speak to you. If you have done your homework, done your character studies on index cards or whatever you do, then they will speak to you. You've got to walk their ground and let it seep into your shoes, into your soul. You have to be there and be quiet, half a day—or whatever it takes. What I want in the end is a work of art that's living, one that throbs with life.

Many writers begin by discovering who and what their characters are all about. Ganz and Mandel are quick to explain, "Our stories are always character-driven. We begin with the protagonist, asking, 'What kind of people would make this thing happen?' Hopefully the events are character-driven."

They also feel the process can be expedited if the writer has some basic knowledge of psychology and a healthy curiosity about people.

It's helpful to be the kind of person who grew up having a sort of penchant for examining people. You do imitations of people. It helps if you can honestly say, "This is the kind of thing that makes me act stupid." Then when our characters are at their worst or their silliest, we can honestly say, "We get like that." We try to write characters we can identify with even when we're not admiring them. And of course we're really big on finding the main characters' voices.

Finding those voices—hearing them—comes about in a number of ways. For Schulman it is all about his main character—a "special" voice who marches to his own drummer.

"I've always been fascinated with iconoclastic people—the mad prophet, the person who has an odd or different view of life—and with teachers who forced me to question." *Dead Poets Society* it was not easy at first. Schulman explains," I worked on the Keating character for a long time. I tried to find a voice for him. I would just write anything that came to my mind and look at it and think, "What is this all about? What is he trying to say? What's this voice in me about?"

Though his more recent films (*Dark Blue, Hollywood Homicide*) have been about law enforcement, Writer-Director Ron Shelton's *Bull Durham* is considered by many to be Hollywood's definitive baseball film. He too, begins by seeking a voice. "I won't start a script until I have my characters' voices. I'll spend weeks or months, but it won't happen until I can hear how they talk and what they are going to say."

Crash Davis is *Bull Durham's* perennial minor league catcher. His first line is "Hi, I'm the player to be named later." Shelton says, "As soon as I heard his opening line, I knew I had him." He explains that in baseball terms, Crash was always the unnamed player thrown in to sweeten a trade. He was never the main player. And his entire character grew out of that one line.

With his own neatly trimmed white beard, burly Bill Kelley always looked a bit like a modern-day Hollywood Hemingway. It seemed logical to probe him about how he created memorable male characters, such as John Book of *Witness*. "I start with the ideal man. Dignity is a very big key to me for the male character. I have to find what a man thinks of dignity, this is the man who is my hero. And he has to have something of an intellect. And then I dress him down. What are his faults? What are his weaknesses?"

Frank Pierson tries to find something in his characters that he can relate to his own personality.

There are those who begin a film by constructing a plot and then try to find characters whose conflict will cause that plot (and no other) to happen. I prefer to begin with a character whose drives touch some unconscious aspect of myself and then proceed to work out a story that dramatizes this character's dilemma, by finding complementary characters whose drives are in conflict.

You have to feel a deep sympathy and alliance, a harmony with the character. The best writing is done when one can literally feel the body rhythms of the character, when one can walk and move and dream like the character. It is a kinesthetic empathy, experienced not in the brain but in the bones and muscles.

Getting It on the Page

Overcoming exhaustion is but one of many obstacles a writer faces. Once a structured story line is complete and the characters are speaking, it's time to get down to the business of "getting it on the page." All writers have their own approach. For many, getting started is the hardest part. Lawrence Kasdan found a certain comfort level grew out of his card collection method. "They were an enormous help for me to get over the big hurdle, which is to start. Once I started I was usually fine—but the trick was to start."

Bill Kelley described the process as, "Part madness, part craft and a very big part is stamina. I'll work ten or twelve hours a day and it will seem like two hours. You make it happen by getting your ass in the chair and beginning."

Writer-Director Barry Levinson (*Diner, Homicide: Life on the Streets*) reveals, "I play music whenever I write. It becomes a little insane. I'll just play the same thing over and over again. When I was writing *Diner* I used to play Peter Townshend's *Empty Glasses.*"

There seems to be no easy way to get through the excruciating task of completing a script. Perhaps that is one of the reasons why some of the most successful Hollywood writers work so quickly. Writer-Director Ron Shelton's sports-related films (*Tin Cup, Cobb*) raised the genre to new heights a decade ago. If you passed him on the street you would probably say he looks like the ex-ballplayer that he, in fact, is. Tall and rugged, the term blue collar somehow suits him. "I generally spend a lot of time mulling, then I write fast. For *White Men Can't Jump*, I started writing on September twentieth. By the afternoon of the twenty-first I had thirty-seven pages; all of them wound up on the screen."

He stops for a moment and smiles a painful smile. "Then the next three weeks...nothing. Not one line!" Like a minor league catcher recalling his glory days, Shelton confides, "I used to be able to write two or three scripts at once. Not now."

Ganz and Mandel have been through the process so many times they can describe their routine effortlessly:

We usually talk it through for weeks before we actually start writing, working five days a week. If we're really prepared, once we start writing, it should not take more than two months for a first draft. We come in at ten or ten-thirty in the morning. We read the previous days' pages. If they don't make us nauseous, we move on. We try to get up a head of steam about lunchtime, talking about what that day's scene is, talk it through for a half-hour or an hour. Eat lunch and then write until four or four-thirty and go home. We average about a scene a day, sometimes two. The rewriting, however, takes about a year!

Sticking to a set schedule seems to work for many writers. Kasdan recalls a time before his first sale—when he was working full time in an advertising job he loathed and feeling very guilty every moment that he wasn't writing.

At that point my wife saved me by saying, "You've got to stop it. You've got to have certain times when you know you are supposed to write and other times when you are free because your free time is very valuable." We had a little boy at that time—our first son. And it saved my sanity.

Shortly after that he did sell his first script, *The Bodyguard*, although it took fifteen years to get produced. Like so many writers, Kasdan also struggles with his own natural inclination to "avoid" writing, even during the hours he sets aside for it. What he finally discovered was a lesson that all writers can take to heart.

> *It took me many years to accept the time that I "wasted" reading the trades and reading the newspaper and walking the halls at Fox or Warners; I felt bad about it. But eventually I would start to write— whether it was twelve-thirty or four and I would usually get a pretty good amount of work done, whether it was two or four or six hours. I finally realized that the walking around and reading time was part of it.*
>
> *I'm not a machine. I had to learn to accept my own rhythms. As long as the stuff came out I was all right. In fact, I wrote very fast. I started keeping track of how long it actually took me to write a script and it wasn't very long. Three months was plenty.*

Schulman describes the process in a way that every writer understands. "Of course, no matter what, writing is still a struggle. It doesn't get any easier no matter how many times you do it. You go into the room by yourself and you turn the computer on and the struggle remains the same."

No Pain, No Gain (No Script!)

It takes courage to create—and a willingness to go deep into the truth. Schulman contends that, "You have to really dig and suffer. The more you dig and connect with those key revelatory moments in your life, the better you write. The key to good writing is to write something where you really know the situation. Choose the assignments that really speak to you."

Bill Kelley always described the writer's process as, "A dredging up of almost all you are, dredging self out of it and trying to get it into another character. You've got to write the awful heart of the matter."

"It helps to have had pain in your life," says Pen Densham (*Moll Flanders* and TV's most recent incarnation of *The Twilight Zone*). "I think that creativity is an evolutionary survival trait, but it also creates worry and stress. I think people write to discover things in themselves. They may not be conscious of it, but it's a therapeutic process."

Kelley agrees. "I've never known a good writer who didn't feel struggle and pain, whether he'd met it or put himself to it through adventures or testing himself. Hemingway would say, 'If you haven't got anything to write about, try hanging yourself. If you succeed, your troubles are over, if you don't, you've got something to write about.'" The best writers feel a responsibility to their art and to their audience. "Writing is holy," Kelley once exclaimed.

We are keepers of the flame. We sit down at our dulcimer and try to steal a little fire from heaven. We are keepers of the word—we must know the word, the proper word. We must know what words mean and we must know if there's a better word. And we are keepers of the gate, we see darkness and we try to light a candle. We try to be proper citizens of what we occupy.

David Zucker says simply, "We are responsible for what we're putting on the screen and what we're saying. And remember, you may get a successful movie with a bad script, but you'll never get a good movie."

From Script to Theme: What's It All About?

How do truly great scripts differ from those that are merely well written? Every classic script is about ideas. It has something to say—about life, about the human condition, about the writer's own insights into "what it's all about." Most writers find that they explore the same themes over and over, even though their stories may be about very diverse subjects. For Ganz and Mandel, the ideas always seem to become entwined with their own interests and personal passions.

Our lead characters are almost always men our age, like in City Slickers *or* Parenthood. *None of our male characters are traditionally heroic men. They're underconfident nice men. Like us!*

We try to find themes that deal with people's anxieties and worries but we always have room for optimism. We are saying that it's hard to be a person, hard just to live, hard to be regular. We're cynical and pessimistic and neurotic and we're worried and we're frightened but we get through our own lives by just hanging on and saying "There's a way somehow."

Many screenwriters tend to find parts of themselves in the characters they create. Tom Schulman observes "What happens is that as you write, you're going through a transformation yourself so the growth of the main character parallels the growth in your own life. I always felt Keating was a character I had inside of me. I felt like I had all these things I wanted to say. And I was also like Todd. I was the shy kid in school. I hardly ever raised my hand. After a certain point in high school, I just closed up."

Schulman reveals how his own high school experience impacted him later in life. "As a writer, I was always hoping I could write a script that was so brilliant that someone would read it and never have to meet me. I wouldn't have to sit in a meeting and talk because I was so shy. In writing this movie I struggled with those issues."

Of course, self-identification and revelation is hardly a guarantee of success. In the back of the screenwriter's mind there is always the fear of failure. Who will really *care* about this movie or its theme? "By the time I finished *Dead Poets Society* I really felt I had an idea of what I was doing as a writer. I felt I could at least express my ideas clearly on the page. I had years to work on craft without anybody watching me." Schulman stops and smiles. "Of course, I still wasn't sure it would sell."

Bill Kelley once studied for the priesthood and his concerns tended to grow out of a lifetime study of theology and philosophy. "I'm drawn back to the same themes again and again. About facing moral imperatives, about reaching for that extra dimension."

The question of theme is a vexing one for Lawrence Kasdan. Twice he resists sharing his own thoughts about "what it all means." Like many artists, he feels the interpretive issues are best left to those who experience the art, not those who create it. But as the question surfaces a third time, he finally gives in with a sigh.

> *Okay, I think all of my movies are about the struggle between ideal and desire. That is really what's going on in all of these movies.*
>
> *The people of my generation embodied in the Bill Hurt character in* Body Heat *had sort of slid through life very easily. When confronted with the real world, they found that things were very difficult. And their desires were not always being met. In order to make the big score, it was sometimes necessary to bend the rules.* Body Heat *is set in a melodramatic form, but the issue is the same—what are you willing to do to ful-*

*fill your desires, no matter what conflict they bring you into with your
ideals?*

In The Big Chill *it's much more explicit, but the issue is the same.
The characters are remembering a time of total liberation where every
desire was acted upon and gratified. They are looking back from a time
in which all kinds of societal pressures and conventions are forcing them
to conform. So the question is—can we lead an honorable life, not just
because of the pressures from society but because of the internal pressures of our own desires? This is the issue for me every day of my life.*

Kasdan continues unraveling the close-knit threads that weave
through a body of work that many feel is one of the best Hollywood has
ever seen.

A friend of mine did an analysis of Grand Canyon. *He said it was
about the tension between responsibility and liberation—if we equate liberation with following our desires and responsibility with being the family man and member of society.*

Grand Canyon *is about other things too, but I believe there is a
subtext, which is that a man who is very responsible is operating in a
world that is chaotic and frightening. The experience he has when his car
breaks down opens a window for him to another world where chaos
reigns. It's all about ideals, desires and trying to control a universe,
which is terribly frightening and random. As random as a bus ending
your life.*

Kasdan surprised many with his decision to helm the "creature feature"
Dreamcatcher, but fear was certainly an element in that decision. And there
were other aspects of the story line that fit right in with his previous
themes. Based on Stephen King's novel, *Dreamcatcher* featured a "memory
warehouse." In an interview with the *Los Angeles Daily News* Kasdan
revealed why that one concept struck him as great grist for the screen.

*When I read that concept in the book, I thought, well that's exactly how
I see my mind. It's too crowded and it's full of crap. It's got all of my past
injuries, slights and insults, every review that was bad.... They're all
piled away there and you'd really like to burn the whole place down.*

Unless the writer can find a theme that connects, the entire exercise can seem pointless. "You have to come up with something that's a resonant theme, something that connects and it has to be clear," Schulman explains. "I know that people go to see movies and they think, 'I can do a script—that looks easy.' So they take a stab at writing. But they often don't write about personal issues and the system doesn't encourage them to dig deep. That's the problem."

Rewriting: Making the Good Script Great

"Writing is rewriting" may be a cliché but there are very few in the trade who would disagree. Rewriting ideas can come from many sources but often screenwriters are their own harshest critics. Tom Schulman remembers his first version of *Dead Poets*.

> *When I first started to write Keating there were no students, just this man talking to this faceless crowd of people, trying to teach them how important ideas were. I wrote the first draft like that and I read it and I threw it away because it was so embarrassing. I felt I couldn't write it. I wasn't up to it.*

Yet as it turned out this particular "embarrassment" refused to die:

> *A year later I said, "I've got to do that story." Then I started thinking about who the students were going to be. I knew each would have his own individual arc and would be affected by this teacher. So I really worked backward, starting with kids who were in this lockstep kind of mentality, each with their own backstory.*
>
> *But essentially they were flowers ready to bloom and the teacher would encourage each to bloom in a different way. One boy would fall in love. The shy kid, Todd, would come out of his shell. Neil was the student who went too far. He was a residue of the notion of doing the story in an acting school—but Neil is the one who seizes upon acting. Remember, in that day and age acting wasn't even considered a real profession. Anyway, each of these kids would find a way to exemplify the theme the teacher was expressing, which was about creativity and conformity.*

With story structure in place, characters well defined and theme woven throughout, the initial wave of pain and anguish is over. The writer's draft of the script is complete. However, the great script rarely appears right away. For a number of reasons this is the point where the collaborative nature of filmmaking begins to come into play.

No matter how good the writer is, it is difficult to be objective about one's own work. Producers and directors may read the script and find that the story is not as clear as the writer thinks it is. Perhaps a secondary character may appear to be more interesting than the protagonist. Maybe the comedy isn't funny, or the action-adventure story lacks action and adventure.

Ideally, rewriting is a process of new discoveries for the writer. With the initial draft completed, the writer may now feel more confident and move to strengthen or sharpen a character. Perhaps a new theme has emerged during the writing process that needs to be expanded. Or maybe it's time to be a bit more outrageous by adding comic elements or reaching for deeper emotional layers during the dramatic scenes. More often than not, the painful rewriting process will yield a script with more depth and greater insight.

Not surprisingly, much of the rewriting will revolve around the nature of the project and who is involved. For Ganz and Mandel there is always someone waiting.

Usually there's somebody to whom we're submitting it—Billy Crystal (City Slickers), Penny Marshall (A League of Their Own), or Brian Grazer and Ron Howard (Splash). They're the first people to see it and they'll have changes to make. That will lead to a second and third draft. Then we do a reading of the script, asking favors of actor friends. This generates a lot of self-imposed rewriting. In preproduction, we get ideas from watching actors read for parts. The director will come in with ideas, or the stars. And if it's being rehearsed for a couple of weeks before it's filmed, that also generates some rewriting.

Given enough time, writers working closely with an actor or director eventually arrive at a shared vision. "For *City Slickers* we sat for a month with Billy Crystal and went over the script line by line," says Ganz. "By the time the production started, he was like a writer on the set. He was our eyes and ears. We felt totally secure that he had the exact same vision we had."

Maintaining the original vision is somewhat easier if the writer is also the director. Given the complexity of his scripts, it is not surprising that Lawrence Kasdan works quite differently from most screenwriters.

> *I will write a scene and write it until I feel very good about it. The reality is that I work very hard on the first draft. Some people find it much more productive to speed through a first draft, so they have something to work on. The thing that is terrifying to them is the unwritten screenplay.*
>
> *It was never that way for me. I wanted to like everything that I had left behind. When I started to direct, the first draft was very much the movie that was going to be made and it has remained that way. Obviously there are deletions and changes and hopefully they will improve the movie, but I believe in the original impulse.*

In practice, unless you are Lawrence Kasdan, it rarely works this way. Writing and rewriting a script for a big studio feature is filled with the kind of frustration that Hollywood legends are made of. Coming from Canada and a documentary tradition, Pen Densham was left aghast as he gradually discovered how the Hollywood system worked.

> *A script is a piece of papier-mâché and everyone else is going to come along and shape it. They'll mold it a little bit one way because Jack Nicholson wants to be in it and pat it flat again because Arnold Schwarzenegger wants to do it and then pump it up this way and bring in the comedy writer because Bruce Willis wants to do it. Then when that doesn't work, they throw it away.*
>
> *Scripts are like chips, pieces of a roulette game. You throw them down on the numbers and you hope they're going to come up. And you try to accumulate enough numbers coming up so you get to make the movie.*

Given all of this, the writer must remember that the act of scriptwriting, like any kind of writing that comes from the heart, must provide its own reward. John Singleton would always put his teachers on notice. "When I was in school I couldn't work on a screenplay that I didn't have my heart in. I would tell my instructors, 'I'm not writing this for you, I'm writing it for me." Pen Densham says that screenwriting carries with it certain basic lessons in "investment theory."

> You have to get your pleasure out of the act of writing it and creating it because if you invest too much in the act of wanting it to be your child, you're going to feel very hurt more times than you'll feel wonderful. Still, you've got to feel about the act of creating a script as if you had created a child. The thing is, you are not going to be the only person who helps it grow up.

Collaboration: Nothing Is Easy

Whether the screenplay is close to its initial form or has been rewritten dozens of times, eventually the moment arrives when it must begin its journey to the screen. For the writer, even the writer-director, that means letting go and that can be painful.

Describing this phenomenon in the *Wisconsin Screenwriters Newsletter*, writer Tom Eberhardt laments, "You should understand scriptwriting is like giving birth, then having the baby stolen by a bunch of dirty thieves and then seeing this thing on the street corner years later." In a scene from Billy Wilder's classic *Sunset Boulevard*, fictional screenwriter Dan Gillis offers this observation on the rewriting process.

> GILLIS: The last one I wrote was about Okies in the dust bowl. You'd never know though because by the time it reached the screen the whole thing played on a torpedo boat.

Screenwriters have espoused such sentiments since movies began. And the truth is that many times, the script will not be well cared for by its foster parents. Yet the fundamental function of the screenplay is not as a piece of literature, but as a guide for the work to follow.

A poem, novel, short story or magazine article is complete or nearly complete when the writer's work is done. In contrast, when a screenplay is finished, the real business is just beginning. A script must serve many masters and accomplish many purposes. Frank Pierson explains that most writers really don't understand the very nature of what they have created.

The screenplay, before it is anything else, is a technical document. It is a different document for every person reading it. To the producer, it is a story that he weighs for audience appeal (or if he's really good, simply as to whether he likes it or not); to the director, it is a progression of images and scenes in a dance rhythm that he or she may want to dance to.

To the designer, it is a list of locations and sets; to the wardrobe people, it is a list of costumes; to the prop man, a list of props; to the actor a list of lines to learn; to the assistant director, a schedule; to the transportation captain, a list of cars, trucks, maps and times.

Assuming they are trained professionals, each of these technical people is astonishingly good at figuring out what is needed from the slightest clues offered by stage directions or the logic of the scenes. You are writing for all these people, but mostly they aren't reading anything except what pertains to them. They read the screenplay like a flea lives on a dog—without caring much what the whole dog looks like.

Ultimately the value of any script always comes back to its role as the plan or blueprint for the film. Densham's advice is deceptively simple.

As a writer you need to tell a story that makes you cry, laugh, feel. You have to validate every step of it. Every element has to have a purpose— the choice of the characters, the choice of the actors, the choice of the music, camera, editing—all must be purposeful.

It's the script that provides the magic that brings together a group of people and it all comes from the imagination of the writer. That's the purpose of a script. In a sense, it's a magic carpet, where everybody you need will climb on board that idea or dream and bring it to reality on the screen.

Frank Pierson's final comments reflect his vision of what the very best scripts must accomplish as they offer various possibilities in the context of the collaborative process.

It is the writer's job to force the director and actor out of merely reproducing a text and into finding themselves in it, thereby allowing some possibility of creating art. The text is meant to be and must be constructed to be interpreted. This is the true meaning of collaborative art.

The collaborative art. Those words keep coming back. When all is said and done, this is what makes the best film writing unique. In the original script the words are the writer's own, as much an original vision as any form of writing. A year or two or ten years later, the lights will go down in a theater somewhere and the audience will finally hear that first line of dialogue.

What happens in between is a collaborative experience like no other; a wondrous collision of art and commerce, a maddening high-stakes poker game played with pictures that "move" and mountains made of the money that keeps changing hands as the vision makes its perilous journey from script to screen.

CLOSE-UP
THE WRITER: AKIVA GOLDSMAN

Falling in Love with the Material

I had read the excerpt about John Nash in *Vanity Fair* about a year before the book of *A Beautiful Mind* was released. I was very intrigued with it, because of my long-standing interest in mental illness. My mother was one of the world's foremost authorities on childhood autism. Our home was one of the first group homes for children who were then called emotionally disturbed.

I was surrounded by children who were diagnosed with childhood schizophrenia or childhood autism. I watched as these children ran from the man in the coat rack, tried to brush fire off their shoulders or stared at horses floating past their nursery windows. People referred to them in those days as being without reason, but the one thing I knew was that they had a reason for everything they were doing.

So, from an early age, I was getting insight into how mental illness worked. The idea of multiple perceptual planes made sense to me. So when I read this excerpt of Sylvia Nasar's book in *Vanity Fair*, it was so clear that John Nash was involved in this other world that nobody else was aware of. And I was very compelled by that.

When the book came out, I read it in galleys, and I took it into Warner Bros. where I had a producing deal. At the same time, Brian Grazer had taken it into Universal through Imagine. Warner wasn't interested, but Universal was. So I went to Brian and pitched my heart out, basically just groveled on my metaphoric hands and knees, asking to write this.

Finding the Angle
In my writing career, I had done a lot of action, so my only calling card for this type of film was a little movie I had written about an autistic boy called *Silent Fall*. When I went to Brian, I presented my approach, which came out of the desire to use the grammar of mental illness in a different way. It was an unconventional approach, because if you read the book, you'll notice that the book is a beautiful reportage of John Nash's external life. But his inner life is almost entirely absent.

So I entirely fabricated this inner life.

I pulled this idea of personifying his delusions from hints in the book and from what I knew about schizophrenia. Very commonly schizophrenia takes the form of religious, governmental or alien paranoia. So I took the political/governmental idea of secrets and then I did a kind of very crude sort of synthesis of Freudian and Jungian ideals. I took the notion of the externalized superego, the judgmental, critical, voice that we have. That became the character of Parcher.

Then I took the idea of a narcissistic id and that became Charles; then I went from Freud to Jung, took the idea of God or unconditional love and that became Marcy. Those were my organizational principles. It's the template I used to delineate the three delusional characters.

When I spoke to Brian Grazer about this, I think he was thinking a movie about "genius" and I was thinking a movie about "madness." I think he was thinking here was an extraordinary mind and how do we put that on screen, and I was talking to him about making the delusions real.

I really wanted this job. It felt like I had potential to be a better writer than I was letting myself be at that point—you sometimes feel like...if you can't do it on this one, when are you going to do it?

Developing the Script
When I got the job I became terrified, and it took me a year to start writing.

Then, I got into a room with Karen Kehela (the executive producer and chair of development at Imagine), who is truly a genius, and sat down and we talked through the movie. I had really thought about the story, to the point that I had a scene-by-scene breakdown.

So we talked through that, turned things on their heads and then went over to Brian's house. I said, "Here's the movie," and I told it to him—and he cried. Which I took as a good sign. And I went and started writing.

It then took me about three months to write the script.

There were several construction dilemmas to solve in this script. The essential question always was, were people going to tolerate two movies? The first story was meant to seem like a straight bio-pic. Universal's idea was never to sell the twist, but to sell the film as a bio-pic. So the audience is thinking they're watching a rather interesting bio-pic with Russell Crowe, about a guy who's going to go crazy, like a monster movie where you're waiting, waiting, for the monster—and then you suddenly realize the monster was on page one. You had been in a monster movie the whole time. He was crazy all along.

We wondered if the audience would stand for being in one movie and then being told that they were in a different one. And when they realized this reversal, which movie were they going to like more? What if one of them was more interesting than the other?

We were always debating where to reveal his mental illness. Now, the audience finds out he's mentally ill right after the midpoint.

Collaborating with the Director

Ron is a visionary, a filmmaker among the best in the world. But he is also a writer's director. He really wants to understand the story and

NASH **POV**
OF
CHARLES + MARCEE (IN MOTION)
HENCHMAN IN F.G.

95-44

the intention of every scene. He's very thorough about understanding why a character does something. He'd get excited and he'd say, "I think you should do this," and I'd say, "I don't think I can do this," and he'd say, "Just try that." And he'd be right. He asked me to write the proposal scene, which turned out to be one of my favorite scenes. I must have rewritten it seventy-five times and each time there were fewer and fewer words. But the scene really helped to find the strength, the fortification of the structure, and then when the script was finished, we sent it to Russell Crowe, and he wanted to do it.

Working on the Set

This part of the process was very atypical of Hollywood. They invited me to casting and then I was invited to rehearsals, and then I was on the set every day. So every day on the set there were the three of us—Ron, Russell, and me.

Russell is in every scene except three, which is very unusual since the film has no "B" plot. Essentially it's a subjective point-of-view movie, except for three scenes from Alicia's point of view. So instead of a film with A, B, C plotlines, here it's an "A" plot almost all the way through the movie.

Russell added rigor and a keen intelligence and a light touch to the script. He knows what his character would do and not do. For example, in the scene when Jenny comes in to meet him in his office to bring back an assignment she's completed Russell looked at me and he said, "Wouldn't it be good if there were something weird but charming?" so I added the weird lines he says when she asks him to dinner: "Table for one. You know how it is. Prometheus, chained to the rock, birds circling overhead." He sorta knocks it out, and it's bizarre, but it's a weird kind of insight and charming.

When you watch the movie all it plays as "You know he said something strange and you know she found it charming." That beat hadn't been there in the script.

Ron was always worried about the hospital scene, where Russell is trying to get the transceiver out of his wrist with a brad from the hospital bed. You couldn't do that in an institution. But Russell noticed that John's nails were very long, so he grew his out. I said to Russell, "let him use his fingernails to cut out the transceiver." We were all having ideas based on the life of the movie as it was actually starting to come alive.

This was the perfect collaborative movie in every way Hollywood says movies can't be. Ron is the captain of the ship, and he's the captain you want at the helm. He asks, "What do you think?" and then really listens, and then decides what course he wants to set. There were a lot of strong personalities here, but Ron is very confident about his choices, so people can be collaborative with him. He's not swayed by the identity of the author of the idea, he's just swayed by the idea. We whipped around all the way through the movie—discussing the structure, a line, the performance, direction, the script—all feeding into each other. Sometimes we totally disagree, but I think we all trusted each other. You know these people—Ron, Brian, Karen, Russell, Jenny—are never going to hurt you to help themselves, because you're all raising the same kid.

The producer is like the conductor of an orchestra. Maybe he can't play every instrument, but he knows what every instrument should sound like.

—**Richard Zanuck**

The Producer and the Long Run

Directors, actors, editors and composers all have well-defined tasks. The producer is another story and the proliferation of titles such as associate producer and executive producer in recent years hasn't helped. Hollywood's most successful producers have grown used to explaining their jobs to those outside the industry. And the explanations, definitions—and tasks associated with them tend to vary from producer to producer.

Brian Grazer is probably Hollywood's most successful producer. His name can be found attached to over forty features, which span an incredibly diverse series of interests. Among them, *8 Mile*, *A Beautiful Mind*, *Liar Liar*, *Apollo 13*, *Parenthood* and *Splash*. What could these movies possibly all have in common?

Grazer attributes his success on all of them to being able to find an idea that connects to the audience. He explained to the *Hollywood Reporter* that, "You have to have the intention of an idea—what its intended purpose is to the audience. You can imagine what the scenes are meant to look like and how to meet the audience's expectations." For Grazer, a great producer must have one thing above all: "Belief and an enormous passion about where you believe you can end up with a movie. If you have a vision and you believe strongly in that vision, you have to be relentless about it and not let anything dilute what you believe can be the endpoint."

Richard Zanuck's *Road to Perdition* is a more recent addition to a growing list of classic films that includes *Driving Miss Daisy, Cocoon, Jaws* and *The Sting*.

People outside of Hollywood and New York don't really have a clear idea of what a producer is or what he does. It's sort of tragic in a way—that this important function doesn't have a clearer image. Most people think a producer is the person who puts up the money, which is wrong. If you're smart, you never put up the money yourself!

David Puttnam is widely respected for the quality of the films he brought to the screen and renowned for his controversial stint as the head of Columbia Studios. He explains the role of the producer in a crisp British accent: "A producer is a marathon runner who plods along, believing against all reasonable hope that at some point he or she is going to go through the tape and actually win!" Coming from the man who produced *Chariots of Fire*, this seems an apt metaphor. The producer's long run begins with an idea that must be moved from script to screen. The rare victory comes years later, when audiences find a film they love and a new classic is born.

Accomplishing this feat means going uphill. "You have to take the long view and keep going. You've got to have patience," says Puttnam. "There's a kind of perfectionism; you can't be too easily satisfied. You've got to keep trying to make everything better. The script can be better. The cinematography can be better. The music can be better. You must strive for an improved product at all times."

From the time the starting gun is fired, Puttnam is thinking about the people out there in the dark.

From Day One the important thing is that you represent the audience— not necessarily everyone out there—but the audience that the movie is being aimed at. If it's a broad-based-appeal film, then those are the interests you represent. If it's a movie with narrower appeal, then you have to represent that interest.

Kathleen Kennedy's first producer credit came on *E.T. the Extra-Terrestrial*. Since then she has racked up an unprecedented string of high profile projects, including *A.I. Artificial Intelligence, Jurassic Park, Back to the Future* and *Indiana Jones and the Temple of Doom*, "I think the role of the producer is defined by what the movie requires," she explains.

> *Each picture is different. It may involve a number of people, a lot of relationships. Or it may be something you generate from a single idea or a book you optioned and you have to decide who you want to become involved. All of that dictates what your role will be.*

Richard Zanuck literally grew up on the Fox lot where his famous father, Darryl E. Zanuck, reigned as one of the last of the old-time studio heads. Today Richard's company, founded in 1988 to produce *Driving Miss Daisy*, now employs his two sons. Zanuck has the benefit of a lifetime spent getting movies made.

> *Ideally, you're the first one on the project, even before the writer— before anybody else. Maybe you don't have the original idea of the story—but you will read a book or see a play and say, "This would make a terrific film."*
>
> *Take* Cocoon, *for example. It came to us as a manuscript for a book that the writer couldn't get published. He wanted our advice. What became the picture was only one small segment of it, but we saw the idea in there. Ironically, after the picture was a hit, he went back and rewrote the book to conform to the movie.*

Cocoon Director Ron Howard joined Producer Brian Grazer to form Imagine Entertainment in 1982. Today the Oscar-winning (*A Beautiful Mind*) producer/director duo is probably the most successful such team in Hollywood. Grazer defines the producer as "the person who must remember what the central vision and goal of the movie is and to try to be fiscally and creatively responsible for that."

All of this speaks to the many roles that a producer might play in bringing a project from script to screen. Richard Zanuck explains the roles producers may play:

> *There is the agent-style producer who plugs in the deal. The other extreme is what we do, which is shepherd the film from inception all the*

way to completion and beyond. In the end everyone else has gone off to do other things, but we're still out there in Tokyo or somewhere talking about the picture and selling it.

Kennedy adds that the producer is often the only one on the project "who is part of the entire creative process. The director might not come aboard until the script is completed and the financing is in place. In some cases the casting may also be complete. The producer is often involved long before and after the actual process of making the film."

The complete producer's role and its relationship to the film brings to mind a famous line from *Citizen Kane*. After Kane's death, his business manager explains to a reporter that he was there "From *before* the beginning, young fellow and now, *after* the end." And that is a long run indeed.

The First Decision

Noted for his ability to bring difficult but exceptional material to the screen, Zanuck says that a producer must begin with a personal commitment, one that can never be taken lightly.

The first decision, to get involved, is the most critical one in the entire process because every decision from that point on can't save you if the first one is wrong. No matter how many stars you put in it—you can get the best director in the world—if the subject is something that people don't want to see, you may make a brilliant movie out of it, but nobody will come to see it.

But what do people want to see? Producers have various points of view. Brian Grazer says "I like warm-spirited movies that have a theme, that are optimistic, with movie stars. You do a concept movie with movie stars, you have a pretty good chance it's going to make money. The movie is definable. You can set up your marketing according to an expectation."

"I never think of the marketplace" says Gale Ann Hurd, producer of *The Terminator*. "If you sit there and are always thinking about 'How will this play in Peoria?' you aren't serving the movie, you're serving the package. I don't think you can serve two masters. A film takes on its own life and you have to be serving that."

Richard Zanuck's career has been spent producing films that seemed to have limited audience appeal. Interestingly, this is precisely what he seeks as he makes that crucial "first decision."

I think the key to it is that it isn't a mainstream idea. These projects have a better chance because people get tired of seeing the same thing, of not having choices. They want something different. Maybe they'll go like cattle to see the latest Schwarzenegger film, but we've proven that there is also a market for pictures that would seemingly have no audience appeal.

You can't just make an ordinary picture—you have to make an extraordinary picture. Find a subject that is exceptional and people are going to be attracted to it because it's unique. I'm actually playing it "safe" in a way by picking subjects that are not mainstream. It doesn't always work. Rush was a failure. Driving Miss Daisy was a resounding hit. There is always a risk.

Once the producer has found the right idea and has committed to it, the long run begins. "The first decision is, this would make a great movie," says Zanuck. The second decision is, "Who will write it?"

The Script: Working with the Writer

If the producer has made the decision to get involved with an existing script, there may be a series of revisions even before a director comes on board. If the project is still at the "idea" phase then one or more writers may be hired. Often this involves adapting the story from a book, play or other medium.

Ed Feldman (*K-19: The Widowmaker, The Truman Show, 101* and *102 Dalmatians*) has worked with dozens of writers over the years. "The writer always feels oppressed," he says with a smile. "But early on, he always forgets to tell you he's the only one who gets paid! He gets his money first. It's a business of uncertainty. If a producer makes $10,000 during a two-year development process, that's a big payday. That comes to about a dollar an hour." Indeed, the long development phase calls for a unique kind of producer endurance. David Puttnam agrees and cites an example, "With *The*

Killing Fields there were two years of research before a page of script was ever written."

In any event, once the script has been completed, it becomes the producer's duty to protect the original vision as the project moves toward production. It's no secret that the preproduction and production processes can take a toll on that vision and on the script itself. Puttnam explains this in terms of a "geometric progression" that he sees as an inevitable part of the collaborative nature of filmmaking.

> *You have to look at it from a geometric point of view. If you start with one idea, be it from the director, writer, or producer, that idea gets seen through a number of prisms. And each time it gets seen, it's 5 percent off. When the director comes in it's 95 percent of what it was, then the cinematographer comes, now it's 90 percent. By the time you've involved everybody the original idea has gone through a prism and it's likely to be 60 or 65 percent of the original notion. A script is a very vulnerable, frail object. It can't sustain that type of distortion.*

As the producer of films such as *Midnight Express* and *The Mission*, Puttnam is renowned for his view that the script is the single most important tool in the filmmaking process. Not surprisingly, he tends to be very protective of what's on the page. "The truth of the matter is that the only reason you are all together making the film is because of that screenplay. You have to remain true to the original vision."

Often it becomes the producer's duty to moderate disputes involving the script. Ideally, producers find a ready-to-shoot script that they simply take to a director. The reality is that this rarely happens. Most often the director will have his or her own ideas about the script and it is a rare project when some sparks don't eventually fly between the director and the writer.

In the case of *Dead Poets Society* writer Tom Schulman intended for his main character, Keating (eventually played by Robin Williams), to be dying of Hodgkin's Disease. Producer Steven Haft was fine with that. Freshly hired director Peter Weir felt differently. Schulman explains:

> *Peter's explanation for it, which I finally came to embrace, was that it was unfair for a teacher, one who knows he's dying, to lead these kids*

into battle when he knows he doesn't have to suffer the consequences himself. It also diminishes what the boys standing up on the desk [cheering Keating] at the end means. It's easy to stand up for someone who is dying, but when the boys stand up for someone who's just like everybody else, we know they're standing up for the ideas that person believes in.

Peter told me, "It's amazing how easy it's going to be to take this out—a simple cut of about five pages." When Robin Williams came in Peter told him we had to lose the Hodgkin's disease and cancer. And Robin said, "Good idea." And I thought, "Okay."

Schulman also explains that Weir had a "golden rule" about avoiding repetition. "As a writer, you're trying to make a point. There's a tendency to want to hit these things on the head and make sure the audience gets it. Peter really goes the other way. He trusts the audience with subtlety. Which is one of the reasons he's a great director."

When it was all over, Schulman found the collaborative process unusually effective. "The whole process on this script was pretty much an ideal situation—the collaboration with producer Steven Haft, Robin and Peter was great. It may never go this smoothly for me again."

The Right "Direction" for the Vision Team

Producers have many different theories when it comes to choosing a director but most agree that once the decision to get involved and the script has been finalized, this decision is most crucial. Richard Zanuck explains that the key is to match the script to the director's interests—but not necessarily to the director's career path.

There's no point in talking a director into doing something that he doesn't quite believe in, because it's going to be a disaster. Every good director has gone through this process. His or her agent says, "You've been making great films and they got good reviews but now you need to break through with a big commercial picture. I've got this picture with a big star attached and your price will go up and you'll go to a whole different level." Every director who has done that has fallen on his ass, because he's going in for the wrong reason.

Zanuck says that producers develop a kind of "sixth sense" about their collaborators.

Whenever someone says, "I don't think this is as sad or as funny as you do, Dick," I start to wonder if I have the right person for the job. You need that connection from everybody—editor, composer, et cetera, though perhaps to a lesser degree. The two key people are obviously the writer and the director.

"If you have a good script, you cast it right and you get a good direc-tor—that's 90 percent," says Brian Grazer. "The good director will hire good department heads so the producer just has to stay out of the way. Of course, I collaborate on those decisions, but directors make the call. You don't want be in the director's face." The director will bring in the produc-tion designer who will hire the crew of people who will build the sets. The cinematographer will head up a group responsible for the lighting and "look" of each scene.

For Kathleen Kennedy, there is always a sense of how every collabora-tor will mesh with the others. "It's a bit like casting, but frankly, you don't always have time to explore alternatives. You meet with people, you make a determination based on skill and you throw them together and hope everyone will get along."

What happens is, over the years, you look at movies and see people's work and you begin to identify with certain people who have clear artis-tic abilities that lend themselves to specific types of movies. Sometimes people tend to want to work with the same people all the time. Over the years we've worked with a variety of people and tend to try to find peo-ple who are aptly suited to the specific project at hand.

The bottom line is that top filmmakers tend to work with the same people over and over again, because once they find collaborators they can trust, they are unlikely to go elsewhere. The hectic nature of film produc-tion means that "training" new people or familiarizing them with the nuances of a particular production style is out of the question. There sim-ply is no time.

For Zanuck it always comes back to selecting the right people—those who can "stay on track."

Even with the right people, this isn't the furniture business or the car business. You have a lot of personalities and a lot of egos; so many factors are at play. It's easy to go astray and very tough to carry the vision through completely every inch of the way—to make it all work. There are economic pressures, time pressures and there are always personality conflicts when you put so many people together. Everyone works for the common cause, but it is an ego-driven business, there's a lot of pushing and shoving going on.

Collaboration, Stars and "The Vertical Line"

Much of the "pushing and shoving" in today's big-budget features comes from the stars, whose vulnerable images seem to rise and fall with the fortunes of each film in which they appear. Brian Grazer doesn't complain about this. He firmly believes in the star system—and in the special something that each star brings to a project. "These people are very gifted. The reason they are stars is because they do a magic that other people can't. They're a little superhuman. So I try to help them maximize their genius."

If you work with movie stars, you have to be attentive to their needs. They are their own businesses. Arnold Schwarzenegger is, who knows?—maybe a half-a-billion-dollar business. So you want to do things to help him maximize his skills on and off the set. If you can help make him feel good and have a good attitude, that's important.

Gale Anne Hurd (*The Terminator, The Hulk*) agrees. "My job is to make sure that the stars have every tool, every element they need to perform as well as possible. When I worked with John Lithgow in *Raising Cain*, I helped find someone to coach him for the Norwegian accent. I made certain that he had the right place to stay, that he was happy with his wardrobe, happy with his hair and makeup—so that he could be free to act."

David Puttnam acknowledges the importance of stars but, in keeping with his comments about the career path of directors, insists that the needs of the *project* are paramount.

What I try to do is find stars who see the material I am offering them as way of making the same point I am trying to make. You make sure that everybody is firing the bullet out of the same gun and aiming at the same target. I've been very fortunate with people like Glenn Close and Robin Williams in this regard. A star who wants to be in a film, but who has his own career agenda for wanting to be in it, is clearly going to distort that movie. It can't be otherwise.

At the same time, Puttnam acknowledges that many producers must temper these ideals with the reality of getting the film made. For better or worse, big-budget features are increasingly star dependent.

Now, it may well be that the producer is desperate for money and bringing in this or that star is the only way to get the picture made. It would be stupid to pretend that this isn't a perfectly reasonable thing to take into account when you are making a movie. But then you have to live with the consequences. The movie isn't going to be what you wanted it to be and you're going to spend the rest of your life apologizing for it.

My experience allows me the conceit of believing that it is the movie that counts, not the star. Clearly, if you make a great movie with a major star, you're going to do that much better. But experience has proven that you can have the greatest star in the world, but if the film is no good, no one is going to come and see it.

Puttnam identifies a crucial but little discussed downside to the collaboration process that has spelled disaster for many a well-intentioned project.

There's a fear factor involved here, because everybody is terrified of having a relationship go bad, because it's a business of relationships. They would rather the film go down the drain than for the relationship to go bad. It might be a relationship with a star, a director, or a studio. In these situations the relationship is protected—but the price you pay is the project.

Puttnam contends that in times of collaborative conflict, "The one thing that is often sacrificed is the material, when in fact that should be the glue that holds it all together."

Once again, successful collaboration is recognized as a primary ingredient in the success of any film. Grazer tells the *Hollywood Reporter*, "I believe in collaboration. I am a total believer in collaboration, that you have to continue to test things—which is the second part of the equation. You have to test the obvious and that's what you do with people. You ask, 'Why do you think this is funny? Why will it be a hit? Why is this actress perfect?' You have to line everything up on the vertical line—exactly."

Other People's Money

If the material is the glue that holds it all together, then money is the grease that keeps it moving down the track. Given today's spiraling production costs, the producer spends a lot of time worrying about where it all comes from—and where it all goes.

Gale Anne Hurd learned her fiscal responsibility lessons by working with Roger Corman, the master of low-budget action films. "We did the most complex, ambitious projects in the world for no money."

> *By the time I was doing* The Terminator *I knew enough to make sure that the film was not so overly ambitious that we wouldn't be able to stay within a small budget. The biggest problem with special-effects films is that the writer and director don't know what's possible or how much things will cost. They don't take cost factors into consideration when they're devising scenes. So it's up to the producer to research expenses, just as carefully as we might research a historical period film.*

At an average of $50-$60 million per picture, Feldman notes, "You could buy a building downtown and it'll stand there for 100 years. But a multi-million movie can die on one Friday night! The technology is such that after the 8:00 PM show on Friday night, you know what the picture will do. They don't even give you a chance to go to sleep and savor it. It's scary."

All of this means that raising money for feature films is increasingly difficult for every producer, no matter what her or his track record. Kathleen Kennedy says that such staggering amounts require a pragmatic approach. "It's not in my wallet. I never see it. I don't sign a lot of checks myself. Because you are not literally counting out dollar bills, it becomes a concept.

You feel a certain responsibility, of course, but I can't say that it makes me particularly nervous."

The Bridge over Troubled Waters

With cast and crew chosen and the money in place, the film gathers momentum as it moves into production. Now it's time for the producer's communication skills to come to the forefront. Every film encounters problems along the way and it will fall to the producer to make sure everything keeps running smoothly.

Feldman explains, "Part of the producer's role is keeping everybody happy. You try to keep everything moving along in a straight line. Make sure the script doesn't run away from you. Keep everyone focused on what the movie is about. That's what the producer is—he's a manager. Some producers are not mediators, they're agitators. That's not my style."

Brian Grazer agrees. "If you can gain the trust of the important principals on the movie—the actors, writer, director—and they believe that your intentions toward the movie are pure and that you will never lie to them, it creates a synergy."

I think of myself as a gracious host all the time. My job is to try to make everybody feel comfortable. As a result, I make sure that meetings are held where everybody is comfortable, where bonding is going to be maximized. I try to make sure there aren't any dark clouds on the set. You have to make people feel good. That's just proper human etiquette.

Is it possible to be *too* accommodating? David Puttnam says that ideally the producer becomes the "unthreatening voice of reason."

The studio or financial source is the threatening voice of reason by definition. The audience, if left to their worst devices, can be the threatening voice of reason. You as the producer, have to be the unthreatening voice of reason. Sometimes 75 percent of the job is to be a peacemaker, to calm everyone down. One of the reasons that so many poor films get made is that the producer has to spend all his time putting out fires. In that case you end up with ashes, a film that is nobody's.

When trouble breaks out on a set and firing someone is not an option, the producer must find a way to reconcile those "creative differences" in a way that is acceptable to everyone. "During the shooting phase your primary job is to troubleshoot," reveals Kathleen Kennedy.

If you see that something is going wrong or about to go wrong, the producer is the one who has to come in and fix it. You have to have strong people skills. You have to figure out how to be the perfect diplomat. If you've got people at opposite ends of the spectrum, you often don't have the time to go through hours of problem solving. It has to be resolved quickly and efficiently.

She also notes that the producer must maintain a certain sensitivity to the nature of a film-in-progress.

Once principal photography begins, the producer steps back and sees where the movie is going. A film is an organic, living, breathing thing. It's not just defined by what's on paper, it continues to change. The creative process continues throughout and out of that comes sometimes the best ideas. But there needs to be someone who maintains a cohesive vision, a focus on the entire picture and not just the individual elements.

Kennedy emphasizes that, as with so many movie collaborators, the producer must rely on instinctive skills that can't really be taught.

I think it's intuitive. The people I run across who are most effective don't really know how they do it or why they do it well. They are just instinctively able to function within this pressure-packed environment. They actually enjoy it. They get along well with people. That's a huge part of it. Communication is always the key.

Richard Zanuck explains why the role of the producer might change dozens of times each day. "Sometimes you have to be a mediator, sometimes a psychiatrist. There are times when you are a ruthless boss—you have to be 'Doctor No.' Sometimes you have to be all of those things. Every day presents new problems and different situations. You have to be a lot of different people."

Producers on Board!

The degree of producer involvement on the set varies. Hands-on types are there from morning until night. "I try to be on the set every day," says Ed Feldman. "I enjoy the set. It's terrific. Somebody gives you a lot of money to play moviemaking! You're also passing out a lot of money. You want to make sure it's being utilized." Since the set is often thought of as the director's domain, some conflicts are inevitable. But effective producers see their duties as complementing those of the director in very specific ways.

Kennedy's collaboration with Steven Spielberg exemplifies what she feels are the best aspects of the producer-director relationship. "He's the one who is the best executor. I can put forth all sorts of ideas, but he's the one who has to maintain the point of view. There is only so far any producer can go before the movie needs to be directed and made, so to have the director as your primary collaborator completes the process in a very satisfying way. Unlike television, film is a director's medium. The producer ultimately services the vision of the director."

Kennedy explains that she and Spielberg often worked on several projects simultaneously. "It's not only the movie we are shooting but everything that we're doing that overlaps into it. Steven and I can be sitting in between shots, discussing four other pictures."

On the set, Feldman likes to concentrate on the actors. "I believe part of the producer's job is to keep the actors happy. You become like a social director. I think it's a question of personality. It's one of my strengths. I like people."

The level of Gale Anne Hurd's involvement on the set tends to vary. "It depends on the project, since every set creates a different set of problems and demands. On The Abyss, I was also the line producer. That taught me a valuable lesson—to insist on delegating. It allows me to have a greater creative rapport with the actors, director and writer, as opposed to worrying about how much every minute of filming is costing. Ideally, I'll be a troubleshooter. I'll stop by the set every day, but I don't usually stay."

Richard Zanuck sees it differently. "I've never had a line producer because that's what I do. I'm there every minute of every day. I have to be there and be on top of everything. You have to know costs, time, have a clear idea about everything that's happening."

Decisions are made every day on the set. These decisions affect money and the look of the picture. You watch everything and everybody. Just being there promotes a certain awareness and alertness. With a lot of people, if the teacher is out of class, then kids raise hell.

The producer is like the conductor of an orchestra. Maybe he can't play every instrument, but he knows what every instrument should sound like. To keep people on their toes, you've got to know everything you can about every facet of the process. There are a lot of tricks you learn that can be used to help a picture and to bring it in on time and on budget.

Postproduction and Studio Relations

With the shoot complete, the film moves toward postproduction. One of the things a producer does during this time is deal with the studio. Invariably pressures mount as the film nears completion. The producer works to make sure there is enough time and budget to complete the movie successfully. Acting as a buffer between the studio and the creative team, the producer must, once again, keep everyone happy.

Ed Feldman explains what is required. "You have to have a strong heart to be a producer. There has to be someone who is focused on the whole movie. That's what they're paying you for. I came up through the ranks, which I think really helped me in this career. I started as a press kit writer in New York. I know the business very well and I know the business of the business as well. So I can see things from the studio's point of view."

If studio moviemaking is the collision of art and commerce, the producer is always the one at ground zero. Dealing with the studios is a process that has changed remarkably over the years, according to Zanuck, a highly decorated veteran of the studio wars.

It's so different now—the composition at the top of the studios has a different mentality. It's lawyers and businessmen and agents. In the days of my father and the Jack Warners—these guys were showmen, real Barnum and Bailey type picture-makers. Now the personalities are corporate. It isn't wrong per se, it's just different and it affects how pictures get made and what pictures get made.

These days there are too many chefs. Every studio has ten would-be Irving Thalbergs in the wings sending in notes. They're not riding on their gut instincts. They went to law school, not motion picture school. So they have to have the marketing research to bolster themselves.

There is no question that marketing research plays an increasingly larger role in studio decision-making at every level. Some producers are comfortable with this; Zanuck is not one of them.

They do all this market research—none of which I do, I never have. You can't poll people about what they will like. They don't know. You can't figure out what fifty million people want to see. This isn't an election. It's a movie. All I can do is figure that if I like it, maybe someone else will too.

The key is to make something different. If you ask the audience after they've seen it, they will tell you they want it again. But that's a trap. You have to go find something else. Audiences have a craving to find new things. Sure, they want to be told what to see, but they also want to discover things on their own. They look for new openings, new horizons, new subjects.

How does the producer discover those new things? Zanuck combines gut instinct with a sense of why the audience goes to the movies in the first place. "I'm looking for things that touch you one way or the other, that move you. Maybe a movie can scare you—like *Jaws*—or it can make you laugh or cry. Those are the things that audiences respond to."

Now well into his sixties, Zanuck understands his own limitations. "The core audience for movies today is what, fifteen to twenty-five? Am I going to try to guess what they want? I'll never know what a fifteen-year-old will think is funny. I've got to go with what I think is funny. Maybe I'll fail, but all I've got are my own feelings and instincts."

Brian Grazer is another believer in the power of producer intuition. "I try to read as much as I can. But when it comes to making a decision, I make a point of eliminating the analytical quality and go by the intuitive quality. One can be lazy with that. You have to continue to inform your brain with information—but ultimately, it's intuition."

Such instincts come into play most prominently as the film nears completion and is tested on preview audiences. The studio looks at audience test scores from "sneak preview" screenings and works with the producer and director to release a film with the best box office potential. In the best of circumstances, this process can help a film. Producer Steven Haft (*The Singing Detective, Strange Justice*) remembers how it worked with *Dead Poets Society*.

Finally it was time for the test screenings. I thought we'd made a picture for adults, a picture about poetry and I had my own doubts about how big the audience was for it. The last thing I wanted was a test screening that showed that people weren't excited about this movie. That would have demoralized the postproduction process. We got the marketing people to agree to stock the audience heavily with adults. We figured that type of audience could provide us with some intelligent comment on what worked and what didn't. We didn't want to pack that first audience with the usual core fifteen- to twenty-four-year-olds, who we assumed would be less interested in a period piece about poetry.

They agreed to hold a screening for teens later with a separate set of response cards. The first screening went great. The cards came back very strong, 89 percent good or excellent. We were very relieved. The surprise came a week later. The teen scores had been even higher, 94 percent!

We all thought we were making a movie for adults, a kind of nostalgia piece. The film covers a period before sixteen-year-olds were even born. What we hadn't counted on was that sixteen-year-olds like to watch other sixteen-year-olds on the screen. The actors weren't wearing tights and they were speaking English. So it wasn't perceived as this "art" film. And, like everyone else, they loved the story. Other than the fact that the cars were dated, the whole picture could have played today. Even Disney wasn't sure until that second screening that this picture would play well to young audiences.

Needless to say, all of this is hardly an exact science. Every picture has its own dilemmas. As Zanuck prepared *Driving Miss Daisy* for its first studio screening, he knew a certain strategy had to be employed.

They wanted to see it in a projection room, but I didn't want them to see it that way. They had gone in thinking this was a Masterpiece Theatre-*type project, but I had screened it privately for audiences. I knew...it would go through the roof. So I made sure they saw it with [an] audience. They were startled. They didn't realize the picture would produce that kind of response. After that they really got behind it.*

To Market, to Market...

Having secured studio approval, the film is scheduled for release. The degree of studio support for any film usually translates to the number of screens that are secured for its opening weekend. A potential blockbuster might be scheduled for two thousand or more screens, while others may open in a dozen theaters. While the producer awaits the verdict of the audience, he or she often has a pretty good notion of how the film will fare. Yet there are always surprises.

Kathleen Kennedy recalls that "When we made *E.T.*, the marketing people told us it was being perceived as a children's film—so we couldn't open in more than six hundred theaters."

Then we screened the movie and it screened off the map and we started getting lots of calls to put the picture in more theaters. But, with the rare exception like The Crying Game, *that just doesn't happen anymore. For the most part the studio decides how many theaters the picture is going to open in, based on the results of sophisticated national market research studies.*

Is it possible to predict how a film will do? Ed Feldman says, "Since I came out of the marketing end of the business, I believe that you can make and sell almost anything if you just give them hope in the final reel."

The Revenue Game

In today's multimedia environment, revenues flow not only from a film's domestic and international box office grosses, but from numerous ancillary sources including traditional sources like TV and cable as well as home video, DVD, merchandising and other promotional vehicles. Product placement (showing specific brand names on screen) is becoming increasingly frequent, but it remains a relatively small part of the financial picture. Merchandising is another matter. From *E.T.* to *Jurassic Park* and *A.I. Artificial Intelligence*, Kathleen Kennedy's films have almost always involved major merchandising contracts.

> *It depends on the movie and what the movie dictates. With a film like* Jurassic Park, *it involved a massive amount of licensing contracts and promotional deal negotiations. The artwork used to sell the movie had to be incorporated into various promotional campaigns. There were point-of-purchase displays to review for merchandising and publishing purposes.*

Kennedy says, "You need to define what the logos are going to be early on. Marketing has become such a sophisticated element of the filmmaking process, it needs to be consistent throughout all aspects of the campaign. The images you choose become the identity of the film through the media. All of this must be in place long before the picture is released."

Kennedy takes a quick mental trip through film industry history and recalls a merchandising milestone.

> Batman *was a perfect example. If you can come up with a strong symbol early on that is identifiable with the movie, it can become a tremendous calling card. Just before* Jurassic Park *was released, the press was full of reports that the $60 million film was being supplemented with $65 million in promotional funds. But those figures can be deceiving. That money is not being spent by the marketing department at Universal. Rather it is the total amount being generated by companies that are involved in selling the picture."*

A recent example of this phenomenon involved Gale Ann Hurd's *The Hulk*. The film's promotional campaign kicked off with a preview during the Super Bowl game, six months prior to its release. Over a dozen "Hulk partners" were already on board. Pepsi sponsored an "instant win" promotion on 150 million packages of Mountain Dew. Hershey Foods offered a sweepstakes promotion involving six of its most popular brands including green colored, green apple-flavored "Hulk Twizzlers." Kraft foods offered sixteen "Hulk products" on 30 million packages. Other tie-ins involved everything from "Hulk Coleman outdoor cooking grills" to Glad sandwich bags and David sunflower seeds "Revved up Hulk Power Pack."

At the End of the Day

From material concept to merchandising contract, the producers are often the only collaborators who oversee the film for the full length of its long run. In fact, it can be argued that with video and television exposure, the long run never really ends. Ed Feldman says all of this places an extra burden on the producer.

You have to be careful of what you do these days because it doesn't go away. It's great to see your name on a picture, but if it's a bomb you don't want to see it too often. Your picture is going to play forever. Save the Tiger was 1972 and it still plays on television. And it's still a very important movie. On the other hand, a long time ago I produced a cult skiing film called Hot Dog: The Movie. Maybe not my best work. But I still get revenues from it every year and send out checks to the people involved. And people still watch it.

Gale Anne Hurd describes the process as a kind of relationship. "You go through this process with every film you work on...early on you think it's the best thing you've ever done and you don't see any flaws." After looking at a rough-cut, she explains, "You realize all the compromises you made along the line and you think it's awful. It's the worst thing that's ever been done. How did I delude myself into thinking this is any good? Eventually your attitude comes out somewhere in between."

Once the film has been released and had its theatrical run, there is finally time for reflection. Hurd learned an interesting lesson regarding the long-term impact of films while traveling in Micronesia.

I was on a boat and I happened to visit islands that are rarely visited by tourists. These people fish out of dugout canoes. But they had this one generator that they would power up a few times each month to provide electricity for a TV and a VCR.

When I found out they had all seen Terminator 2, *it was terrifying. I didn't want to invade their culture with something that would impact them the way it did. Here were these peaceful people living in paradise, but with no running water, indoor plumbing, or telephones. And they had all become fans of Arnold Schwarzenegger and urban, action-oriented entertainment.*

At that moment I realized that whatever you may think your responsibility is, it's overwhelming. It changed my perspective on the influence that I have as a producer. There are very few places left in the world that will not be impacted by films.

For better or worse, the producers' legacy can be found in the films that bear their names. Like writers, directors and all other film collaborators, this is what they will leave behind, forever. "The ultimate satisfaction is putting the finished movie up on the screen and being able to watch the audience respond," says Kennedy. "Very few people get to have a job where you create something that generates immediate feedback. That's quite unique and that's what's addictive about this business."

In the producer's day-to-day world, there is little time for such reflection, but the most caring and successful producers have thought long and hard about what it all means. And each of them has an agenda of her or his own. "I won't do any pictures where women are debased," says Ed Feldman. "I find it appalling in this business today—graphic depictions of rape at knifepoint—there are people sitting out there in a dark room watching and you're responsible for that." He leans over his desk for emphasis. "All these high-minded depictions about how life doesn't imitate art. I don't buy it. I think we are very responsible for what we put out there. You have to be very careful."

Such sentiments are sure to spark a debate among filmmakers and David Puttnam would like to see more of it.

I used to talk quite a bit about the need for debate. It still hasn't happened. I find it staggering that such illustrious organizations as the Motion Picture Academy or the American Film Institute have no ongoing format for debate or the clash of ideas on what cinema is and what its role in society should be. By not having those debates, we're allowing the media to do it for us. Whether it is the liberals or the conservatives that are attacking us—we should be ahead of them about values. We should be taking the lead in that debate and not merely responding to it.

For his part, Richard Zanuck worries most about the films the audience never gets to see.

There are lot of pictures that never get made because people don't have the courage to make them. A lot of the pictures I've been associated with were very tough battles to get made. There's a real audience out there, starved for these pictures. When one sneaks through, people respond by saying "Finally, there's a picture that we want to go see!"

What is a producer? What should a producer be? "In fact, we are paid seducers." David Puttnam laughs. "Our job is to seduce audiences, but to seduce them in ways which I believe are user-friendly, as opposed to ways in which it can be damaging."

I want to make films that don't attempt to pretend the world is a simple place—because that's one of the things I find most damaging about many of today's pictures. They're selling the audience a bill of goods because they pretend the problems of our society are not complex and that the application of brute force by two buddies on the police force can solve them all.

For the best film producers, the stakes are high; yet it's not about money but something of far greater value. "Yes, life is complex," Puttnam concludes, "but at the same time it is also worth living. I want to show people that if you actually apply yourself, you *can* make a difference. That's what it's really all about."

Steven Haft takes a particular pride in the enduring impact of *Dead Poets Society.* "The movie affected people in powerful ways. Every time I went to a party and someone introduced me as the producer of *Dead Poets,* there would be another story of a person who saw it and left a job, or made some serious life change."

And at the end of the day, every producer seems to long to secure a safe journey from script to screen for a film that will make a difference in the lives of those who see it. As Haft reveals, sometimes that realization that success has come at last can happen in a single special moment.

I can remember the moment when the film's impact really crystallized for me. My wife and I were in New York, walking down the street with Robin Williams and his wife, Marsha. This middle-aged man came up to Robin and simply said, "Thank you," for Dead Poets. *Robin bowed to him slightly and turned to me and smiled. He told me there was a definite difference in how people approached him about this film versus his other work. Usually people say, "Hey, great film," and so on. And that's fine. But with this picture it was always "Thank you." That's a very gratifying reward for our efforts.*

CLOSE-UP
THE PRODUCERS: BRIAN GRAZER, RON HOWARD AND KAREN KEHELA

Finding the Property
BRIAN GRAZER: Ron and I were interested in doing a movie about the mentally disabled, specifically the subset of schizophrenia and John Nash's story worked really well as a vehicle to speak for the mentally disabled and to try to shed positive light on the subject. The book of *A Beautiful Mind* was out, written by Sylvia Nasar, but John Nash didn't want to sell his rights. Then Sylvia wrote an article for *Vanity Fair* about John Nash. Graham Carter, the editor of *Vanity Fair*, called me and said, "I think this would make a good movie."

The book has a different style and tone than the article, but *Vanity Fair* captured enough of the story that I knew I wanted to do it. I asked Universal to buy the book for Imagine, which they did.

RON HOWARD: I was doing two films back to back, so the timing wasn't right for me to do this movie when Imagine first got the rights and I didn't want to hold Brian up. Later, the script evolved to a place where Universal was interested, so it all came together.

Finding the Writer

BRIAN: Karen submitted a list of possible writers to me and we sent the book out to a few of them. Around this same time, Akiva Goldsman had submitted the book to Warner Bros. but they passed. Then he came to us and said that he wanted to adapt it. He was on our writer's list, but we hadn't yet sent it out to him.

Akiva and I and Karen Kehela had a meeting, then Akiva and Stacey Snider from Universal had a meeting. We all listened to his particular approach to the material.

Akiva came up with the idea of creating a reality for the viewer, so that for two thirds of the movie all the people you encountered you believed were real—allowing the audience to experience schizophrenia the way Nash did. Akiva wanted to do it so badly and he had a take on it, to get you inside the mind of mental illness. So we hired him.

I knew that I didn't want the movie told in a linear fashion. I didn't want the "womb to tomb" story. I also wanted something that glamorized mathematicians during that time. In the 1940s, these people were the rock stars of their era. It wasn't a group of nerdy guys with pens in their pockets.

When the movie opens, we hear Judd Hirsch saying that mathematicians won the war. I mentioned the film *Top Gun* and how you looked at those guys and thought they were the coolest guys in the world.

Once Akiva was hired, he and Karen then went into a conference room and spent nine days breaking down the story.

Developing the Script

KAREN KEHELA: Besides being the executive producer of this film, I'm also the co-chair of Imagine Films. Brian sets the direction and I work on the development of the script with the writer. Akiva and I went into that conference room day after day and every day we would start by going back to the beginning and re-telling the story. We knew what we wanted the first act, second act and third act to be and I worked very closely with Akiva in building that structure.

We played with the idea of starting as an old man and then going back, since the book starts with Nash as a child. We had versions where he was a little boy, we had him doing a mathematical trick, but eventually those things went by the wayside in the screenplay.

In another version, we plotted it out as an escalating thriller. We knew that John was going to be recruited by the CIA in the person of Parcher. We talked about the first time he meets Parcher and how Parcher is appealing to his ego. So we wanted to tailor the story to this. We knew that eventually it's going to get scarier and scarier and scarier, but we also knew that John believes all of this is real.

We knew that we were juggling a couple of things. Nash needs to meet Alicia after he's already had his first conversation with Parcher. Then we would juggle what's going on with Parcher while at the same time juggling this burgeoning love story. We knew the love story had to come in by the beginning of the second act because, at its heart, this film is a love story. With every idea, we'd keep asking, "What's going to happen after that?"

We knew it would be difficult when the audience is informed that none of this is real. Eventually, we had to have the scene in the kitchen when Nash asks, "What do people do?" Even in editing and dealing with the structure of the script, we knew for sure that there was very little that the audience could tolerate before he stopped taking his medication. We were never 100 percent sure, until we were cutting the movie, how much could be tolerated, how much made sense, how much John and the audience would put up with.

We asked, "How did he know that none of it is real?" so we came up with the idea that Marcy never gets older. So all these decisions happened over the course of creating what was eventually a ten-page outline.

From Outline to Script

KAREN: While Akiva was writing the script, I didn't really get pages, but he would call me when working on a very difficult scene. At one point, we talked for quite a time about the scene right after John discovers that Marcy never gets older. They're sitting at a table and we wanted to include Alicia in the process and we wanted to make it clear that Alicia was part of the solution, so there was a lot of dialogue written about Alicia putting two and two together. Basically Alicia suggests that if you choose to focus on this reality, you can force yourself to be better. It's a very abstract idea.

So Akiva wrote many versions of that and would read them to me over the phone, so he'd call me and say, "I'm struggling with this, here's where I am," and we'd talk that through. Eventually I read much longer versions and then would edit them. We were also always fighting the fact that we knew the secret and the goal was to make sure the audience didn't know the secret until after the midpoint. Sometimes I told Akiva that I thought Parcher sounded too spooky and so he didn't seem real. So we'd change that. We were so protective of that secret in developing it, that we were hypervigilant about it.

Researching the Math

KAREN: At one point in the development, we sat in to observe certain math classes. It isn't that you get lost in the lecture; you *start out* lost. It's like coming into an advanced conversational French class when you don't speak French. We all had college degrees, we had all taken certain math classes, but it didn't matter.

It was clear to us that we were completely out of our league, but they are cool guys, they weren't a group of nerds. Mathematicians see something that is not understandable to us, so we had to make the audience think that these were a group of cool guys. So it was an intentional effort to make the audience connect.

Preproduction

BRIAN: I really believed in the story and believed that actors and directors would want to do it. Once the script was completed, we sent it over to our agent at CAA to package it. They decided not to send it out, but to let people come to the script. There was a lot of interest and eventually there was interest from Robert Redford as director and Tom Cruise as the actor. Around this same time, Ron read the completed script and decided he was interested and agreed to make the movie. Once Ron got involved, we talked about how we saw the movie. Eventually, we reduced this story into a sentence or two that we followed throughout the film.

RON : We were all sitting around a table—Akiva, Karen and me— and I had this idea about adding a proposal scene. We talked about this idea about Nash saying, "What if I wanted to marry you?"

KAREN: Then I suggested, maybe she should say back, "How do you know I want to marry you?" Because I wanted to make sure that Alicia wasn't a kind of wallflower. We wanted to make it clear that she's a match for him.

RON: We talked about showing the struggle for verifiable proof of love. How do you know it's there? You don't. Akiva would say that there are several ideas to this scene—that Nash is awkward with women. He's a mathematician who thinks like a mathematician even in his feelings about love.

Casting Choices

RON: I wanted someone with nerve to play John Nash. I saw an intelligence with Nash and whoever played him had to have that intelligence. Russell Crowe is intense and smart, so I arranged to meet with him. I was convinced immediately.

BRIAN: We read hundreds of actresses. We needed an actress who would challenge Russell so he'd stay at the top his game.

RON: There was a tremendous interaction between Jennifer and Russell as actors. So Jennifer was cast.

On the Set

KAREN: I was on the set every day, but not full time. Akiva was also on the set, so there were rewrites going on during rehearsal and filming. Russell was very specific about putting a lot more humor into John and suggested a line like, "There's a mathematical explanation for how bad your tie is." We wanted to soften Nash up and warm the audience to him so he wouldn't be so remote. So Russell would add lines and Akiva would go back and rewrite.

Todd Hallowell was the other executive producer on the film and he was more of a line producer. He was in charge of all the physical production and shot the 2nd unit on the movie as the director.

The Film Is Released

KAREN: After the film was released, we would see it with audiences and we were surprised at some of the reactions. When Dr. Rosen (Christopher Plummer) told Alicia that Nash had imaginary delusions and she said, "What kind of delusions?" and he responds, "One that we know of, an imaginary roommate named Charles," we kind of expected an "Ahhh!" but instead, there was complete silence. People would just stare.

And he goes back and forth, talking about how the records show that he didn't have a roommate at Princeton, etc. There were some audience members who didn't believe that he was sick until Alicia went into the shed. It was a complete shock.

The Collaborative Roles

KAREN: The driving force is Brian.

RON: Brian provides a safety net. He understands the big thematic values, the big picture. I get fascinated with details. Brain has distance and the objectivity, so he's like that first audience. When we agree on something, that becomes a strong choice.

BRIAN: Was it hard to make? No. My movies aren't really hard to make—what is hard is to find exactly the right artistic elements that would be the foundation of the movie.... That is hard. The making of the movie is less hard—if you do the foundation right. If it's wrong, then it's a mess anyway.

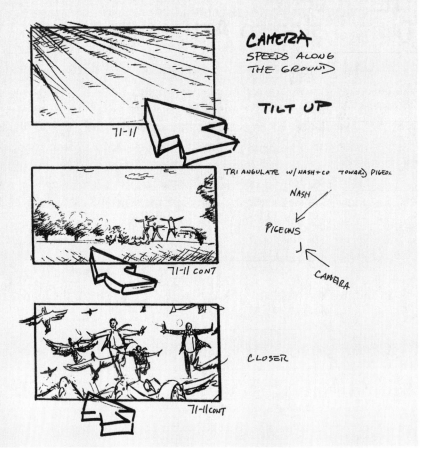

*Every film has its
own life, its own
destiny that must be
guided. The reason
we make films is that
films are forever.*

—**Norman Jewison**

The Director:
From Vision to Action

Look carefully at Ron Howard and you can still catch a glimpse of Opie, the character who so captivated us on *The Andy Griffith Show,* or Richie Cunningham of *Happy Days* fame. Mayberry is a distant memory, but Howard's experiences as an actor left an indelible mark. He begins by explaining how they helped shape his decision to become a director.

> *As a kid I loved hanging around with the actors, but I also loved hanging around with the crew and it didn't take me long to discover that the director was the one who got to play with everyone. That's what I feel like. There's something very electrifying, energizing and very rewarding about being at the center of all these creative discussions.*

In an interview on CNBC, Howard reveals that he faced the same kind of problems as any would-be director:

> *You know, people were downright patronizing when I said I wanted to be a director. I wasn't just dreaming. I wasn't being a dilettante. I was going to film school. I was making films on my own. I was writing scripts. I was thinking about it virtually every waking hour.*

Howard's directing career has spanned over two decades now and from his first film—A Roger Corman action film titled *Grand Theft Auto*, to his trip up to the stage to collect his Oscar for *A Beautiful Mind*—the modest, soft-spoken director always seems to find more praise for his collaborators than for his own efforts.

Asked about *Mind* he explains, "It was a very inspiring and unusual story. It features incredible performances by Jennifer Connelly and Russell Crowe. That's a great combination. A fresh, original, exciting, story and great action." He pauses for a moment and smiles. "Maybe the director did his job in there somewhere too."

What is a director's job? What is a director's "role?" Roland Joffe's first feature was *The Killing Fields*. "Being a director is like playing on a multi-layered, multi-dimensional chessboard, except that the chess pieces decide to move themselves."

But do they? Director Norman Jewison (*Moonstruck, The Hurricane*) has a contrasting theory. "The most important thing is to manipulate. Some people call it communication or inspiration. I call it manipulation. The director is constantly manipulating people, whether it's the actor, cameraperson, sound, lighting, composer or writer. They're trying to manipulate everyone to conform to their interpretation, their vision."

In an interview on Canadian television Jewison elaborates. "You have to have a good rhythm, good timing. I think directors should know a little bit about everything." He pauses and adds "And I think you should find a good pair of shoes. It's hard on your feet!"

A director's footprints must lead to the collaborative spark, that electric energy that drives a classic film from script to screen. Along the way a series of creative discussions must be held. At the center of virtually all of them is the director, who is the person who functions as a kind of living touchstone around which all other creative decisions swirl. And there's always the danger that ego will get in the way.

In an *Esquire* interview Robert Redford confides, "I never even think of myself as a director when I'm directing. I think of what I'm trying to say."

And the director is also a team captain, forming the troops into a cohesive squad. Ron Shelton agrees that the director's ego must never get in the way of what's best for the picture. Instead, he thinks in terms of the egos of his collaborators. "You don't want to crush the egos. You want to max the egos. You want them to be all they want to be, yet it's a team game."

According to Director's Guild of America President Martha Coolidge (*Rambling Rose, Introducing Dorothy Dandridge*), "Any director needs a strong male and a strong female side, an ability to move the film along with a nurturing side." Amy Heckerling (*Fast Times at Ridgemont High, Clueless*) agrees with a grin: "You have to know about painting, music, literature and costumes, but most of all, you gotta have heart."

With younger and less experienced directors there is always the danger of intimidation. Working on only his second film, Sam Mendes (*American Beauty, Road to Perdition*) found himself directing Paul Newman. But in the end, "You immediately have a working relationship with them...and it's as simple as that," he explains.

Mendes tells CBS' *Early Show* that the key is to at least *appear* to be in charge. He came from a theater background and was used to "exploring" with stage actors and asking questions. But all of that changed when he moved into film.

> *If you say, "I don't know," on a film set it's like, "Well, if you don't know, who does? You're the person who's got to know!" So even if you don't know you have to pretend that you do and just keep going until you've got something to cling to.*

Scripts and Directors: "Choose Me!"

In the beginning there is the word. Hollywood is full of scribes trying to create "the write stuff," scripts that will attract the attention of top directors. Contrary to popular belief, there are a *lot* of well-written scripts out there. This fact alone does not guarantee that they will find their way to the screen. Barry Levinson explains this rather contradictory process in terms of the personal challenges a script provides.

> *I'll read some scripts and say, "This is a good script but I already know it and I don't know what else to do, it's all just there." I've got to find something that ultimately challenges me to the point where I don't know if I can make it work.*

Is there a magic formula for attracting a top director to a script? Sometimes it seems that there are as many answers as there are directors.

For those whose success has given them a large measure of freedom in choosing the projects they pursue, interest in a script can stem from a set of values and experiences that stretch as far back as childhood.

Martha Coolidge read the script for *Rambling Rose* and was struck by a visual description that connected her to a personal memory.

You're always looking for a metaphor that is extremely visual and dramatic so that it becomes a picture and not just words on the page. In the script there was an image of sunlight coming through the window in a kitchen, this vivid light hitting the fruit on the kitchen table. And I realized that Rose brought love and light into that family. The metaphor came out of the writing, but the visual image gave birth to the design of the entire film, the way the cinematographer lit it, the production designer's color scheme, everything else.

The image was just like a memory that I have of my grandmother's house. I actually made a documentary about my grandmother, which has a lot of things in common with Rambling Rose. *So there was this connection to my feelings about my grandmother's house.*

Oliver Stone remembers his own childhood and how it led him to the kinds of "civic minded" projects (*Born on the Fourth of July, JFK, Nixon*) that have become his trademark.

My father always talked politics and ideas at the table. I grew up in that tradition of talking and writing and discussing ideas. So, many of my movies are issue-oriented. I try to show the cause and effect of the world around me.

Norman Jewison is another director whose enthusiasm is driven by the social terrain that a story explores and his conviction that "films are forever."

First of all, it has to be a good story, but I'm looking for an idea behind the writing—political or emotional or a thrust of truth. Somewhere along the line, hopefully the film is going to affect thinking, your concept of life. It's the idea behind a work of art that perhaps makes the work of art enduring.

For Roland Joffe, the challenge of transforming real events into feature films yields the most enduring art of all.

I love taking a true event and asking, "What was it like to be inside it?" The Mission came from a true-life story, Killing Fields from a magazine article, City of Joy from a book. I like to put myself in a situation where you're confronted by the fact that it is true, it is real. I try to make it like a life experience, to give it the same volatility as life and some people are very uncomfortable with that.

Director John Singleton emphasizes that from the beginning he was trying to give voice to stories that have not appeared on film before and remain true to his own experience. "I'm a black male living in America. I have to draw on that to make films," he says. "It's all I know. It's not that I am trying to change the world, but good film work will always find its way into the culture. You put the movie out, then it's on its own." He cites his first film as an example.

Boyz N the Hood was a street fairy tale. It was a story that a lot of people have lived, it was a lot like their own lives. So they rallied behind it. They felt, "Hey, that's my story, that's my experience." And they don't see that story on the screen very often.

Of course not every classic film is driven by the burning need to make a social statement. Even Singleton went on to make *Shaft*. But most powerful films explore some aspect of human behavior that is "real" in the sense that it resonates within the director and the audience as well. Ron Shelton describes it a quest for "honest moments." Like Stone, he can trace it back to his roots.

I'm interested in doing films about real human behavior. Even a pratfall is an honest moment if it's earned and it's utterly dishonest if it's not earned. My mother used to say, "Give people their dignity and you'll be amazed how many times they rise to the occasion." She treated everyone the same and I'm sure some of that rubbed off on me. I start by embracing the characters because I identify with them.

Creating an unforgettable character in a script can be the key to winning the heart of a director because so many directors begin by considering how the character's journey through the story will ultimately affect the audience. For Ron Howard this is the single most important consideration.

Everything is changing all the time. If you're trying to maintain the status quo, you're probably going backward. I think there is some sort of force within us to be better people. We have it within our power to actually phase out certain behaviors, such as violence, and create viable alternatives.

Directors like Howard tend to seek out material that will confirm their own worldview. More often than not this involves an attempt to carefully select the kind of stories that will have a lasting and positive impact on the audience.

With his penchant for hard-hitting real-life stories, Roland Joffe sees the differences between life as it is and life "as it should be" as a source of persistent inspiration. "To me, life is very volatile, chaotic, complex. There is an immense difference between the world people want to inhabit and the world we do inhabit. And that fascinates me."

And then there are those projects that simply "call out" to the director. Peter Weir explains:

In the end I don't choose the material, the material chooses me. You get an emotion rather like the way music can affect you. And then you know you are going to do it. With any project, the challenge is to put that initial emotional response that you had at that first reading on the screen.

You can't define the emotion because it's like a ripple through your body. It's like describing how you feel when you hear Mozart—moved. Touched. It's something so strong that it can sustain you for a minimum of twelve months of production and dealing with hundreds of people and practical problems.

What conclusions are possible regarding the kind of script likely to attract a top director? In the end, patterns begin to emerge. Mendes, Joffe, Stone, Singleton and Jewison all tend to seek out the difficult political and social truths. Barry Levinson searches for scripts and stories that challenge him to make them work. Martha Coolidge seeks visual metaphors. Ron Howard prefers projects that are life-affirming. Ron Shelton tries to find the honest moments. Peter Weir wants to be moved.

And of course everyone wants "a good story" with "strong character development." Put these reasons all together and they offer a good overview into the kinds of scripts that are likely to attract the industry's most respected and successful directors.

Research: Getting Inside the Material World

Once the director has settled on a project, the development process goes into high gear. Since the story may be based on a book, real-life event, existing script, or some combination, research is usually required to get inside the material.

It's hard to imagine a more formidable research job than that employed in the making of *JFK*. For Oliver Stone, it was the Herculean task of gathering written, film and video material from hundreds of public and private sources and then weaving them together into various story lines.

> In *JFK*, *there are four threads—the Garrison story; the Oswald history, which comes from a combination of public sources and* Crossfire, *the Jim Marrs book; there's the reenactment in Dealy Plaza, which is based on Marrs plus public sources and witnesses that I talked with. The fourth part of the screenplay is essentially the Mr. X story—the Fletcher Prouty story, which he told me when I interviewed him in Washington.*

Getting inside the story often requires a kind of "method direction" as the director goes into the field to share in the lives of those who are to be portrayed on the screen. It's easy to imagine the kind of research that would go into a "real life story" about mental illness (*A Beautiful Mind*) but what about an action story like *Backdraft*? Ron Howard began by getting a taste of what it was like to be a firefighter. "The writer had been a firefighter. And I spent some time with the firefighters. I spent a night in a firehouse, went out on some runs with them."

Shooting a film set in another country carries with it a special set of research challenges. The director must learn enough about the other culture to present it honestly on the screen. In these situations Roland Joffe is not one to cut corners.

> For City of Joy *I went to Calcutta several times over four years, traveling on a bus, staying in villages. Most people see the India of the gurus, or the India of the Taj Mahal, but that isn't the truth about India. The truth is the teeming immensity of the struggle of life.*

Martha Coolidge says, "Good research is very critical," and explains how it often leads her to important information she uses in her films. In a crucial scene in *Rambling Rose*, a sinister doctor suggests to the rest of the family that Rose's sexually charged nature could be surgically "taken care of" without her knowledge.

> *I found out that ovariectomies and clitorectomies were commonly done in the 1930s. They were doing a lot of experimental psychological surgeries. That related to the attempted "castration," so to speak, of Rose. To say nothing of the contemporary metaphor of a woman's right to her own body. I learned as a documentary filmmaker that in reality, in the truth, you find much greater and more interesting images and a variety of details than you ever would find in something that you made up.*

The best research is that which yields a true vision of the arena in which the story takes place. Ideally this means going beyond the cultural clichés to create a dynamic and insightful script that will result in an honest movie.

Shaping the Script

As research nears completion, there is generally a need to reshape the script to get it ready for production. Virtually all directors will provide input at this point. Sometimes this results in major changes. In the original *Dead Poets Society* script, the Robin Williams character was dying. In *Alien*, the Sigourney Weaver character was a man.

Then there are minor revisions that may involve changing locations, seasons, or transforming a scene on a bus to one on a train. Some directors will do rewrites themselves, becoming a co-writer on the script. Others spend hours working with the writer to achieve clarity in the story and richer emotional nuances in the characters. During this crucial period, Oliver Stone likes to work directly with the other writers. At the same time, he maintains a discreet but discernible distance.

> *I co-write the script but I believe in sitting there alone. I never work in the same room unless it's an audio experience, like with Richard Boyle in* Salvador. *He told me stories, but I basically shaped them...dramatized them. With Ron Kovic (Born on the Fourth of July), mostly he talked. He talked. I shaped. I often overwrite, almost deliberately. I'd rather shoot more and shoot a little more intensely and overdo it and look to come back in the editing.*

There is a tremendous variation in terms of how directors shape scripts as production nears. Peter Weir notes that his scripts become "rainbows" since each revision is done in a different color.

> *The script is a living thing. I will be constantly changing things. Most of my scripts are blue, or blue and pink and green. There are really very few of the original white pages left. The original pages to me are only a guide. I keep changing them—it could be visuals, the order of a sequence of a scene, it could be an idea, any of those.*
>
> *I collect pictures and magazine photos, a lot of visual references, which are a personal inspiration that carry the film. These go in the back of my script and some of them will get hooked up into individual scenes. When all is said and done, eventually you get to a place where everything seems fine. It seems like there is nothing else you can possibly do. It's just right.*

Yet, for Weir, there remains one more period of adjustment and it is now that intuition comes to the forefront.

> *Then a couple of weeks go by and all the experiences, all of your antennae are active, you're extremely intuitive. Talking to the crew, dinner at a restaurant, a man you saw standing at the bus stop, the plane flight over, the stop in Hawaii—all are going through your computer banks and being sorted and translated for anything that might be useful to your*

story. I think the whole process of directing has to do with this heightened sensitivity that one has during that period of time.

For Norman Jewison the art of revision begins with a series of notes.

I make a lot of little notes about how something should be said or what that person is feeling right at this point. I'm constantly reading the scenes and performing them. I read the scenes out loud and I play some parts and the writer plays the other parts.

With any luck, the process eventually begins to reveal the essence of the story. Like a sculptor slowly chiseling an obstinate piece of granite, Jewison "romances" that stone by seeking out the distinct emotions inherent in each scene.

I'm looking for the secret of the revelation of human emotions. I'm looking for comedy, the humor that's in life. Every day I laugh, almost every day I'm brought to tears. Laughter and tears are two very basic emotions that must be in every single story and in almost every scene. It's the yin and the yang because there's something constantly touching us and pulling at us.

Keeping the emotional content of the story uppermost in mind, Jewison shapes the script into its final form.

I work with the writer to make the script as revealing as possible through honest behavior. The transitions from one scene to another must be absolutely seamless so the story flows with a certain rhythm and an ease. This is the art of screenwriting.

Every Picture Tells a Story

As the script nears production, the director begins to "see the movie" in visual terms. At this crucial juncture the art of directing comes to the forefront. The very best directors will make creative visual choices that enhance the script and breathe life into the story. Ron Howard explains:

By the time I'm committed, I'm already starting to make little notes, lit-
tle visual ideas in the margins. Generally that first round of ideas gets
thrown out. They can be as simple as drawing a line along three-quar-
ters of a page of dialogue between two characters and saying, "This
should be a two-shot because it's overlapping," or, "It would be great if
all this played in a full-figure shot because it's important to let the audi-
ence know that these people are part of a world and to show them that
world as part of the background."

The location might be written "backyard—day" and we ultimately
might find that the scene would play better in the subway at night. It
might be something as simple as, "I need a powerful image here." I might
not know what it is.

The search for images is unrelenting. Ridley Scott's work in *Alien*
established him as a Hollywood director with a definite visual style. You
can glimpse his background as a painter as he describes the process. "You
need to keep an overall image in mind. I think in terms of light, visuals,
sound, texture."

The ability to think in pictures and intuitively sense when a shot will
work is something that all the best directors seem to possess. As Scott
describes the now-famous opening title sequence from the widely acknowl-
edged classic *Thelma & Louise*, you begin to see how the process works.

I had no idea how to start the movie. So while I was in Utah, I was
standing on this perfect road that went to a mountain and somehow the
whole thing represented freedom. So I banged off a six-minute shot
knowing that somewhere I'd use it—and I ended up using it on the open-
ing titles.

Sometimes a single image might serve as a metaphor for an entire story.
Roland Joffe found one for *City of Joy*. "The rickshaw is a central metaphor
for the whole movie. It's the freedom of work and the enslavement of a burden, it's power, but under the power of others. It contains all the complex-
ities and paradoxes of India. Notice it is also a kind of family member, they
take it inside with them when they sleep."

Perhaps one of the most powerful uses of the "image as metaphor"
school of thought came during *Dead Poets Society* when Director Peter

Weir decided to include a number of isolated shots of small birds. He recalls the shoot:

There were a lot of birds around because of the harvesting of the various crops in the area. They moved like schools of fish. I've never seen so many small birds! They almost formed a shape and they would swirl and it would look like a question mark. I'd sometimes stop the car when I saw them on the ground to go and startle them to see how they would move. I said to the main unit cameramen, "Let's get some shots of those birds because I like them." Later I said, "If you see birds on the way to work, you should be late."

So the birds became a motif and they seemed to be full of hidden meaning. They're like those anonymous kids at the school, everyone is in uniforms, there's no individuality. Keating is sort of naming the birds. It's talking about individuality and finding your own individual voice and so forth. Not swirling and moving with the group. In editing, we placed the birds next to the image of the boys coming down the stairs, the image of this freedom and flying versus this very contained space. I always thought of the boys like birds, just moving in a group, without individual shape and focus.

Whether it's a visual image for the entire film or for a single scene, each decision must be thought through carefully, with an eye toward building layers of meaning in the film.

In *Bugsy*, Barry Levinson's imaginative use of a blank screen shrouds the two central characters who appear as shadows. This visual device, used in their first love scene, provides one of the film's most memorable moments and offers a kind of visual commentary on the "Hollywood syndrome."

Bugsy Siegel and Virginia Hill wanted to be movie stars. He had a screen test made. He saw himself as a leading man. So here were these two people who wanted to be movie stars who never made it. I thought it would be interesting for these two lovers to end up on the wrong side of the screen, to play it as silhouettes behind a blank screen and end up as a negative rather than a positive.

A different kind of visual predicament faced Ron Howard in *Backdraft* when he decided to go with four major fire sequences. How to keep from being redundant?

I wanted each of them to evoke a little different sort of feeling or reaction from the audience. Visually, I didn't want us to be repeating ourselves in the fire, so I tried to come up with four different styles.

The first fire, which the child observes at the beginning, we did as a more dreamlike fire, from a child's point of view. The second, as the fire character begins to evolve and grow, we turned into combat footage. We have a rookie firefighter and we stay pretty much with him and it's a sense of how hellish, how violent, how chaotic and how terrifying the whole experience could be.

Our next major fire sequence is the haunted fire, the supernatural. Doors breathing. Firefighters would talk about the fire as a creature, an opponent. We shot this with a Steadicam, a lot like Alien. *Where was the fire going to pop up? Lights flickering, that sequence was more like a thriller, a monster.*

The last had little camera movement. When it was moving, the movement was broad and sweeping. That sequence was shot more traditionally, more operatic. More like a western, a mythical confrontation.

Myth and Meaning

Envisioning mythical confrontations and finding appropriate visual metaphors for them is at the heart of the directing process. Ridley Scott reveals that with *Thelma & Louise*:

The mythical dimension really begins on Louise (Susan Sarandon) as she sits outside while Thelma (Geena Davis) is robbing a store. And she looks at an elderly woman who's staring back at her. It was a moment where she starts to [put on] make up and then decides not to and throws the lipstick away. And there's a moment when she looks at the woman who is staring back at her through the window and that to me is a way of saying, "You better make a decision about your life before it passes." And then Thelma comes out from robbing the store and says, "Drive," and from that moment on they pass over, they cross the line, they leave their old reality behind.

As a director who built his reputation on action pictures, Scott is acutely aware of the pitfalls of the genre. "I think dynamics are not car chases or people shooting each other but story and emotional dynamics, the exchange of information." Of course, it all begins with the script, but it's the director who needs to find the image, build it, clarify it and give it form.

You can take a great script and just shoot it. Thelma & Louise was an excellent script, as good as you're liable to get. But the choice becomes, "What do you want an audience to feel at the end of it?" Do you want to take this script as a straight-ahead story and treat it as a docudrama, or feel marginally mystical at the end of it, since these characters become two mystical figures in a way?

Many contend that the decision to go with the mystical ending transformed the film from a well-executed genre piece to a groundbreaking masterpiece. Scott modestly concedes, "The journey of these two characters became a slightly more elevated experience than just two girls in a car being pursued by the law."

Hear It Now: The Inflections of Film

A director's decisions involve an intuitive process that seeks out the basic rhythms in each scene and story. This process applies to the characters as well as to the film as a whole. Norman Jewison sees, senses and *hears* the rhythms. "Certain films have a slow lyrical style, others a more staccato rhythm. *Moonstruck* is an opera: Loretta (Cher) is the lyric soprano, Cosmo (Vincent Gardenia) the bass, Ronny (Nicholas Cage) is the tenor, Johnny (Danny Aiello) is the baritone and the mother (Olympia Dukakis) is the contralto."

John Singleton focuses extensively on the language of his characters, what they say and how they say it. His gritty visual style provides a perfect match for the stories he wants to tell.

The whole thing about black cinema—about films produced by black people for a black core audience—is that you must do it in the language of the culture. You don't try to water it down any more than you would try to water down Japanese culture if you were producing films for a Japanese core audience.

If you get it right, it comes out like strong coffee and it keeps you awake. If you water down the language with cream and sugar, it won't have the same effect.

My films are not about people I have seen or have met. They are about people I know. My characters say things that ordinary people say, exactly as they would say them. Sometimes they're funny. Sometimes they're dramatic. But mostly they are real.

Getting in touch with the reality of each script invariably involves listening carefully for the inflections inherent in them. It's almost as if they have a life of their own and it becomes the director's job to "tune in." Oliver Stone explains:

I've always found that I have different rhythms for each film. And it has dictated the pace of my life, the tone of my life, the editing room, the music, it becomes like an acting job. You live inside that rhythm—that wheel—for that year or two years or whatever it takes. Every film has its music. A visual rhythm.

The Casting Quandary

While directors "tune in" to their scripts to discover the life within them they must also think about choosing the right cast members—those real-life human beings who will physically bring the script to life. How important is this process? Ron Howard fondly recalls the day Bette Davis told him, "Ninety-five percent of directing is the script and the casting. Once you've done that, the rest is knowing how to stay the hell out of the way and still get the movie shot."

Ron Shelton's experiences with the audition process reveal a fundamental and oft-cited casting quandary.

I'd never been in auditions until I started casting Bull Durham. *So suddenly I'm sitting with a casting director and actors are coming in and I don't know what to say. I said, "That's great, read it again." Pretty soon I realized how terrifying the experience is. If the actors succeed in passing that terror—then they have the real terror—now they're onstage and in front of the camera.*

For White Men Can't Jump *we read over three hundred guys. Ten of them were great basketball players. I'd look at them in the outer office flirting with the secretary, nervous energy, couldn't sit down, up and down. Then they'd come in and they'd be just deadly, dull. Something happened when they walked through that door—they had the part out there. I would call them back, some of them four times, trying to figure out how to get "out there" in here, trying to help them get rid of that baggage.*

Part of Martha Coolidge's reputation has been built on discovering young "unknown" actors. She often conducts casting workshops. "It's a critical, painful, but very creative part of the business," she explains. "For me it's very rare to see an actor and think that they could never play the part. It's like most actors have the part when they walk in the door, but they lose it in the reading." How does she know when she has found the right person?

Acting talent has to do with a subtext that goes on in the individual that the camera will see. It's often connected with a kind of power that is quite frightening. Some people come in the room and scare me because they are so real or so different or so quiet or angry; these are really good signs.

Another paradox involves how much the actor needs to fit the director's operational vision of the character. Norman Jewison begins with the physical characteristics.

I'm looking for the actor that has the same sound and look and body language—height, weight, age—all those things that I see in my mind. I've been living with these characters for so long. I know them better than the actor at this point because I've lived with them. At the same time, occasionally an actor will come in and he may not look right for the part but he will give something to the character, a dimension that I hadn't even considered. And it will jolt me and then swing me over.

With *Moonstruck*, Jewison ran into a major casting problem immediately.

Cher didn't think she could play the part of Loretta. She said, "I'm not from New York. I don't know how to do that accent." I explained to her that she was a singer and all accents and dialects are rhythmic.

I put her with an Italian lady from Brooklyn to work with her—Julie Bovasso, who played the aunt. I told Cher she was going to be surrounded by people from New York and surrounded with the reality of that sound, that the accent would come. And the dialogue in Moonstruck is so real that you can't possibly go wrong if you stay with the script.

In the most ideal of circumstances, the director may know from the beginning who will best serve the role. In a CBS interview Sam Mendes reveals that when he first received the script for *Road to Perdition* someone said, "'I think Tom Hanks might be interested.' So he was in the back of my mind when I started reading it. And by the time I got to the end he was in the front of my mind. And that was who the part was."

Rehearsal: Searching for "Slightly Unrealized"

Once the major roles have been cast, rehearsals can begin. In today's Hollywood, there is increasingly less rehearsal time and its duration varies according to director preference, the availability of the actors and countless other variables. Generally it will take two or three weeks. Ron Shelton defines what he tries to accomplish during this time.

We spent two weeks rehearsing for White Men Can't Jump. *We'd rehearse in a room and tape off the floors of the sets that we knew. I tell the actor, "I know nothing about blocking. Here's the chair, here's the wall, let's just block it from scratch." The blocking comes out of rehearsal.*

I encourage input from actors. I'll say, "If you don't believe your line of dialogue, let's find a line of dialogue you do believe in." I wrote this character, I know more about this character than anyone, but I want the actor to surprise me. I rewrite the scenes during rehearsals. If we play out a scene and I don't believe it, I'll say I don't believe it and we'll change it. Or if an actor says, "I don't know how to say that," I'll work with him and we'll change the lines.

Like Shelton, Norman Jewison sees rehearsal as an opportunity to get to know his actors and to establish the boundaries of the collaboration. "I love rehearsal. It's very important that you meet and talk about the character. You tell the actors how you see the character. If they disagree with you, then you allow them to prove it."

Of course, every story and location presents special challenges. Often these can be resolved as the rehearsal process evolves. Ron Shelton's films provide a good example.

For White Men *and* Bull Durham, *we had a basketball and a baseball camp that was run by professionals. They would work out all morning and then we'd rehearse all afternoon. All the plays were choreographed. I gave the actors the playbook and they had to learn the plays. Ten to twelve hours a day on asphalt. Over and over. The trick is to make it look unchoreographed.*

Oliver Stone is a firm believer in the rehearsal process. "We rehearse a lot. We rehearse wherever the base is for a week or so and then on location. And then we rehearse the day of the scene—when we start a new scene."

Some directors take their cast on location so they can experience the environment in which they will work. Stone set up a kind of boot camp for *Platoon*. Francis Ford Coppola took his cast to the Philippines for *Apocalypse Now*—a long rehearsal for a legendary shoot that ran more than two hundred days.

It should be noted that not all directors require or even desire rehearsal time. Some prefer to bring the actors to the set and rehearse just before shooting while others simply opt to shoot it all, hoping to catch something unique as the actors play a scene for the first time.

Spontaneity is always an issue. Ron Shelton adds a final note of caution. "One more thing about rehearsal: when I feel it's about there, I quit.

I always get nervous when we nail it in rehearsal. I'd rather leave it slightly unrealized until we shoot."

Lights, Camera, Action!

With rehearsals complete, the lengthy preproduction process finally comes to a close. At long last the time has come to actually shoot the film.

Permits are issued and an armada of hundreds moves into place. Catering trucks roll, wardrobe assistants scramble to dress everyone for the first day's scenes and dozens of production assistants sporting walkie-talkies seem to appear out of nowhere.

In the midst of the chaos the director of photography (cinematographer) works closely with the director to set up each scene. Their collaboration will result in a visual interpretation of the script that will ultimately determine the success or failure of the film.

The late Robert Wise, an Academy Award-winner for *The Sound of Music* and *West Side Story,* had probably been through this process as often as anyone in Hollywood. In one of his final interviews, he revealed his thoughts about a number of crucial issues facing the director on the set of every shoot. Above all, he always stressed preparation and flexibility.

> *Although you have worked out much of the blocking in your mind in the office and may have storyboarded many of the scenes, you don't want to lock yourself in to those shots. Frequently when you're on the set with your actors, you'll find new things you can't anticipate in your office.*

In the simplest terms, it begins with a single question: where to place the camera? The director has a number of options. The camera can pan back and forth or up and down. It can also move, as with a hand-held camera or Steadicam. The cinematographer can follow the actor, or dolly.

Most directors begin with a master shot, where everyone is included in one take. Then the scene is shot again and again as the camera moves in to focus on medium shots, two-shots, or close-ups. During the editing process each take will be screened and creative decisions made regarding which will appear in the final version.

Asked what the director needs to keep in mind during production, Wise began with his own thoughts about the master shots.

You will probably be shooting some master scenes that go on for several pages. The whole scene is done with the camera in one place. You'll need to have a fairly wide shot to show the entire scene. Of course, even while keeping the camera on a stable tripod, you can still tighten a little bit, pan back and forth, or move up and down.

While there will always be debate about the *best* possible place to put the camera, there is a consensus on the worst place. Wise quoted John Ford, who once told him, "An eye-level camera is a dull camera." He explained that the scene is always more dynamic if it's lower or sometimes higher than eye level.

Next comes "coverage." The director will "cover" the scene by shooting it again from various angles and perspectives.

You need plenty of coverage so you have a number of shots to choose from. You have two-shots and close-ups and over-the-shoulder shots in order to have a lot of choices so you can build the scene rhythmically and dramatically. You want to have enough coverage in case you need to fix a scene in editing. When the film is previewed to an audience, maybe there's a laugh line that doesn't work or a line you have to remove. You might decide to use the over-the-shoulder shot so you can dub in a different line.

Despite all of the technical considerations, Wise stressed that the director must never forget what the process is really all about.

The most important thing is the scene itself. Get that scene up there. Get it building. Get it playing. You still always start with the emotional moments—with the actors in the scene. But you're also thinking of how the scene will look within the frame.

I want the image to fill the whole screen. If you add space on the side, you lose the dynamism of your composition. So if I have three people in the scene, perhaps shooting them in a medium shot from the waist up, they'll fill the entire frame—no air on the side.

The Moving Camera: A Matter of Degrees

Now that the camera is in place, the next question is: does it move during the shot? Wise recalled legendary director John Ford's simple philosophy. "He didn't like to move the camera. He liked to move the actors."

In a way, the eye of the camera represents the eyes of the audience. To keep the natural look of a scene, Wise stays away from too much movement.

I don't like to overdo it. Sometimes people take the camera 360 degrees, which makes you conscious of the camera. Try to make the moves fit the action so you're not conscious of the camera moving. The audience should be as unconscious of the filmmaking process as possible.

David Zucker agrees and resents the trend toward epic shots that call attention to themselves. "I don't move the camera unless it's natural to. I'm not proud of great camera moves. They're only great if they help tell a story. If you have to move the camera because the script is boring, you're in trouble."

In fact, Zucker points out that it may be the framing process—rather than the camera movement—that is crucial, at least when shooting comedy. "Comedy happens in the frame. You need to be very exact about what is within the frame, not only making sure that the frame shows the whole joke, but also being aware of the depth of the image."

In *The Naked Gun 2 1/2: The Smell of Fear*, Leslie Nielsen and Priscilla Presley make love on a bed while the traditional fireplace flickers in the background. Look carefully and you'll see a skewer of meat and vegetables slowly turning above it. Zucker explains, "What's going on in the background of a shot might be just as important and as funny as the joke in the foreground. Sometimes the best joke might be in the background."

Technological breakthroughs over the last twenty years have made it more tempting than ever to keep the camera moving. Most notable is the invention of the Steadicam—a camera with weights around it to, literally, keep it steady. It gives the director many options that were unavailable under the old "dolly" system since the camera can move in any direction with no discernable jarring effect.

Historically, one of the most memorable uses of the Steadicam was in Martin Scorsese's *Goodfellas*. The long, breathtaking shot follows the main mob character (Ray Liotta) as he walks down the street and into the side door of the Copacabana restaurant. We journey with him through the kitchen as waiters swirl around, then into the dining room where a table is set up awaiting his arrival. He's seated and Henny Youngman comes onstage and tells a joke—all in one long shot! Michael Ballhaus's cinematography in the scene helps convey Liotta's sense of power and prestige as he is greeted by those he encounters along the way.

A similar approach came at the beginning of Robert Altman's *The Player* as the camera moves slowly across a movie lot, catching various producers, writers and executives pitching projects, gossiping about who's in and out, making lunch plans and opening their mail. Such examples illustrate how camera movement can be essential to the story and theme of a film.

Though the Steadicam has made such breathtaking shots easier there remain those from an earlier era that have left their mark in movie memory. For example, do you remember the scene in *Gone with the Wind* in which Scarlett is surrounded by dying men at the train station? As the camera moves relentlessly back and up and the frame widens, we get an increasingly devastating view of the horrors of war. By the time the long shot is over, a tattered Confederate flag is seen in the foreground and we understand why she runs away, devastated. A spectacular shot and, again, one that was essential to the theme of the film.

Recalling one of his most memorable moving shots, Ron Howard reveals that he had the audience's point of view uppermost in mind.

The last shot of Far and Away *was the first shot that I had thought about for the entire film and it was while we were still writing. I hadn't seen that shot in a movie. So we used a moving crane shot, starting low on Tom Cruise and then quickly moving high. The wide lens on the camera also made it feel like you were really going up there.*

At this point the audience is convinced that the Cruise character is about to die. Howard explains with a mischievous grin, "I thought it would be great to push the audience right to the edge of thinking that we were actually not going to allow a happy ending."

Problems, Problems

Any director—no matter how powerful—sometimes finds the camera at the mercy of actors who simply won't take direction. Amy Heckerling discovered this while shooting *Look Who's Talking*—a film where much of the crucial dialogue came "out of the mouth" of an actor still wearing diapers.

> *The hardest shot was always of the baby sleeping. The baby wouldn't fall asleep with all the commotion on the set. So we'd have the entire crew working with their shoes off in the dark, so the baby would stay asleep as we set up the shot.*
>
> *For the newborn baby, when we wanted it to cry, I'd snap my finger on the bottom of his foot. The nurses do this to check the baby's reactions and to make sure the baby is okay. We could do that with a baby, but if we had an animal on the set, we wouldn't be able to do that. According to animal rights rules; you can't upset a rat!*

By the time she got around to shooting the sequel, Heckerling had picked up a few tricks.

> *We used five different babies, representing different ages. In* Look Who's Talking Too *the toddler, who was about two years old, was very responsive, very intelligent. There's a whole montage where he has to be jealous of his sister and I was able to talk him through the shot by having him mimic me—to look angry, jealous, or to be thinking mean thoughts, or to say, "I hate her." I'd be making the faces and he'd be looking at me and imitating them. He had a wonderful sense of how to react.*

After working with real babies, plastic replicas would seem to be easy. "Not so," says Heckerling. Like any props or special effects sequences, these had problems all their own.

> *We constructed this puppet—the baby inside the womb—but the baby kept breaking down. The plastics and the materials weren't lasting the way they should and there were all these different moving parts on the puppet's face: expressions—one eyebrow, the other eyebrow looked the other way, twist the mouth. During the course of any reaction there's a lot of muscles that get used and usually they wouldn't all work together.*

Each part was controlled by a different puppeteer. They all had to be timed so it might take a few days to set up the shot and we might need to have twenty-five to fifty takes of every movement.

Ready on the Set?

In the midst of the chaos that is the shoot, the director attempts to establish a set where creativity can flourish. Of course, every director has a slightly different approach. In the end, the "tone" of every set is determined to a great extent by the director's personality. Amy Heckerling admits:

> *I'm not the kind of person who gets everybody to sing camp songs or fly paper airplanes. I'm pretty quiet and insofar as I set the tone, it's like I'm not a leader-type person.*
>
> *I like actors a lot and people feel that and feel I'm really happy they are there. They are always free to try something and be silly. They need to be comfortable and not feel like somebody is going to be bothering them and judging them, particularly if they're messing up. Even if I'm not this bandleader type—I want it to be a comfortable place for them.*

Oliver Stone agrees, "I try to feel myself in the shoes of the actors, to feel what they are going through and understand and support them. Because they do need emotional and moral support."

Asked about working with actors, Norman Jewison echoes these sentiments and responds with an obvious and genuine warmth that radiates outward as he speaks.

> *You have to be totally simpatico with your actors. I feel closer to the actor than I do to any other aspect of the film. You really have to like each other, depend on each other, trust each other. The actors must feel that I will protect them, that I am their best friend, that all I want is for them to be wonderful in that role.*

Actors: The Number One Storytelling Tool

The actor is the most vulnerable person on the set and it's up to the director to bring out a great performance in the midst of the actor's uncertainties and insecurities. As Jewison sees it:

> *If there's a problem with the actor, I'll take him or her aside. But if you've had enough rehearsal before you shoot, a lot of the problems will have already emerged. Sometimes it's a wrong line or a problem of behavior or understanding or conflict. It's a matter of talking it out. The last resort is giving a line reading, although I have done it.*
>
> *There have been times that I cleared the set of the crew, closed the picture down, took everybody through a scene and just kept working at it until the right rhythms were there and until I was satisfied.*

Ron Howard often draws on his own acting experiences to achieve those elusive "happy days" on the set. Not surprisingly, he sees a lot of parallels between the two professions.

> *The processes of directing and acting are quite similar. The actors are looking for the honesty in a scene, some breakthrough that is going to allow them to play the scene in order to tell the story.*
>
> *Like the director, they have to be aware of tone, rhythm, the desired result. Is this a comedy? Laugh line? Are people supposed to be crying? Good, creative actors find ways to make that dialogue into something a little more than just straightforward.*
>
> *Directors pretty much have to do the same thing. It's a great advantage to be able to talk to actors. They still are the number-one storytelling tool. You can shoot it wrong, you can have lousy sets and crappy lighting, but if the writing is good and the acting is good, chances are the whole scene will still be effective.*

Howard gazes out the window to the city below as he considers what he is saying.

> *My theory is, if you know where you're supposed to be going with a scene and each character's course within that scene, if the actors can find*

their own way to get there, they will accomplish what they're supposed to accomplish.

Sometimes the only thing an actor needs from a director is "nothing"—to be left alone. Otherwise you impose a lot of ideas on the actors and you're not allowing them the freedom to create. Some actors want to be given a line reading, they want to be given a result. Other actors freeze up when you start talking about a result. You have to be able to talk to the actors and they'll make the adjustment.

Knowing what actors need in order to accomplish their best work is, of course, easier said than done. And there are those rivalries and jealousies among cast members that can sabotage a project. It's times like these where the director must take charge.

Peter Weir recalls that in *Dead Poets* he had seven boys in the ensemble cast. "Most of the boys were getting their first major break in a movie with Robin Williams. And there was a tendency, initially, for potential tensions to show because some people had "better" parts than others. Will they get their close-ups?" The solution, Weir says, lies in a kind of environmental management. "...I had to create an atmosphere where we worked as a group and they almost lived their characters."

We began by getting them into uniform haircuts. Then I held three or four classes, where I played a teacher. We had desks set up. I told them, "This is an imaginary school and I'm the drama teacher and the English teacher and we're going to put on a Christmas show. You have to stay in your character."

Since it was in the 1950s, I gave them a list of words that they couldn't use, such as "keen," or "it was really amazing," or "aaah, yeah..." all those broken-up sentences. I had them acting as reindeer and carrying packages, abysmally childish. Throughout the process the boys became younger, sillier, funnier and lighter.

Of course each set—each cast is a new challenge. Getting the best emotional response from an actor can be difficult for everyone involved. But the payoffs can be enormous in terms of what winds up on the screen. Norman Jewison remembers a particularly difficult night while shooting *Moonstruck*:

The big love scene was shot at three in the morning. Cher did not want to do the scene because it was so cold and she was in a light dress with high heels and no protection from the cold. Actors have a problem when it's cold. They have a problem giving this natural believability to the performance because physically they are so cold that they can't control their body.

So I set up the camera…and what happens is she is so cold that she starts to feel totally uncomfortable and tears almost come to her eyes. But because she's so tormented in that scene and can't make up her mind and is moved emotionally, the physical problem ends up working for the performance within the scene. By forcing it we got a wonderful performance.

Creative directors constantly seek solutions. The best ones always seem to find them. Another kind of problem was encountered while Ridley Scott was shooting the crucial climax scenes in *Alien*.

In the last seventeen minutes of Alien, *there's no dialogue, so it's Sigourney trying to emote without any other actors to play off of. And that's very difficult. So I was always trying to cook up ways of helping her. I even had three- or four-inch speakers lining the set, which I used to play Tomita's "The Planets" for her. And it used to help her because she had everything going rather than doing the whole thing in silence.*

In order to make each scene become as real as possible, the director must overcome the fact that the story is being shot out of sequence. Norman Jewison sees the director's vision as the essential tool he uses to get the best from his cast in these situations. "You try to take the actors back to the moment emotionally, they must be quite aware of where they are in the story. The director is making this seamless story in his mind, but he is usually shooting it totally out of context."

While the director labors to make sure everyone on the set achieves his or her best work; it is the actors who invariably receive the lion's share of attention. Ron Howard strives to provide "a set where people interrelate, where people respect the actors and what they're doing."

The Collaborative Art

By the time the shoot nears its final frantic days, chaos often reigns. In this heady environment, the director's intuitive instincts become more important than ever. For Ridley Scott, the set is like a big kitchen where the final results are always unpredictable.

Creating is like a stew...frequently you don't really know where you're headed. It's all by instinct and intuition. You can rely on a few logical elements, you know that you're going to move in a certain direction because decisions have to be made and you've got to move on. Because unfortunately filming is all against the clock. So it's a constant battle between commerce and creativity.

Oliver Stone stresses the collaborative function of all involved:

It's all the same soup. The writing, editing, directing, acting. We're all in it together. Directors are actors to a certain degree. Writers are actors. You act it out on paper. The fun of movie collaboration is that you really work with a lot of people who are different from you and you learn a lot from them. People you don't like. But you learn to live with them. It teaches you tolerance.

The need for mutual trust, respect and affection between all the collaborators can be seen in all phases of production. As the shoot nears completion, the struggle between commerce and creativity accelerates. Whether soup or stew, the contributions of each and every collaborator along the way will, it is hoped, merge to become one seamless celluloid experience. For Ron Howard, it's a three-step process.

I try to come in every day with a plan that is solid enough to provide a foundation for the movie. That's where it starts. Next you look for ideas and inspiration from your collaborators: actors, cinematographers, production designers and others. Then there is a kind of editing process where I sort through the ideas, weave them together and apply them to my original overview.

You look for things that will embellish on that fundamental point of view and elevate the storytelling quality of the film to help take it to the next level.

Martha Coolidge begins by asking collaborators, such as the director of photography and production designer, if they have images or ideas that connect with the script.

It's very important that everybody is making the same movie, so I want to know if their first instincts are similar to mine, both on a visual and psychological level. It's a collective vision but it's the director's vision. That's the vision that is shared or interpreted by the artists working on the picture.

She emphasizes that at the end of the day, it is the director who must accept responsibility for what winds up on the screen.

It's about choices. You choose the cast, you choose the sets. You decide how to shoot it and which takes to use. You sit in editing and every single frame on that screen is yours, it's up there because you picked it after looking at it hundreds and hundreds of times.

The amount of attention that goes into every shot means that nothing is in there by accident. So you must take responsibility for it and that includes taking responsibility for what doesn't work. It's painful, but it happens.

If films were physics, directors would be the fulcrum, the axis around which all the immutable laws of the universe hum. Ron Howard's journey may have begun in Mayberry and brought him to the Oscar stage for *A Beautiful Mind*, but his evolution as a director has taught him a deep appreciation for the infinite mysteries of collaboration.

The buck does stop with the director, but there are so many others involved. I think the sooner we all see the same movie in our heads, the sooner the collaborative process works and the film benefits from the valuable ideas coming from all those different areas of expertise.

Caught up in his own enthusiasm about the spirit of collaboration for a moment he shares a final thought. "You know, there are a lot of very creative, intelligent, people in this business."

CLOSE-UP
THE DIRECTOR: RON HOWARD

Choosing the Material

Brian and I were both fascinated by this paradox between the remarkable genius and the mental illness of John Nash. We thought we had a great film character and a powerful dilemma to deal with. We had already developed a couple of projects that dealt with characters coping with mental illness. But they hadn't gotten made, since each was problematic.

Akiva created the storytelling device of externalizing the delusions that gave us the opportunity to make a really extraordinary and surprising movie and not a straight docu-drama. I felt this approach offered greater insight into the nature of the disorder on a very personal level that we were able to achieve in our other scripts. So it was a really creative, powerful, story.

It was that particular dilemma of mental illness that interested me. It so misunderstood and it represents such a huge human trial. Mental illness is such a disorder and so debilitating, not only to the individuals, but to the entire family. I felt like this was really rich, compelling territory for a human drama.

One mathematician explained to me that with every generation there's a kind of line into the unknown, into the darkness. Geniuses gravitate toward that line, but there are just a few who are bold enough to be the real warriors who are able to cross the line. Nash was one of those.

Choosing a Character Drama

In a sense, A Beautiful Mind was a natural part of an evolution of my directing. There have been elements in many of my films that have been pure human character drama. Skyward with Bette Davis, which was my fourth film, made in 1980, relied on nothing more than simple, truthful, human drama and I always enjoyed directing those sequences. I try to develop my range of directorial experience in such a way that I don't have to latch on to a particular genre or style. At this stage in my career, I feel I can execute whatever is needed for the film. That said, I realize that I have never really done a film that was first and foremost a character drama from start to finish.

Every film has its challenges. *A Beautiful Mind* challenged me to a cinematic approach that would offer the audience the experience that Nash was enduring, including being duped by the delusional characters and the betrayal when he realized that these characters were delusions. It was well scripted, but from a director's viewpoint, it needed to be able to be photographed in a way that would not draw attention to itself but would be consistent with that cinematic idea.

Creating Images to Externalize the Story

One of my overarching images was of patterns. I did some research dealing with theoretical mathematics and discovered that mathematicians don't just deal with numbers, but with relationships and pattern. They think about shapes and relationships, designs and interactions.

I don't know much about math and Russell Crowe doesn't know much about math, but I know something about writing and Russell knew something about music. And I could connect with the character and his passion because I can relate it to something I understand—the creative journey.

To make this mental illness and the mathematics visual, I began to think about mathematical symbols as words on a page or notes on sheet music and I then began to try to find a way to visually present that to the audience.

I wanted to show Nash picking up shapes and working with them and playing with them so we could visually establish his point of view and the unique nature of his mind and how it worked.

To figure out how to visualize this world, I started asking a lot of these mathematicians what they visualized when they were daydreaming or thinking or working on a problem. Some could articulate it, some couldn't. I looked for visual patterns and shapes everywhere we could find them—such as the tie reflecting in the glass in the first scene or the arch of Princeton that Nash runs through. Sometimes the shape was directly symbolic of something and other times there were shapes that he was constantly observing.

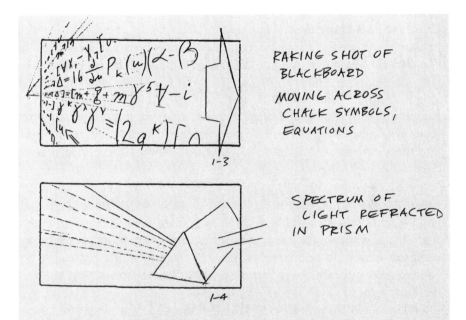

RAKING SHOT OF
BLACKBOARD

MOVING ACROSS
CHALK SYMBOLS,
EQUATIONS

1-3

SPECTRUM OF
LIGHT REFRACTED
IN PRISM

1-4

Creating the Human Relationships

Akiva always talked about connectedness, emotional connectedness, and this character's problem was that he was unable to connect on a human level. And I thought that that was interesting, because math is all about trying to piece together the elements of the universe and create connection and understand where the connections are.

And one of the first things I was able to articulate for myself was that mathematicians are trying to prove the existence of entities or structures that human beings actually cannot experience. But in proving they exist, they're expanding our knowledge and solving a mystery. It gets back to human relationships and how mysterious they are.

I tried to introduce the characters, both real and delusional, from Nash's point of view. So we never cut to a wide shot of characters walking up. We introduced all of them from Nash's point of view.

Sometimes we tried to remind the audience of that world that Nash was constantly observing. We were talking about emotional connectedness and his character's problem was that he had difficult connecting emotionally.

Creating the Themes

I try to identify a number of personal and social themes because you can always have more than one theme going. Then I try build a structure around them that can be expressed so the audience can understand them. I look for ideas that can be moved by action and expressed by character. *A Beautiful Mind* is a kind of good versus evil story, with the disease as evil and particularly Alicia Nash's goodness and the goodness of others as a positive force that helps to actually defeat the evil force.

Creating the Character

Some of my friends read the script and they were concerned that Nash was not going to be sympathetic, but I felt that the journey itself was so noble and heroic—that it was important that he be a complicated guy and that it would be far more interesting if you were really put off by him.

He was just charming and entertaining enough to help you keep within the movie, but you were always kind of thinking, "This guy is a bit of a jerk." Yet you understood later that you couldn't justify holding him responsible for any of that.

Part of making that character work was the collaboration. Akiva wrote a great script and was there during production. And Karen at Imagine worked long and hard on the script. There weren't massive rewrites going on in production, but there are always small things and new ideas.

Working with the Actors

As far as the actors go, I've learned more and more to try to engage them and help them find what works for them. I encourage research and an on-going discussion, not to bog it down, but to lift them.

If you can help the actors find themselves in the characters, then you've accomplished what you need to in the rehearsal. In addition to trying to solve the story problem, construct the staging, try to get all the questions out on the table, I've learned to create an environment where actors can find things in themselves that are consistent with what I'm going for.

I learned that many of the affects of this disorder are physical. Russell and I evolved a kind of menu of effects by watching videos—mainly documentary footage of people with schizophrenia. I told Russell to find the things that he could work with, whether small or big.

We tried to let the audience think of these gestures as eccentricities or tics and then later they realize they're part of the disorder. So I thought it would be interesting if you thought his behavior was quirky in the first half of the movie and then you realized it was a symptom of this painfully debilitating disorder—schizophrenia.

The Most Important Idea

At the end of the script, Akiva said it so well—it's about finding the equilibrium. He has Nash say, "I have always believed in numbers. In the equations and logics that lead to reason. I was wrong. It is only in the mysterious equations of love that any logic or reason can be found. Perhaps it is good to have a beautiful mind. But a better gift is to discover a beautiful heart."

You don't just deliver the line; you think about it. You dream about it. You connect with it in very personal ways. If you're successful, you have something to bring to the party.

—Leonard Nimoy

The Actor and "The Kindness of Strangers"

When Jennifer Connelly was interviewed on *Today* after being nominated for an Oscar for her role in *A Beautiful Mind*, she did what any modest thespian would do: she made it sound like a stroke of good fortune. She made it sound easy. "I just try to do the best job I can. I have had some good turns lately and, you know, good luck. I'm very grateful...for the opportunity to work on this movie and in the movies that I've done in the last few years."

But how "easy" is it, really?

"People think that acting is walking and talking and so they say—'Hey, I could do that!'" Acting teacher Nina Foch laughs. "But acting is very difficult. The best succeed precisely because they make it look so easy. Maybe if you're an actor your whole life long, you might do one or two scenes completely well."

It begins with vulnerability. For actors to do their best work, they must be willing to be totally open, to experiment and allow all that is inside to be exposed. To accomplish this at the highest levels requires tremendous discipline. Actors work with their emotions, their experiences, traumas, feelings and memories. Bodies and voices become finely tuned instruments that express and convey the character.

Since the actor *is* the instrument, he or she is in a very different position from film's other collaborators. The writer projects an inner life onto a piece of paper, the composer uses notes, the producer has contacts, the director a vision. But actors stand alone. It's not about the work, but about *them*. And it's very personal.

Veteran actor Peter Strauss has dominated television movies and miniseries since his performance in the highly acclaimed *Rich Man, Poor Man*. More recently he starred in *A Father's Choice*. He says a certain trust must develop between actors and their collaborators.

> *Ultimately, most actors have to walk on the set like Blanche DuBois in* A Streetcar Named Desire *and say, "I have always depended upon the kindness of strangers." Because you may be dressed in the scene, but trust me, you are naked in front of a lot of strangers. And you are ultimately depending upon their kindness.*

This is exactly why actors are so vulnerable to criticism. When the critic says, "The script doesn't work," the writer says, "Well, it's just a script, it may be part of me but it's not *me*." The actor can't displace the criticism. There's nowhere else for it to go.

The critics have been kind to Mary McDonnell. Her performance back in 1990 as Kevin Costner's co-star in *Dances with Wolves* brought her an Academy Award nomination. Another came for her starring role as a recently disabled ex-soap opera star in *Passion Fish*. Response was also positive to her role as Claire, the "woman who found the baby" in Lawrence Kasdan's *Grand Canyon*. In 2001 she costarred with Drew Barrymore in the critically acclaimed *Donnie Darko*.

She feels that the experiences that help the actor or actress perform can be traced to childhood. "I think that most actors had a difficult time growing up because of the level of their emotional response," she says. "They had no control of themselves and were often seen as overly dramatic or negative. They have these tremendous emotional responses and other people say 'What's the problem?'" McDonnell points out that actors live in a different world from that of their fellow collaborators.

> *Actors are part of a certain percentage of people on this planet who have an emotional vocabulary as a primary experience. It's as if their life is experienced emotionally and then that is translated intellectually or conceptually into the performance.*

In Search of Magic

Like the best directors and producers, successful actors and actresses must choose from among the many projects available to them. As with the other collaborators, it all begins with the script. "It was the script that first attracted me to *Dead Poets Society*," explains Robin Williams. "It was quite powerful. The philosophy of Keating was combined with a spirit and intelligence. There was grace, dignity and a lot about the creative force. These are all things that are quite near and dear to me."

Peter Strauss feels that a certain attitude is necessary.

> *I always try to approach the script with great excitement. I go find a quiet corner and open up a screenplay with three anticipations. First is the truth. I don't care if the script is funny, sad, black, yellow, about politics, love, death. I want to find the truth. I look for insight in the writing, depth, the courage to go behind closed doors—I want the writer to be daring. The next thing I want to find is the magic. Why do this movie? Does it shimmer? I want to be transported by the screenplay. To go to the movie, to be in the dark and have magic happen.*
>
> *Finally, I need to know that every day coming to work will be a challenge. I don't want to be doing reality. I want to go above it, to raise the meter. I look for passion, aliveness, hatred, rage, fear, pain, joy, bigness. I want to feel big, I want to be angry big, feel sad big.*

The inherent artistic challenges of any script begin with the actor's initial response. Is it to the story or the character? Edward James Olmos's career (*Miami Vice, American Me, Stand and Deliver*) has been characterized by stories that speak to universal truths. "For me the most essential aspect is the story. Character is secondary to the story. I look for the intent, the subtext. I believe that intent equals content and therefore it doesn't matter how intensely buried it is, the intention will inevitably come out."

Mary McDonnell's roles in films by Lawrence Kasdan and John Sayles have afforded her the opportunity to work with two of Hollywood's most renowned storytellers. Not surprisingly, they have also influenced the way she approaches the script.

> *What I respond to is a good story and then I look at the role. If it's a good story, usually the role is going to be a great one, no matter the size of it.*

It's a story with a structure to it that you understand. It involves what I perceive as an honest reflection of the human dilemma. If I read something that I feel is false, it seems to be placing itself out of the realm of humanity.

What gets me charged is being in a situation that connects to the general population. To connect myself to the world is a big part of what drives me. It's important for me to know who those people are in the audience. That we're sharing a common experience.

John Lithgow's distinguished career has included performances in some of Hollywood's most interesting feature projects, including *Terms of Endearment, The World According to Garp, All That Jazz,* the cult classic *The Adventures of Buckaroo Banzai: Across the 4th Dimension* and *Shrek* as well as its sequel. As he describes his approach to the script, you begin to understand why those career choices did not happen by accident.

I want a story that grabs me and a character who travels a journey. The action of the story affects the character and he changes, going from one point to another as the story unfolds. Also, the character has to have something new about him that surprises me. It might be the way he uses language or a different look or accent—some surprising behavior that I want to try to pull off.

Character behavior always seems to be an issue. In the fall of 2002, Strauss found himself being interviewed by a reporter for the *Saskatoon Star Phoenix.* He was there on location for the Pax TV series *Body and Soul.* What drew him to the part of crusty Dr. Issac Braun? "This character I adored the minute that I saw him on the page. I adored his flaws, I adored his pomposity. I adored his commitment and dedication to medicine and his absolute refusal to believe in anything that's not provable by science."

Graham Greene is best known for his role as the Sioux Indian who befriends Kevin Costner's Lieutenant Dunbar in *Dances with Wolves* and more recently starred in *Skins.* He has his own novel approach to the script, one that begins with an examination of the character he has been asked to play.

I take out all the pages that pertain to my character. I read them first and see if the thread is good. Then I take the rest of the script and read it sans my character and see if that thread is good and try to match them up. If I can't understand what the script is about, then I can't make somebody who's watching it understand it.

It's hard to think of another actor in Hollywood who is more renowned for his ability to recognize a great script and a great character than Dustin Hoffman. In an interview on *Larry King Live* he emphasizes the scarcity of really good scripts. "There are probably one or two scripts that I read every year where the structure is sound." And the character?

With Hero I didn't hear the character and I had to talk to the writer for a long time. I said, "I would like to play this guy because I like the way he interacts in terms of the story, the narrative, but I can't say I hear him." And it took me about two or three weeks to find something fresh about the guy for myself.

At the same time, Hoffman reveals that his penchant for finding "something fresh" in the character occasionally prompts him to turn down roles he wished he hadn't.

I read Close Encounters of the Third Kind *and I thought, "This is a great script. It's almost a perfect script." But I turned it down because I was naive and I thought, "I don't know how to do this part in a fresh way." Now I know how rare it is to get a really good script with a good director. And even if you don't know what to do with the part, you take it.*

This was precisely what happened to Mary McDonnell when she first read *Dances with Wolves*, but getting the script—that was the problem!

When I first heard about Dances *I was in New York and my agent called me and said, "You've got to go down to this hotel and read this new Kevin Costner script." I asked what it was about and she told me it was a Cowboy-and-Indian movie. I said, "No way, I'm not interested." She said, "I know, but there's something really special about it."*

> I asked why I had to go to a hotel to read it and she said, "They're not letting it out." I remember that I had a horrible reaction to that. You can go to the library and get Shakespeare, Shaw, Ibsen, but not this script? Right.
>
> So I went with an attitude and they gave me the script and about fifteen pages into it, it just knocked me out. I was on fire. Kevin had come to New York because he said, "I want a woman, not a girl." He said he wanted somebody older, someone who "had a few lines in her face." As it turned out, that was me!
>
> I also think he was looking for a level of skill necessary for the language. It's rare to have so many challenges in one script because you know there won't be one moment of dissatisfaction or boredom. Just the very act of being asked to pull it off is a gift.

Sometimes actors seek the right kind of "balance" in a project—something that suits their personality. When John Lithgow returned to the stage for the first time since 1988 in *Sweet Smell of Success* he explained to a reporter from the *Milwaukee Journal Sentinel* that the role of a corrupt gossip columnist was just the ticket.

"I really feel well cast in this part because I have a bit of a light touch." And what of the reputation gained from his work on *Third Rock from the Sun?* "People know there is a little bit of comedy in me. They even know there's a little bit of heart in me. It's like a dish that needs a couple of essential flavors or you just are not going to want to eat it."

Finally there is the question of career moves. Many were surprised when Robin Williams accepted his dark role in *Insomnia*. During an interview on *Good Morning America* he explained "I wanted to play different characters. You want to keep the range open. If it changes people's perceptions and allows me to play...more characters like this, great! Make it interesting, keep surprising people."

My World and Welcome to It

With the question of artistic challenge settled, most actors begin to reflect on the themes of the script. How will it affect the audience? How does it reconcile with their personal worldview? For Edward James Olmos it's "about the clash of cultures—sometimes they clash, sometimes they're bonding, but it's all about culture." At the Golden Apple Awards Geena Davis exclaimed, "I choose roles that honor women and give them something to root for."

Usually the writer will originate a story, or sometimes it begins with a director or a producer. Yet it's the actor whose image will forever be associated with the story. What's more, the performers will spend the rest of their lives being approached by perfect strangers who want to discuss the values and philosophies inherent in the story.

Olmos is still invited to speak to educational groups all around the world as a result of his role in *Stand and Deliver*. And of course there are few performers who have experienced this phenomenon more frequently over the years than Actor-Director Leonard Nimoy. Though his feature directing credits include *Three Men and a Baby* and *The Good Mother*, it is his role as Mr. Spock on the *Star Trek* franchise and feature film projects that have brought him worldwide recognition. Whether he is doing a public appearance or shopping at the grocery store, *Star Trek's* enduring philosophy is always a hot topic among those who approach him.

> Star Trek *was certainly entertainment, but time and again people ask me what its longevity and durability are all about. I think part of it is because you can revisit the shows and films and experience new levels.*
>
> *An eight-year-old will respond to certain visual and audio elements. But that same person at twenty will see something else. They may discover the ecological themes or find something that relates to a novel they just read. It's all about connections and over the years they add up.*

Frequently asked about the impact *Star Trek* had on his career, he appears to have come to terms with it. In a 2002 interview in the *Sunday Mirror* he explained, "I don't consider it a millstone, it's possible that I might not have had this career had it not been for Spock." Though the original series run ended in 1966 "...I've never been out of work since. For an actor to say that after so many years is remarkable."

When the Write Stuff Is the Wrong Stuff

Ideally, actors will commit to a good script they can believe in and they'll go about the job of helping bring it to life. However, as we have seen, the

Hollywood filmmaking process often means the script will undergo a number of changes along the way. Whatever the situation, the actor's performance will depend on the script and very often that script will not be as good as it could be. All experienced actors encounter this problem. John Lithgow reveals how it impacts on the performance.

If the script is not a very good piece of work, you need to struggle to give it some emotional authenticity. Sometimes you do too much to try to puff it up. The hardest roles to play are poorly written or underwritten, where you don't have enough information to create a multidimensional character. The ones that are effortless to play are well written. Terms of Endearment was a perfectly written script. At first glance the scenes seemed prosaic, but you didn't have to do much with them. In the end they were extraordinarily moving because of the good judgment and writing of Jim Brooks.

Nina Foch says certain other problems tend to crop up in scripts, most notably in the dialogue. "What you want from the writer is a storyteller with an ear, one who can hear the way people talk. In addition, the actor can work with the director to cut out the extra lines that don't need to be spoken."

Graham Greene acknowledges that like everyone else, writers have their good days and their bad days. "Sometimes you get a really good script and the dialogue just jumps off the page at you. Other times, it's just syntax. I say to myself, 'It definitely must have been ten to five when the writer wrote this!' I like to bring a little humor to most of the roles that I do. Very few writers demand that you say exactly what they've written."

Like most actors, Peter Strauss finds it easier to start with a great script. "I love subtext. I love colors in a character. The more that's there, the less I'm going to have to do." As for the problem script, Strauss uses an interesting visual metaphor to describe what it can do to the actor's performance.

It's a nightmare for the actor when the screenplay doesn't work. Sometimes I know in my gut that this scene could be a great dramatic scene—and I ain't got the words for my character. And I'm banging my head. If it's a good skeletal frame, the actor will blossom. If it's a man where his legs are sticking out of his ears, that poor actor is going to be suffering up there. Now, it's the actor's job to know that. The more you dig and demand, the better it's going to come out in the end. My job is to keep fleshing out the character in the direction the writer intended.

Leonard Nimoy points out that there are also times when the actor knows the character better than the writer does. This occurs most often on television, but applies increasingly to features, thanks to the sequel phenomenon.

Sometimes a performance characteristic that I'm not even conscious of sneaks into the character. The writers will pick up on it and ask you to do it again. "You raised your eyebrow when he said this to you. That worked. Let's do that again."

The problem is I didn't know I would be doing it for the next twenty-five years! It becomes such an identifiable characteristic. Now all of a sudden every seven or eight pages it says, "Spock raises an eyebrow." So you have to say to them, "We're going to lose the value of this if we keep using it as a way out of every situation. Let's find something else. Don't make it so cheap."

Scripts and Tips

Whatever the ultimate state of the script, actors must eventually move to try to make the characters their own. This is accomplished by manipulating the script in a variety of ways.

Mary McDonnell likes to know her territory. "In *Matewan* I mapped out the material. It was like a graph that showed the evolution of my character, what might occur when, what she might feel, page by page. Then, when we started shooting out of sequence, I could just review my notes."

Leonard Nimoy reveals that, "Science fiction calls for a certain kind of theatrical imagination. Sometimes it comes from me, a personal experience that might be applicable. I make notes to myself, or I'll hear about something on radio or TV that's topical, a thematic idea that becomes useful."

Nina Foch recommends that her acting students stay in touch with the totality of the script.

The actor does everything the director does: breaks down the action, the intentions, the props, every little beat in the scene should be broken down. I advise actors to take their part out of the script. Take the actual pages out and put the rest in a drawer. Then read their pages at least once every day. You need to know what's required of each scene and how to help it be better.

Nimoy explains that a successful actor finds the best in every script and adds to it.

The best actors bring something to a character. Perhaps it's based on personal experience or the lives of others. They get the best out of what the script has to offer by discovering ways to illuminate the ideas in it. Perhaps it's an attitude, a posture, or a gesture, so the audience can see more than a character and say, "I know who that is."

You don't just deliver the line. You think about it. You dream about it. You connect with it in very personal ways. If you're successful, you have something to bring to the party.

Research: You *Are* the Details

For Peter Strauss, part of making every character effective and each scene better involves research. Given today's high-pressure production schedules, though, research is a luxury. "An actor who gets to research gets really excited about the opportunity to bring color to his work." He demonstrates how this can involve anything from in-depth character analysis to something as simple as holding a gun.

Every time a weapon is in the script, I'll go out and practice so I can be comfortable with it in my hand. Most characters who have props in their hands handle them without it being a meaningful event. But when an actor gets an Uzi in his hands, it's a meaningful event!

Today's roles require research. If you get to play an AIDS victim, you've got to spend time learning how an AIDS victim dies. At Northwestern University they taught me that if you're going to play an English king, you need to know English history. I buy that.

Hollywood lore is replete with stories about the extensive research Nick Nolte brings to his roles. While shooting *Farewell to the King*, Nolte transformed his hotel suite in Borneo into a war room worthy of Patton. There were battle charts, arcane historical accounts of Allied objectives in the Pacific theatre and a frayed copy of the script into which the relevant pages of the adapted novel were inserted for background. Several sources report that director John Milius took one look at the chaos and barked, "What in the hell does any of this have to do with acting?" To which Nolte replied, "Everything!"

For *Down and Out in Beverly Hills*, the actor disappeared for several days into Los Angeles' skid row. While there he drank cheap wine and slept in vacant lots. By the time he appeared at rehearsal, Bette Midler and Richard Dreyfuss were dumbfounded because he literally stank. Of course, that was exactly what the script called for.

Director Paul Mazursky says, "Nick would never be so pretentious as to call himself a method actor. He just does it." In a *Premiere* magazine interview Nolte explains, "Preparing for a role is when I get to indulge. To me an actor's technique is about learning so that he'll survive. Only then can he deal with his insecurity and his fears."

Bio Research

Research becomes increasingly complicated when playing a real-life character. For *Stand and Deliver*, the true story of extraordinary teacher Jaime Escalante, Edward James Olmos was able to spend time with the entire Escalante family. "I talked to Jaime for hundreds of hours and watched him for hundreds of hours. I would stay there from early in the morning until late at night. I would just watch every behavior and ask questions."

Jack Nicholson's Oscar nominated role in *About Schmidt* served as another reminder of his versatility. But there is a lot of hard work behind that seemingly effortless acting style. Some years ago, in a *Los Angeles Times* entertainment section interview that coincided with the release of *Hoffa*, Nicholson revealed his own research methods to writer Hilary de Vries.

I look at endless tapes, a lot of books. We also shot in the towns that Hoffa worked in and there are a lot of people still living who knew him. I met his son and I talked to the prosecuting attorneys in both cases where Hoffa was tried. There are some parts that you say, "I could play this and I sort of know how," and then there are some parts—and Hoffa is one—where you say, "Jesus Christ, look at the size of this. It's like a huge mountain." You know you will do it but you don't know if you can, because you don't know how exactly.

Hoffa was an especially interesting case because, as with JFK, no one really knew what happened in real life. Nicholson found this somewhat liberating.

It's not a biography, it's a portrait, and there is a difference. Because no one really knows what happened to Hoffa, it gives you license to do a lot of guessing with other things, too. I had a certain amount of license in my job as an actor to have an inside interpretation of the guy.

An actor's interpretation of a character can be formulated in any number of ways. Graham Greene likes to prepare a mental biography that is rich in detail.

I work out the background of my character in my head. Each one is a little different. Is he married? What does he like? What kind of clothes does he wear? Does he even care about clothes? What kind of house or car does he prefer? How much money does he have in the bank? Who are his friends? His allies? Who hates him?

For Edward James Olmos it is a matter of moving "forward into the past," but there are always larger implications.

The past is what we look for in building the story. How far back can we go to develop a bible that allows you to understand what this character's choices have been? What happened to him as a child? How does that permeate itself inside the character? I think that you must understand the backstory before you can move forward. It's like trying to understand yourself as a human being without understanding your past. That's why most of us have to really look at ourselves and our civilization and understand where we come from, so that we can understand what motivates and drives us in the conscious mind today.

Accents: Say What?

Talk with actors about the challenges they face as they prepare for a role and sooner or later the subject of language and accents comes up. Often this is accompanied by a sigh, groan, or similar disparaging remark.

Mary McDonnell laughs as she recalls how the meticulous John Sayles gently corrected her fledgling Louisiana speech patterns in *Passion Fish*. "Mary, you're no longer in Louisiana, you just entered North Carolina!"

Regional American accents are something of a specialty for Peter Strauss.

Language has eccentricity. It has some rules. But stand in a room with fifty Americans and you have fifty dialects. So there isn't any American dialect. There's just a way of speaking. It's flavor, subtlety. For the television movie The Trial *I played a southern sheriff. I had dialect work to do. I did it with videos. I had the film commission send me videos of the newscasters and local talk shows.*

The task becomes more difficult as the geography expands. John Lithgow's experience in *Raising Cain* is typical. "I worked with a Norwegian linguistics professor at Stanford and I got his accent. I had him teach me the accent and we sang Norwegian lullabies."

For *Dances with Wolves*, Graham Greene had the most difficult semantic assignment of all.

We had to learn the Lakota language. I couldn't retain any of this, it was so foreign. I've learned a number of languages phonetically, but this was completely different. To learn it, I sat in my hotel room for eight hours a day. We had tapes, but they were slowly pronounced, and we had a dialogue coach who was with us and was on our case every second.

It took two weeks to learn all the dialogue and then I'd work in my hotel room until two in the morning, going through the speeches. Next morning I couldn't remember any of it! I was nearly in tears. So I'd go back to the beginning and slowly it would come.

Mary McDonnell's role as Kevin Costner's interpreter in *Dances* put extra pressure on her, but also taught her a deep appreciation for the intricacies involved.

There is a real modesty in Lakota speech, there was no aggressive quality to it, rather a kind of musicality. It's gentle, nasal and economical. When I was learning Lakota, I found myself becoming very nasal. One day Kevin said, "You're starting to sound a little Chinese."

When a scene called for her to switch from Lakota to English "for the first time in twenty years," there were emotional barriers for her character to overcome. What's more, they had to be reflected in just a few halting syllables.

The implications of giving up her primary language are so painful that when Graham Greene's character asks me to translate for Lieutenant Dunbar [Costner] I say, "I don't think I can do this." What I'm really saying is that I don't think I can remember. What I'm feeling is completely emotional, I'm threatened by the possibility of having to go back and retrieve that traumatic memory.

The Inside Trick

Mastering accents, doing research, imagining biographies and back stories—all of these represent an attempt to get inside characters and bring them to physical life. There are as many ways to accomplish this combination of mental and physical challenges as there are roles to play. Edward James Olmos defines the two basic theories.

The English form of study teaches you to go from the outside in. You do the behavior and it starts to seep inside. The Stanislavski method teaches you to go from the inside out. You begin with the feeling and memory and those feelings begin to affect your behavior. In other words, some people will turn around and get a limp and then figure out where the limp came from. Other people have to figure out why they have to limp before they can do the limp.

Nina Foch sees the two basic theories increasingly merging into one.

The fact is, everybody uses both. You see a limp, you steal it, you put it on. By doing it, it begins to become organic. By adopting the outside behavior, it affects the inside.

John Lithgow's experiences in *Ricochet* illustrate the process.

I developed a limp based on the fact that this character had been shot in the knee early on. The moment he'd been shot was a moment of humiliation and defeat which he carried around with him bitterly for the rest of his life. I thought about the limp. I figured the knee had been frozen up a bit so I put a knee brace on my knee.

Graham Greene found a rather unconventional way to get inside one very unfamiliar character. "I had to play a fifty-six-year-old man who had no teeth, was loud as sin and had bad posture. I put a slice of bologna in each shoe. I needed something slimy in my shoe to make it work."

John Lithgow has achieved a considerable amount of fame for his ability to get inside characters. He begins with the physical accoutrements that accompany each role.

A lot comes from external trappings. Wardrobe fittings are extremely important. You try out your ideas with the costume designer. I go through a personal process; looking in the mirror, seeing how the clothes are beginning to characterize this person. Then there's the haircut, maybe you grow a beard or wear some peculiar makeup prosthetics, all that plays a part.

When asked to recall his most memorable challenges, Lithgow cites three very different characters and reveals how he brought each to life.

For Buckaroo Banzai I was an Italian scientist. Forty years ago his body had been inhabited by a tyrannical evil alien from another dimension. He was still inhabited by that alien but he was forty years older. The idea was to figure out how forty years of being inhabited by an alien changed you. I put a lot of thought into this and came up with some very striking physical devices.

Since he fed himself on electricity and sugar, I hit on this idea of red hair as a sort of shock wig, the hair going straight up as if I had been electrified at least once every day of my life.

On another occasion, Lithgow discovered a simple way to get inside the diabolical mind of a tortured killer. "I gave myself a milky contact lens in one eye. This was a bizarre, sadistic horrible character and I liked giving him a couple of characteristics that made him loathe himself or made him self-conscious."

Finally, there is the challenge of how the actor's own physical identity must be sacrificed to create an unforgettable character. Lithgow learned more about this from George Miller, who directed him in a segment of *Twilight Zone—The Movie*.

> *Miller wanted me to dye my hair black and I told him I didn't get the point. Then he said, "How about a cold sore on your mouth?" I asked him what he was driving at and he said he wanted to think of something that would throw me off my image of myself.*
>
> *That stuck in my mind because now that's always something I look for. It was a gift from him to me. For Twilight Zone I ultimately decided to have a three-day growth of beard and my hair was full of grease. I looked very, very haggard and I wore a black suit and a brown shirt. I certainly was not my image of myself. And it's somehow liberating because it facilitates the whole process of becoming another person.*

One of film lore's most famous transformations came when Dustin Hoffman assumed the role of a woman in *Tootsie*. In his *Larry King Live* interview he confessed, "All I can say is that we did seven months of makeup tests and I really wanted to look as beautiful as possible. But I was shocked when they told me that this was as beautiful as they could make me. I thought Hollywood could do anything!"

The physical stamina required to act for hours and hours and do what is physically needed can be considerable. During a shoot the actor might routinely rise as early as four in the morning. Several hours of makeup may be required, hours more may be spent sitting around waiting for the first cue. But when the camera rolls, the actor must be totally there, totally present. It's all right for the director to be a bit tired, or for the costumers to yawn, but the actor must be totally alive.

All of this becomes more complicated when the role calls for the actor or actress to assume a character who is severely disabled. In *Passion Fish*,

Mary McDonnell's character May-Alice spent most of the film reconciling herself to an accident that had left her paralyzed from the waist down.

It was clear to me that I had to start physically. I needed a great deal of upper body strength to do the role in order to pretend that I didn't have it. Because if I had been as weak as May-Alice was, I would have been very sore and run down. I worked with a trainer to build up my strength so that I could lift myself into my chair and crawl on the floors and do what I needed to do without looking like I was in training. At the Rehab Center, I worked with a therapist and a counselor who was a paraplegic. They put me through rigorous training. It was frustrating but it helped lead me into some of the emotional aspects of the material.

The physical demands of a role may also include developing certain skills that must accompany it. Harrison Ford's use of the bullwhip in the Indiana Jones movies was certainly central to his character. Ford explains how he did it in an interview with *Playboy*.

I do all my own whipping. But it's not a skill I keep up between films. It's a bit like riding a bike. Once you've learned the basics, you remember them, so that you're not lashing yourself about the head and shoulders as you did when you were beginning. I have bullwhips in various lengths and practice with them on posts and trees. Now it all comes naturally—wrist action, you know. I must say, though, that it was hard to find somebody to teach me. Amazingly, there aren't that many expert hands with a bullwhip.

Being There

Acting is not just about doing, it's about *being*. It's about making the moment ring true so the audience really believes the actor is the character. For Nina Foch, the "doing" comes from the actor's own ability to completely comprehend what is happening in the character's inner life.

Understanding leads to doing, which leads to emotion. How do they eat? How much do they care about their bodies? Do they wear tight clothes?

People who live on Big Macs and beans probably break wind a lot. People who don't take care of themselves are constipated.

I can't even walk through the door unless I have an idea of what I had to do to get to the door. All of this understanding has to occur, to know the preparation for the entrance, or any scene.

Robin Williams recalls the process he went through to "become" Mr. Keating in *Dead Poets Society*.

To prepare for a role, I use anything that works. With Keating I was combining teachers that I had, there were probably two or three of them in there somewhere. You try to put together people you've known and kind of synthesize them into yourself.

I started with my own beliefs about what is creative and then those were combined with the poetry. I usually write some notes on the script, scene by scene and overall notes for the whole piece. They are often notes about things to remind me of the different points in the scene. You don't have to knock the socks off of every scene, you just need to know where you are in the whole piece. That's the key.

Graham Greene explains that "Film is internal. As an actor, internalizing is about listening, relating."

Peter Strauss has to ask the six basic journalism questions: "Why, when, who, where, what and how? Who am I? What am I? What drives me? Why is my character like this?"

Dustin Hoffman's description of his approach in *Tootsie* strikes a similar chord. "What if I was this woman? What if I looked like this? How would I have been different in terms of my own personality?"

The trick seems to be in developing the ability to transcend the self and the task at hand—the "doing" part—and to become the character, literally, the "being."

Nina Foch teaches her acting students to use their own physical selves to become the character. "You have to know how to use your body and voice as an instrument so you can call on it and use it easily. The actor must learn how to play that instrument. That requires getting rid of your own tension."

"You Must Remember This"

The use of personal memory to convey the appropriate emotion in a scene is a tool that most actors find useful. This is most often accomplished by a journey within. "Everything is inside you," says Foch. "There are only eight emotions: love, loss of love, pleasure, loss of pleasure, fear, grief, rage and impotent rage."

For Robin Williams there are many different paths that lead to an emotional performance.

> Sometimes you're tapping into your own experience and other times you find different things that put you into the scene. You may be thinking about something that's very personal for you, but you don't tap into something if you haven't learned to deal with it. If you're tapping into a recent painful memory, you're not going to be able to handle it as an actor. It becomes some kind of method madness.

For Peter Strauss the truth of a performance is one way to measure the actor's ability. "You have the truth in your gut," he reveals. "That's the magic of the good actor versus the bad one. The bad one doesn't know the difference between truth and falseness. The good actor does. And the exceptional actor gets in touch with truth on screen and is unafraid of being in touch with it."

Actors must be fearless when it comes to the delicate issue of dredging up their most painful personal experiences. Before achieving success on film, Mary McDonnell's career flourished on the stage. It was there that she learned performance and pain often go hand in hand.

> All actors possess an ability to project disaster and drama on situations. I remember one time I needed to make an entrance and accomplish a certain emotion on stage. I started to think about something that was very terrible on a personal level and I had a tremendous emotional response to it and walked out and played the scene beautifully. But afterward, I was upset with myself for tampering with this. I had to rethink. Do I want to do this my entire life? What are the boundaries in terms of what I'm willing to tamper with on a psychic level? Because as much as I don't think I control anyone's destiny or fate, I do believe that thoughts create energy. So it makes you wonder....

Peter Strauss acknowledges the role of pain in these situations. "You always will have the pain. Pain won't go anyplace. You've got pain in the bank. The next step is to achieve openness as a human being. As an artist, you've got to be prepared to explore another person's point of view."

Good actors tend to take a personal experience and somehow let it gleam. I had this discussion with an actress. She was sitting there with her husband. He wanted to know how she managed to be in such pain in the scene. She said, "Well, I imagined that our child was dead." The husband looked at me dumbfounded, disturbed. Finally he said, "That's really sick!" I wasn't sure how to respond. She got very intense and said, "No, that's our gift."

It's a bizarre thing to do but actors do it all the time in order to turn their pain into something positive. They take people they love and kill them, beat them, cut their hands off, make them sick, lose them, divorce them. To some people on the outside looking in, that's neurosis, but to the actor that's a gift.

Can actors afford to be neurotic? The press is full of stories about how this or that actor or actress threw a tantrum on the set. Strauss acknowledges the thin line between emotion and neurosis, but sees a key difference.

There are actors who say "I don't want to go into therapy because if I make myself happy, I won't have any pain to draw from." I used to think that way. It's the most grievous error I ever made. Ultimately, it is when you begin to understand yourself that you are more open and willing to exploring the scene from a whole new perspective.

In the end, every actor or actress develops a personal method. "As an actor," Robin Williams explains, "you have to find the right level of response. Too much is sentimental, you need just the right amount. You're looking for the perfect tone, you need to have something in mind, but it also has to fit within the context. Preparing for this type of response, you use things you have in your mind but you never want to talk about them. You don't want to give away all the magic."

Rehearsal: The Self-Discovery Channel

As the project nears production, there is usually some rehearsal time. It is during this crucial period that performances begin to gel and the elusive "magic" begins to be discovered. John Lithgow explains how the process works.

I want about a week of rehearsal time. First we'll have a cold reading. Then, as a group, we sit down and break the script down scene by scene. We read the scene through once, with the assistant director reading every word of the stage directions to remind us of them. And the very reading of the material triggers ideas from the director and actors.

Then we put it on its feet, spending time in a rehearsal room. We've taped down the basic set, which is very elaborate. Beyond that, we set up four or five chairs to represent the interior of a car or bus or restaurant.

It is only after the physical situation is set up, Lithgow maintains, that the real business of rehearsal begins.

Then we discuss what the character is going through and what the scene is about. It's easy to forget little details in one scene that affect events in scenes that occur five or ten minutes later. Just by rehearsing you pick up on those things. Inevitably the shooting schedule is going to jump around. It's only by rehearsing that you keep the sequence of events straight, exactly where you're supposed to be on the time line. You don't want to over-rehearse, but I think it's great to get to the point where you're playing the hell out of a scene even though you may still have a script in your hand.

For the actor, rehearsals are not just about "nailing it" or "figuring it out" but about discovering if there will be chemistry between the actors. Most prefer to keep the rehearsal process quite fluid in order to experiment. Peter Strauss reveals, "To me, rehearsal is where you really discover scenes." Mary McDonnell says the process differs significantly from the common misconceptions about it.

It's not about finding the answers and then showing up on the set some-day and executing the choice. I respond creatively to a rehearsal situa-tion where you are opening up opportunities, starting to see the myriad aspects. You try to see different things and you start to get comfortable with the idea of experimentation with the other actors.

Often the nature of the material will have an impact on the rehearsal process. McDonnell recalls that for Lawrence Kasdan's *Grand Canyon*, a probing portrait of the nature of contemporary urban life, the cast began by discussing what life in Los Angeles was like for them and how it affected their own daily behavior. "Larry Kasdan's rehearsal processes are filled with exploration. He told us he was excited about directing *Grand Canyon* because he was going to witness everything as a director that he couldn't know about as the writer."

McDonnell also contends that the best actors are the ones who aren't afraid to make mistakes, no matter what the stage of the performance. "A very wise director once told me before opening night in the theatre, 'Go out there and make some mistakes. You can make some beautiful mistakes. They're so *interesting*.'"

In fact, the relationship between the actor and the director seems to work better if they are both willing to gamble a little. When Robin Williams rehearsed with Peter Weir on the *Dead Poets Society* set there was always something going on. "During filming he would play music before a scene to get us in the mood to try different things. One of his favorite things to say was, 'Try something,' which is very freeing. And he would also say, 'You don't have to do anything.' Peter is so confident that it just allows you to feel safe even when you're doing nothing."

Dustin Hoffman points out the fundamental differences between rehearsals for theatre and film.

In the theatre, you have a chance to rehearse every day. You can get out there and find that character over a period of weeks—even during pre-views, even after you open.

Many times, actors say to each other, "Don't come see me until three months after opening night." You can grow into a part. You can't do that on film. Sometimes there is no rehearsal time. Once you start shooting, you are trying to find the character, but it's all on film. And if you improve that character too much, it doesn't match at six weeks what you did the first two weeks.

Mary McDonnell had the luxury of a relatively long rehearsal for *Dances with Wolves*, but then again, there was so much to learn.

We rehearsed for three weeks out on the prairie. We would get up in the morning and pile into a van and then they'd put us on horses. Then we went to language class to learn Lakota. Then we would get fit for these costumes. I was being asked to learn very quickly and I started to understand about the adaptations one makes in trying to survive and conform. So, rather than being familiar with everything, I focused on the unfamiliarity and what that made me feel like. And that helped me understand what created this little girl who was without a family. The guilt. The sense of aloneness.

Invariably, actors discover something about themselves as they move through rehearsal. McDonnell fondly remembers the scene where her character passes out and must be carried home across Lieutenant Dunbar's (Kevin Costner) saddle.

I remember when we were rehearsing the little ride that it felt so comforting to have someone take me physically and care for me. My character probably hadn't felt a lot of that. And I had a sense that she hadn't had a really connected physical life with another person for a long time. So I started imagining what happens to a being even in that unconscious state.

The next time she meets Dunbar consciously, there is obviously something in the unconscious that she doesn't necessarily want to face. She is quite happy with the Indians. But the presence of this man brings up for her a whole level of desire. There's a need for emotional connection that's been denied for a long time. Then it starts to surface when she is around Dunbar, the chemistry begins.

McDonnell is enthusiastic about the discoveries that she makes during rehearsal. "Often I discover some amazing things. I make notes about it." At the same time she stresses a low-key approach because of the ego factor.

"I keep it kind of vague. You don't want to pay too much attention to your-self. It's more like: What was the experience? What was the territory we stepped into? It's a stimulation, a reminder."

Ready on the Set: From Script to Scene

With rehearsals complete, the actual filming begins. There are a number of strategies for dealing with the pressure-packed atmosphere of the shoot. John Lithgow relates that if the rehearsal process was successful, the actor has something he can take with him to the set.

> *You have this memory of having gotten it right at least once before in rehearsal. You've found the essence of the scene. Then you may shoot the scene from four or five different angles and with each angle you may have seven or eight takes. That's forty times you're doing the scene. In addition you may have camera rehearsals and maybe you've run the lines with the other actors. You've had lots of opportunities to get it right.*
>
> *Once the master scene is complete, you have to cling to that basic version of the scene. You can't start messing around outside of those parameters. But you certainly can fine-tune different inflections, differ-ent rhythms, different intentions. And a good director is very watchful. He knows when you're going too far, he has you try it different ways. He gives himself lots of choices.*

Actors begin by familiarizing themselves with their surroundings. Graham Greene relates that in a project with the scope of *Dances with Wolves*, even that simple process can require some formidable adjustments.

> *It required me to literally divorce myself from civilization. I would get into my costume and walk around. Finally it became livable. As an actor you have to get used to that set. You can't walk around stumbling on rough terrain. Whatever is there, you've got to get used to it.*

Mary McDonnell tries to pay attention to her own responses as the shoot continues.

You put yourself in the scene and start to pay attention to some of your responses because it leads you to the direct response you're having to the scene. I may have disregarded the fact that every time I played a certain scene I have my arms folded and I was scratching my face. But now I pay attention because it helps me understand my emotional response.

Some scenes are easier to play than others. The problem always involves how much to trust your own emotional response and how many adjustments need to be made. McDonnell recalls the scene in *Grand Canyon* where she finds the baby. Many felt it was one of the most powerful scenes in the film. Even at the script stage it had a direct effect on her.

I pretty much left that one alone. When I read it, I was blown away by the experience of finding this child. I had such a strong response reading it. I was in touch with all my maternal feelings as soon as I read the scene. They came flying to the surface really quickly. I thought, don't even tamper with it, don't get too used to it.

Graham Greene advocates a zen-like concentration coupled with an ability to relax.

The only thing that's important to me is the scene at that moment. I found that napping between scenes is very important. I kick back. Sitting is recharging my batteries to get another go at it. You have to ignore everybody else. Sometimes it's difficult to focus and concentrate, but it's my responsibility. My responsibility is to be there and do the job I was hired to do. Not to gripe about why there's no banana on the craft service cart. It's not my damn business. My business is to stand in front of the lens when somebody says, "Shoot."

Like Greene, Leonard Nimoy emphasizes a certain work ethic. "You do an honest day's work. You don't do shoddy work. You try to make it better and walk away with a sense of accomplishment." Nimoy explains he learned this during his childhood. "My father was a barber—and there was a sense of completion when he'd snap the apron off the guy and say 'Next!' He'd done a good job of cutting the man's hair."

Dustin Hoffman commands a kind of respect on the set that few actors do. He reveals that much of what he learned about the process came from his first film acting job.

> *The Graduate was my first movie and it still is one of the richest experiences I've ever had, in terms of a director who was so thoroughly prepared. One day, apparently I was dogging it a little and Mike Nichols said something to me that stuck with me. He said, "You're never going to get a chance to do this scene again for the rest of your life and it's going to be there and you're going to look back on it one day and you're going to say, 'I could have done better.'" And I must say, his words stuck with me.*

The challenge of maintaining intensity throughout the production is crucial as the same scene is shot over and over again. First the master shot encompasses the entire scene. Then the director moves in for the tighter shots and finally the close-ups. Graham Greene explains how this translates to the actor's performance.

> *You can do anything you want in the master, but you earn your money in the close-up. That's where you have to convey a thought. If you don't have a line and they cut to you and you're sitting there blank—it just doesn't work. But if you're thinking seriously about what the other actor is saying or doing, maybe he did something really neat in the master. You bank that, you put it away.*

His fellow actors also appreciate Greene's ability. Mary McDonnell worked with him for many months in *Dances with Wolves*.

> *A part of the skill involved in movie acting is acting with authority. Graham Greene has an incredible facility that way. There's a learned ability to make a discovery in one lens and know how to reduce the role or exaggerate it for the next lens. In a sense the master shot is like the last rehearsal.*

For Dustin Hoffman the peculiar needs of filmmaking lead to a kind of schizophrenia for the actor.

If you're stage-trained like I am, even though you are making a movie you really feel like you're rehearsing a play. But when it comes time to have opening night, you've already finished making the movie. And now you want to start to play it, but it's too late. It's over. Movie making is like rehearsing.

Jack Nicholson contends that the special demands of film require a kind of intensity that is very different from other forms of acting. "Movie acting is harder than stage acting. No one could play Hoffa on stage for three hours—the amount of energy that's telescoped—they'd die."

Also, in film, you have to see your work yourself. In the theatre, you give a rotten performance, twelve people say it's great. But in film, the mind knows this—or at least my mind knows, "Ah, I'm going to have to see this." I've done a lot of film editing and I know that at a minimum, at least half of what you do every day on a shoot stinks. It's the worst that it could be.

Peter Strauss's favorite "Jack story" is illustrative of how Nicholson approaches filmmaking. It involves the advice he gave to one of Strauss's friends, actress Mary Steenburgen.

They were working together and one day he said, "Okay, this time do the scene and kill the darlings." In other words, kill the things you know will get you through, the little grimace, the grin, the tilted head, the raging look, all the things you do in almost everything you do. These are the things that reflect your stereotypical but generally salesworthy moments.

Energy and Synergy: Collaboration with Other Actors

Since actors rarely work in a vacuum, it's not surprising that they benefit from their experiences with one another. What finds its way from script to screen is often the result of their on-camera collaboration. Leonard Nimoy compares it to a tennis match.

You begin to interact with other actors to see what kind of rhythmic exchanges you're going to have. You can only do a character alone for so long. Then it's time for the tennis match. You have to know what kind of balls are going to be hit at you and start thinking about how you are going to return them.

How is she going to play this scene as your wife? Is she angry? Is she sad? I've got to see her face, her body, hear her intonation, so I can respond to that specifically. You can't bring a rehearsed performance to the set and refuse to change it. You have to be flexible. Acting is all about chemistry.

Graham Greene uses the same word to describe the collaboration process.

The director has to make the judgment about how it's going to work with all these actors together. Sometimes it doesn't work and you find yourself with another performer who becomes an adversary on the set. Although at times I've worked with people who I didn't get along with and it showed on the screen. And it worked! It's chemistry.

During the shoot, any number of things can happen, even though they may not be in the script. The actor needs to be able to maintain the flexibility to go with them as they occur. In *Grand Canyon* Mary McDonnell's Claire had one long scene with Steve Martin that became one of the film's most memorable moments.

I was surprised at the deepness, the tone, of the scene with Steve. She kind of gets a kick out of him. She disagrees with him on everything and that's okay because they have a great love for each other. I had thought of Claire as a sort of contemporary woman with a clear head about facing the trouble in her marriage. But as we did it, I discovered this was an opportunity for her to touch those feelings that she'd been afraid of. And when she actually talked it out with the right person, someone who was safe, it just all poured out. Suddenly she was sad, terrified, threatened by the potential loss.

Another kind of synergistic challenge comes from playing a supporting role. Graham Greene says simply, "It can be really tough. Supporting is a big word in my mind. You're boosting that character." He chooses his words carefully. "You can't overact; don't be stupid, don't steal the scene. You can act your face out in your scene, but in someone else's scene, be supportive. There's no shame in being a bit player. It's like they say: there are no small roles, only small actors."

Jack Nicholson became one of Hollywood's superstars by specializing in supporting roles. In his interview with Hilary de Vries he explains:

> Film acting is different from stage acting, when you get just three scenes, which was the case in A Few Good Men, you couldn't play through the entire production at the intensity that I played them for two weeks. I was quite spent at the end of those two weeks.

No doubt it was a tumultuous two weeks. The result was his tenth Academy Award nomination, in this case for best supporting actor.

Large roles or small, it all comes back to the way actors function together on the set. Their collaboration can help make the film flourish, if all the elements are right. Dustin Hoffman says simply, "There is a synergy that takes place and for a moment, you feel like you're in a jazz group."

In the best moment, actors can bring out wonderful performances in one another. Robert Sean Leonard, who played Neil in *Dead Poets Society*, remembers a key scene with co-star Robin Williams.

> There's a scene with Robin in the schoolroom where I lie to him and tell him that my father gave me permission to be in the play. He says, "Did you tell your father? What did he say?" and I say, "It will be fine."
>
> The scene was only about five lines and then I was to get up and leave. But when the camera was on me, instead of letting me leave, Robin repeats the questions again, "Really, you really told him?" In my mind I'm thinking, why aren't we cutting? What's happening here? We're completely off the script and why aren't we cutting? Robin says it again, "Really, you told him what you told me?" And he looks in my eyes and I'm terrified. I say, "Well, he wasn't happy," and then I mumble something, which I don't think makes any sense, like "He'll be in Chicago, so it won't really matter."

I totally made that up as the camera was rolling. Robin just tortured me. He kept repeating all the questions and I had to improvise different answers. I'm totally on the spot. And of course it comes across wonderfully that I'm lying.

Peter said, "Cut," and, "Perfect," and that was the take that was used. Robin made that scene work and that was his strength. He's incredible on his feet....

Collaboration with the Director

During the course of a film, a special relationship forms between the director and the actor. Each is dependent on the other. Each must learn to trust the other. What does the actor need from the director?

Peter Strauss says, "First and foremost, I want a protector of the integrity of my work and a nurturer of courage." For John Lithgow, "A good director helps you move in new directions, makes you feel comfortable, liberates you."

Mary McDonnell explains that "good directors are in touch with their masculine side, they have a sense of balance. They know how to give orders and have a heady sense of the whole picture. Then they turn around to the actor and have their feminine side—they become a reflector and emotional supporter. It's a remarkable thing to see a director with that kind of balance. You just feel great and want to be there."

Most often actors want a director who will protect them while transforming the set into a space where creativity can flourish. For Peter Strauss, it is the actor's willingness to risk that is at stake.

Actors are only good when they're daring and if you're afraid to be daring, you're dead. In order to be daring, you have to have a fertile place to work, a place where your work is given a place to fail. You don't want to be ridiculed or frustrated by time elements. You want a director who insulates you and protects you from everyone else on that set.

The notion of being protected on the set is something that actors mention again and again. Why is this so vital? According to Strauss:

The actor has to please. He comes through the door, the scene calls for him to be in tears and to accost a girl and walk out. Some directors will say, "Let's go, Peter, come through the door, just get through the door, I've got to get the shot." The director of photography might say, "Peter, when you come through the door, get out of that light, come in at this light." The costumer says, "Well, I wish he would wear his tie closed as opposed to open. And the prop person is saying "Do you want a brown suitcase as opposed to a black suitcase?" In that case, you're dead.

And how might a good director solve problems like this? Is there any way the director can help the actor cope with the chaos on the set? Strauss says:

Sure. Another director will say, "Okay, I want the props, costume, sound and makeup to talk to Peter now, get your problem solved. Is everybody happy? Good. Now Peter and I are going to work." Then the director takes me aside and says, "What do you need to get you through that door with tears in your eyes? Because I'd like to start on a close-up."

Or he will say, "Look, I need coverage, so I'm going to start on a master, don't blow it, take it slowly, we'll work up to it. Do you need a minute of quiet backstage? Are you capable of doing this? Do you want me to help you? Would you like to try it and I'll let you know how I feel about it and what it looks like?"

Much was written about Robin Williams's "transformation" as an actor after his performance in *Dead Poets Society*. Critics said that the wild and chaotic comedian could never pull off a dramatic role but he proved them wrong. Much of the credit went to director Peter Weir. Somehow he knew exactly how to "handle" Williams.

"Peter did have me do each scene in three different ways," Williams explains. There was a "straight" take right from the script, an "outrageous" take where the actor was allowed to improvise in any way he liked and one take that was a kind of combination of the two. "Sometimes we'd do the outrageous take first, sometimes last, like dessert," Williams recalls fondly, "It lets that instinct out. Otherwise it can back up on you. At least you get it out so you don't feel like you didn't get a chance to do it. Sometimes it works, other times, no."

Williams does recall one spontaneous scene that wound up in the film. "At times we got really outrageous, as in the classroom with the Shakespeare bit. Some teachers perform for their students, so we kept in the part where Keating talks about classical performances of Shakespeare done by Brando and John Wayne." As it turned out that was probably the only "outrageous" take that ended up in the film, but Weir got what he wanted. And Williams was nominated for an Oscar.

Another aspect of the director's job is to keep the thread of the story in mind and to correct the actor if something is out of sequence or if his or her emotional line doesn't track. Mary McDonnell has worked with some of the best directors in Hollywood.

> *A good director keeps you in tune with the thread. With all four directors I've worked with recently—Larry Kasdan, Kevin Costner, Phil Robinson and John Sayles—each has come up to me at a very important moment and said, "I think we lost the thread of something." I wonder how they can do that? I only keep track of this one little [character] and they keep track of everyone. I'm blown away by what directors have to keep in mind every day.*

A good director can make the shoot a great experience for the actor. Then there are the other kind. Leonard Nimoy says, "I am most comfortable when I see myself as a workman. I consider myself a laborer." Working for the director, he tries to "build" the best possible performance.

> *Less-than-competent directors will force actors or actresses into unworkable situations. They will ask you to deliver a chair with three and a half legs. And when you try to point out that it will fall down, they will say, "Just do it." So you do it. And sure enough, it falls down.*

Nimoy says his background as an actor has certainly influenced him as a director.

> *I think the biggest edge for actors who become directors is that we understand the actor's problems. We're aware of what the actor's contributions*

can be. We're not threatened by it, we invite it. You know because you've been there.

Peter Strauss feels that most directors could use a little more understanding when it comes to their actors.

You need a mentor figure who understands the creative process and knows how to nurture it and protect it. And most directors don't know that. They'll know how to move the camera through your nose and around the corner to catch the glimmering sunlight, but they don't know a thing about your dilemmas.

You can sense the frustration in Strauss's voice as he describes what happens so often on the set.

In the end, you're on the set and you're looking around grasping at straws half the time, hoping you'll get some clue that will help you get the emotional content right. Maybe the actress will be so damn good that the scene is going to work because you're touched by her great ability. And the director might have told you a story at lunch and you think you can use it.

You're on the set and it's a whirlwind of activity based on economics. And you're hopeful. You've gotten your homework done as well as you could to get through this quiz. That's all the time there was. The problem is that it's not the quiz, it's the final.

Clothes Encounters: Love and Sex Scenes

A particular kind of trusting collaboration is needed between the director and the actor during love and sex scenes. Playing a love scene with the likes of Tom Cruise or Sharon Stone certainly sounds appealing. "Not so," says Peter Strauss. "There's always a degree of discomfort. It's uncomfortable for the actors, for the director and for the crew. Why shouldn't it be? Here we are at our most intimate and we're supposed to forget about these sixty bored technicians standing around watching us. I've done a great number of love scenes and, believe me, actors are rarely oblivious to the world around them."

It is up to the director to reduce that discomfort. Strauss explains that this can be done in a number of ways. "First of all, the director can reduce the number of people in the room who are watching. Secondly, it's important that the director create a trusting place to work so that the performers feel they are being protected. These scenes depend on the professionalism and the sense of humor of the principals involved."

Methods for the creation of a comfort zone can vary from director to director. Nina Foch recounts how director Philip Noyce did it while shooting *Sliver*. "He played a scene nude himself and showed it to the cast in dailies so they could see what would be expected."

Strauss and Foch agree that actor preparation is similar, whether you are doing an eating scene or a love scene. But on-screen lovemaking requires a little more thought. Foch emphasizes that there needs to be some attraction to the other actor, even though it might not exist in reality.

> *You have to know what the scene is about, know what you want from your partner and you have to decide why he or she is attractive to you. In most cases you are not attracted but you have to say to yourself, "This will be over within a few days. I can find something in this person that's attractive for the length of the scene." If you're really playing the scene and are clear what you want from that other actor, then you have no time to think about the fact that you are exposing yourself.*

On the other hand, real attraction between performers can also create a problem. "The ultimate terror for an actor is to get turned on," says Strauss. "With a man this demands a kind of mental control that generally would not exist in that kind of intimate moment." He smiles. "It means that the actor has to do a little more acting than usual."

> *In these situations actors have to protect themselves. You should know exactly what's going to be required and it should be in your contract. You need to know how intimate the scene should be, how much will be shown. There's also the question of allowing still photos and who has photo control. You consistently hear horror stories, particularly from actresses who didn't know there would be a still photographer or how the camera was going to be positioned.*

Widespread use of still photos on the Internet has only exacerbated these fears. Despite all of this, the actor must be ready.

Mental and physical preparation is a good idea for those intimate scenes. "Have massages, have a facial, be sure that you are your best self," says Nina Foch. "That's something you have to do in any picture, but particularly for a nude scene. Know that you've done everything you can and then forget about it."

Beautiful bodies don't happen by accident. "The personal trainer and the dentist are always visited before films," says Strauss. "You find actors suddenly showing up at the gym six weeks before their big scene, expecting miracles."

Are there *any* advantages to playing love and sex scenes? Strauss admits to a few. "Hey, I get to be intimate with someone and get away with it. If there's a halfway respectable relationship with the actress, there can be a kind of warmth to the experience. Besides, I'd rather play a scene that says, 'He kisses her passionately' than a scene that says, 'He rescues the horse from the raging river'!"

Generally we think about how sexually explicit scenes are handled by the two players, but what happens when a third character enters the mix? That's exactly what happens in *One Hour Photo* when Robin Williams' character interrupts a couple in their bedroom. "Nude scenes aren't great, they're really uncomfortable," he tells Philly.com. "They're basically naked in front of you and you're threatening them with a knife. And I think more emotional, it's pretty hideous what you are making them do."

Williams does remember some nude scenes more fondly than others however. He played one opposite Maria Conchita Alonso in *Moscow on the Hudson*. How did it feel? "If you're going to be nude, she's a good person to be nude with!"

Collaboration and the Actor:
The Kindness of Strangers

In the best of films, the spirit of collaboration seems to extend outward in every direction. John Lithgow feels the actor can contribute through a willingness to form relationships with as many collaborators as possible.

I try to think of every single person on the set as a collaborator in several ways. Because I come from the theatre, I count on an audience, a feeling that people are watching me. And I always like to treat the crew as my audience and to get them interested in what we're all doing. I try to have a specific personal relationship with every one of them, first because it's more pleasant and also because you're collaborating with them in very specific ways.

If you have a working relationship with the dolly grip, you can work with him in timing your moves. You can tell him when you're going to pause. If he's dollying along next to you and he gets to know that movement, that can save you a couple of wasted takes. The same thing with the focus puller and camera operator, or gaffer. It helps to have a first-name working relationship.

The spirit of collaboration can even extend from the set into postproduction, to the unseen faces of those whose needs may be anticipated by the actor. Lithgow cites the actor's relationship with the editor as an example.

The editor on Twilight Zone—The Movie *said he was amazed I had been able to stick with continuity even in the midst of these scenes where I was tumbling through the air, screaming, behaving totally irrationally. I was always still in frame, exactly in focus and he was able to use almost anything in my performance.*

He said, "You have no idea how I've had to save actors' performances [when they] don't pay any attention to continuity." Well, I don't want to ever do anything great that nobody can use because it doesn't cut. And in order to do that you really have to get everybody working with you.

With the shooting over, the long postproduction process begins. It is interesting that so many actors acknowledge that this final stage of the film will determine how their performance will be received. By the time postproduction gets under way, they will be on to the next job. Most often they will not even meet the many men and women whose job it is to make the film work and to make the actor look good in the process. This is why Peter

Strauss emphasizes that actors all must ultimately rely on the kindness of strangers.

> *You are depending upon the kindness of an editor who doesn't know you at all and may not know how hard you worked for that subtle, subtle nuance. For him, it may be a longer take and he needs to go to the shorter take. Or he looks at it and doesn't catch that moment that you built your entire film around. He still goes through that footage from his point of view; the composer is looking from his.*
>
> *Ultimately, everybody's in their own little world and the director is supposed to coordinate all these roles. But he or she has to deal with the ramifications and repercussions of all those strangers. And, of course, so do you.*

If it all comes together perfectly the result can be a rare masterpiece that will transform everyone who was involved. Robin Williams still remembers when he began to feel that *Dead Poets* was special. "I knew that this film had a feel to it which was very powerful. I knew it about halfway through. You just felt something wonderful was going on and you didn't want to talk about it too much because you don't want to mess with it. Just let it be. Let it grow. Don't water it too much, just sit back and experience it. It's a moving event."

At the end of the day for Williams, the project was all about life lessons. "*Dead Poets Society* tapped into an essential feeling we all have about finding that passion, that bliss that comes from doing what you love to do." Sure, people ask him about the film but William says his favorite comment was "One day in New York, there was a garbageman who saw me and he yelled out, 'Hey—I *loved* that dead man thing!'"

Asked to summarize the importance of the collaborative process, Peter Strauss pauses for a moment, reflecting on the difficulty of transforming a classic film from script to screen. All of these strangers, millions of dollars...How does it happen? "It's amazing when we make a great movie." He smiles. "It's so easy to make a lousy one."

CLOSE-UP
THE ACTORS: RUSSELL CROWE AND JENNIFER CONNELLY

Responding to the Material
RUSSELL CROWE: I tend to make my decisions pretty much the same every time. And it's all got to do with the material. I got a call from my agent, George Freeman. And then I got another call from Jeffrey Katzenberg, both of them enthusing about a particular script called *A Beautiful Mind*. So I sat on the back porch on one of those really steaming, hot Texas summer nights. And I read it and I had a very big reaction to it. I call it the "goose bumps" factor.

JENNIFER CONNELLY: I loved the script right away. It was one of those rare scripts that you read and it just seems to have all of the elements. It was a beautifully written story. It's very compelling. All the more intriguing because it is based on a true story. It had everything going for it—an incredible story, Ron directing it, Russell in it. I really wanted to do it. I thought, if only I get to do this, I'll never ask for one of these special parts again.

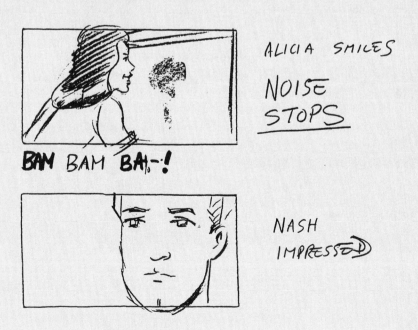

Developing the Character

RUSSELL: I'll begin to play the character. I'll begin to make decisions like, "No, I wouldn't say that, I'd say it like this." I just start working the script. So, at the end of the first reading, there are already notes. And I actually have had a physical reaction to it.

There's an old-fashioned attitude that some actors have...that you must love the character. Well, I've played a variety of different characters, some positive, some negative. And so I think you get into a problem as an actor if you love the character, because when you love something, you lose your objectivity. And the whole point of it is exposure. And you can only really expose the emotional workings of the character if you are objective and you are willing to say, "Well, at this point of time maybe he's not in the best of lights, but that's his humanity." I love characterization. But I don't necessarily love the characters.

Acting, particularly in feature films, is really an instinctive thing. You can either do the gig or you can't. I do apply things that come out of Stanislavsky or Stella Adler or whatever, but I am not a student of a method or The Method. Whatever I can use, I grab.

Researching the Role

RUSSELL: I didn't feel that Nash as he is now is a true template of Nash the young man, because he has undergone around thirty-five years of medication and hospitalization. I decided early on I couldn't get everything I needed from Nash, so the priority of sitting down with him sort of slid down the list.

JENNIFER: Even though our version of Alicia is fictionalized, I still wanted to meet her. I felt—it just felt right to me. I asked to meet Alicia before we started shooting. I went out to Newark, New Jersey where she works and had lunch with her.

I just personally wouldn't have felt comfortable doing this project if I hadn't at least talked to her. I wanted to say, "Is there anything, in representing you, that you would like to see me convey—or not convey—about you, that I otherwise might?" I was looking for some gem of wisdom and insight and inspiration. I felt it was really important that she be human and plausible and not turn into some impossible martyr/hero. Ultimately, I took more of the biographical information from the book and sort of made my own character.

RUSSELL: We weren't setting out to make an absolute biography, we were dealing with the spirit of Nash's life, so we have very large touchstones. Playing Nash was a much scarier journey [than my part in *The Insider*] because there were whole big patches of stuff we just couldn't really get information on. Even though he was noted in academic circles—mainly for his eccentricities, I might add, and [for] his analytical mind—there was no footage of him and not a single piece of film showing him as a young man, showing how he walked. [There was] no audio to hear how he talked. You have to take the facts of his life and look at what you can really use. I had to take photographs and I had to take really big, broad-strokes facts and say, "Okay, he was born in West Virginia. No matter what he talks like now at the age of seventy-plus, I'm going to make him a West Virginian."

You've got to take the facts of his life and look at what you can actually use given the facts of the script. So, really, at a certain point in the research the only place we have to move from this point is deduction and intuition. All of us are, really, false witnesses to our own lives. A man in his seventies remembers certain things. But the types of questions I was asking initially were kinds of feeler questions to see how reliable he could be as that witness [to his own life]. "Did you ever smoke cigarettes?" "No." "Brother, I've got evidence that says you smoked cigarettes for so many years." Nash cannot remember whole periods of his life...so I can't use him.

Ron videotaped John doing a lecture at the blackboard and I noticed that his hands were really graceful and he had very long tapered fingernails. So I started growing my nails. You have to be slightly more careful when picking things up with long nails, so it immediately gave my hands more grace and that's what I was looking for.

Mathematics and I parted company when I was about fourteen...In conjunction with a fellow called Dave Buyer, who is the mathematics consultant on the film, what I am scribbling on those windows and chalkboards is a series of problems and conjectures that mathematicians will enjoy working through. They are genuine equations. However, every now and then, I would just throw in a completely incorrect number, just for balance.

Someone asked me about the research I did and I said, "I'm living in Manhattan. I just go for a walk every Sunday." There were certain people in Manhattan I would visit regularly. There's a bloke up on

East 92nd street who would have a conversation with half a dozen imaginary friends whenever he was packing his bed up in the morning about how nobody ever helps with the chores. He was kind of a particular favorite.

Playing the Love Story

JENNIFER: It's a powerful, moving love story and a very adult, human love story. I know that, for Alicia, she had her sights set on him for a while; he was a big man on campus. And he was a man whose greatest pursuit was an original idea and I think that was incredibly intriguing to her. It's a story of genius and struggles with mental illness and marriage and ultimately triumphs.

RUSSELL: The amazing thing about Nash [is] the romance. The romance that is built into the story, the fact that these two people are still together. That was what made it important. We have genius, madness, a Nobel Prize—and then, what was more important to me—a romance that spans fifty years and a very full, deep, nurturing and caring relationship between John and Alicia.

JENNIFER: Specifics of their lives have been modified in our film, but I think the essence of it has been preserved, which is that they had this remarkable marriage and she was so devoted to him and committed to him and was really kind of a pioneer of helping him in his recovery.

Very few people knew how to manage Nash's eccentric behavior and Alicia really did, so I felt that I really needed to embody that. Russell was kind of perfect training for me. Russell has a very charismatic, strong personality, which can be overbearing. I've seen a lot of people falter when trying to talk to him. I felt strongly about not letting that happen.

I was really happy that you see her delve into her own chaos and struggle. You see her kind of wrestle with her own grief and self-doubt. I loved that section of the movie. I think without it, you wouldn't have stayed with her or believed her choice to stay with him. It's a love story and it's a story of human triumph and of human will and the miraculous recovery.

Collaborating

RUSSELL: Ron Howard, it seems to me, has got everybody in the world fooled that he's some kind of simple bloke. He's one of the most intense filmmakers I've ever worked with. But he does it in a gentle fashion and that's because he's organized and he knows what he wants.

JENNIFER: I loved working with Ron. He really respects his actors and thereby commands a lot of respect. I never felt that I came away from a scene not having been able to explore something I wanted to. Russell is great to work with as an actor because he gives you a lot. He's very spontaneous, he's very present, he's very available. He's thoroughly prepared but then likes to, sort of, refine things as he gets on the set. For me it was really exhilarating because nothing was ever the same, nothing was ever predictable. It was like nothing was ever just on paper. The room was always very dynamic.

*You'd be surprised
at how much detail
goes into even one
little piece of film;
it's much more than
anyone could
possibly imagine.*

—Robert Grieve

Behind the Scenes:
Collaboration by Design

The curtains open. The lights go down. Audiences settle into their seats and munch on their popcorn. The opening credits roll by. Two hours later the movie is over and the end credits scroll across the screen. By the time they are done, the theater is virtually empty. Empty popcorn boxes litter the floor. The clean-up crew hurries to get ready for the next showing. Everyone else is headed for the parking lot.

While little noted and often quickly forgotten, film credits nonetheless provide a story all their own. The opening title sequence lists the studio first; the final three credits go to the writer, producer and director. By contract and custom all the rest go to various collaborators whose contributions remain a mystery to the average moviegoer.

You have probably never heard of Production Designer Wynn Thomas, but if you saw *A Beautiful Mind* or any of his many other projects, then you have seen his work—and been moved by it. Like so many of the "Hollywood collaborators," his "role" in the creation of a classic mainstream film may not get a lot of press, but it remains crucial nonetheless.

"What I try to do as a designer is to provide a visual concept that provides a journey for us to go on as we travel throughout the movie," he explains. "And generally what will happen is once I formulate those ideas, I will take them to the director and see if it's something he agrees with and then sometimes he or she will embellish my ideas and take them one step further."

Many of these collaborator roles have earned their own Academy Award category—and rightfully so, for their contributions elevate the film experience. Meet the "collaborators by design"—the women and men literally and figuratively "behind the scenes" of every major motion picture.

Production Design: "Dream a Little Dream"

The late Ferdinando Scarfiotti was one of film's best-known production designers. When he died in 1994, he left behind an impressive body of work, much of it in collaboration with Director Bernardo Bertolucci. The results can be seen in such visually stunning films as *The Sheltering Sky*, *The Conformist* and *The Last Tango in Paris*. They won Oscars for their efforts on *The Last Emperor*. It was Scarfiotti who received warm critical praise and an Oscar nomination for creating the eccentric visual world seen in *Toys*, despite its lack of box office success. In one of his final interviews he revealed the "interior world" of production design.

The production designer is really the production dreamer, quite literally, the one who dreams. When I was working with Director Nicholas Roeg, he would always tell me, "Dream on! Dream on!" My dream team includes the art director, the set decorator, sketch artists and construction people. They all work under me and are part of my department.

Generally I start preparation for a film about three to eight months before filming. With Toys *I stayed on the movie almost two years. It was a very elaborate production to prepare, but I got a break when Barry Levinson decided to do* Bugsy *first. So I had all that extra time, but I think that was essential because that was not a movie I could have rushed through. There was a lot of research. Practically every scene had to be illustrated with a color sketch so the director knew exactly what kind of world I was creating.*

It was just the opposite situation with The Last Emperor. *I came into the picture quite late in the process. I barely had enough time to design the first two or three sets before shooting began. Then I was designing during shooting, which is never easy. I think I had about three months of prep, total; for a movie like that—a big period piece—three months is nothing.*

Every film is different and requires something new. In Love Affair we had to design a Russian cargo ship that was supposed to be in the South Seas. Imagine building this huge boat on a stage! I'd never been on one before, so there was lots of research. Every film is a whole new world. You have to explore that world and give it your own sense of style. Because it may be a Russian cargo ship, but it is your Russian cargo ship, you know?

On Being a Production Designer

There are no formal requirements to be a production designer, but most of us are people who have some background in the arts. I studied architecture for four years in Rome, which was very useful for me. I've been interested in the arts since I was a kid. I was always going to the museums and making drawings in bed as a young child. My choice of architecture at the university has helped me with the technical background, which is really my weakest part. I rely heavily on my art directors for that, but still you need to know about structure and building. You have to know how to read a blueprint, to read technical drawings, otherwise you'll be in trouble. You also have to have a good sense of color. I feel at ease with color—this is one of my strengths.

From Script to Set

When I first read a script I generally try not to think about anything, I just let it flow through my head. That has always been a crucial part of the process because most of my ideas come from the first reading. Very seldom do I get other ideas from a second reading. So I have to be really relaxed in order to let the images emerge.

If it's a contemporary story, then you need more from the director in order to define the characters and know what their lives are like. If you're designing a house for a character, then you need to know more about that person.

Of course, we do go through the script many times, with the director, art director and all my other collaborators. There are so many meetings that by the time that you finish your work and design the whole thing, you know the script very well. There are little details, little changes. But the first impact is generally the one that counts for me.

Preparation

I begin by designing in my head. Then I'll do some very loose sketches. If the sketch needs to be a bit more elaborate, I use illustrators who do it very fast because I would take too much time. I have a group of set designers who make blueprints and technical drawings. The art director and I will supervise these. Out of the drawings come the models. I build them more for the director than for myself. Many directors are ill at ease when they have to read a blueprint or technical drawing. They don't know what they're looking at. You'll catch them looking at it upside down. So a model is really the best way to show the space and how the camera can move around inside it.

With Toys we tried a new computer program that can animate a whole set. You feed the computer a technical drawing with a floor plan. Then the computer builds the room on the screen—inside, outside, upstairs, downstairs—everything. Then you can move figures inside and outside, make every camera move you want.

To me it sounded like a dream. I got this computer wizard to feed all the sets into the computer for Barry to look at. But he didn't seem much interested in it so we dropped that idea. One day it will work, but at that moment it seemed like a cold way to envision the scene. So we ended up having a traditional storyboard artist illustrate the scenes.

You must do whatever research the movie requires. So I research, but then I try to close the books and do my own thing. The style usually comes from me, but it's also open to discussion. If it's a period movie you already have a sense of the style because of the period itself. You tend to see the script through the period if you know the period.

The Last Emperor

I knew very little about China. Because of the political situation, very little was available. Since there are very few art books in China, most of the research was done in Italy and London.

There is one excellent book on the Forbidden City that was helpful. And I researched Chinese architecture and Chinese artists. The subject is very vast but we were dealing only with the last few years of Imperial China and the coming of the revolution, so that made it easier. We also used the book written by the real-life English tutor, who was played by Peter O'Toole in the movie. It didn't have any photographs but it did convey how people lived at that time.

When we went to China for location scouting I met some of the men from the imperial family. There were two brothers of the emperor who had family books and photo albums, which proved very valuable to us. They had pictures of the houses, which don't exist anymore. There was this Palace of the North where *they were raised. It's now a clinic and you can barely see what it once was. Even buildings of the 1920s are very hard to find. They've been buried under concrete or rooms have been added to them.*

Then there were the color problems. Imperial yellow is a special yellow that could only be worn by members of the imperial family. No one else could use that yellow. It's quite a true yellow, very gold. And there's a special red that had to be re-created for the set.

I brought a team of Italian painters and sculptors with me. We had to decorate all the ceilings with really thick decorations, as they used to do, especially in the Forbidden City. It was funny; the Chinese were in total awe of these people who were able to paint "authentic" Chinese decorations on the wall. There was no one left there who could do it in the correct way. After the Cultural Revolution there was this backlash against art, artistic expression and freedom. Many of the techniques used earlier in the century had been lost or forgotten. Finally we found some students from an art school. The challenge was enormous.

We were allowed to film in the Forbidden City in the courtyard, but not indoors. So we built all the interiors. Most people thought that everything was shot inside the Forbidden City but it's not true. There was only one interior given to us at the last minute after a great deal of negotiation—the place where the little emperor was crowned. They let us in for half a day but with only five people. We couldn't bring lights inside because they were terribly afraid of fire.

Originally the script called for the interior with the door closed and then the door would open and the little emperor would come out and everybody would see these zillions of people outside. But if we had closed the door we wouldn't have been able to see anything. As usual in movies, when you have some problems they stimulate you to do something bizarre that you never would have thought of.

So I came up with this yellow curtain in the scene because that was the only way to light the place without closing the door. It was a canopy and you could lift it up. It worked wonderfully and had beautiful movement. I was really proud of it because it became a real focal point for the movie.

Toys

When I first read the Toys script I realized it had so many possibilities, it was totally open to interpretation. Barry Levinson left me completely free, so I thought of an old 1920s French play by Roger Vitrac, who was a member of the dadaist movement. It was probably the only play written by a dada artist. There was a very surreal style that seemed to fit somehow.

From there I decided to use the European avant-garde art of the twenties and thirties, which was quite famous but hasn't been used that much in movies. I thought of the surrealists and the futurists and the Russian constructivists, as well as the modernist movement of the early twentieth century.

Actually, the artist that I used the most is an Italian futurist called Fortunato Depero—one of the most important artists of the futurist movement. Research like this provides inspiration, but then I try to go off on my own and depart from the research.

There was an extraordinary series of events involving the outdoor locations. The script takes place in a heavily wooded area. But when you set a film in a forest, no matter how beautiful it is, there's always something very real about it.

I wanted something different so I envisioned this absolutely naked landscape, with really nothing but hills of grass. My idea was to find something like the Sahara, but instead of sand, have grass. So I drew it that way, but I wasn't sure such a location actually existed anywhere.

When it came time to find the actual location, we happened to find the exact look in Washington State, in a region near Spokane. There it was: no billboards, no telephone poles, nothing. Farmhouses maybe every ten miles. The rest was green hills, green hills, green hills. It's a farming community; they grow wheat, millet and barley. So there were different shades of green and we controlled it a little, telling them what to plant so we would have a kind of uniform look. The planting had to be done twice because the picture was postponed for a year.

It had never happened to me where I designed something out of my head and then found the reality exactly as I dreamed it. It was a miracle.

Costume Design: The Lines of Illusion

Costume designer Marilyn Vance's résumé reads like a definitive bibliography of Hollywood studio filmmaking. Among her credits: *Pretty Woman, Die Hard, Predator, The Breakfast Club, Romancing the Stone, GI Jane* and *Mystery Men.* She was nominated for an Academy Award for her efforts on *The Untouchables.*

When I first read the script, I'm looking for the setting and the story and what that story encompasses. I want to see how many people I have to deal with in my head. How many important characters are there? How do they relate to one another? Will they be driven apart?

Then you start asking character questions. Where would they live? How would they live? What's their income level? How would they represent themselves? Would they wear jewelry? Would they have a piece of junk on their wrist? Earrings? Makeup? You try to develop a sense of the kind of character they are. A mean, nasty, killer—he's looking one way. If he's blue collar, he's looking another way. The personality of each project can be found in the script.

For the costume designer, everything in life is psychological presentation. We all express ourselves through what we wear. I do character boards, which are like storyboards. I lay out the feeling and the look I'm going for. A lot of people know me for those character boards because they are a communication device. I can present them to the director and the actors and they have something specific to respond to. Or maybe we'll take photographs of the actor or actress to see which colors are best suited for them and their personality. Very often the actors are appreciative. Other times it's too much for them. They'll say, "Oh, I suppose the next thing you'll do is act it out for me." It's always different.

Research

Research is always important. I'll start with traditional sources: books of costumes, art books, anything pertaining to the subject. I'll look at paintings. It depends on the project. You do whatever it takes.

For Pretty Woman I went to Hollywood Boulevard to look for hookers, but I couldn't find any. They had cleaned up the street! And I needed the visual look to get it right. Then one night [Director] Garry Marshall was driving around and saw this hooker wearing an old fifties' or early sixties' band jacket. It was perfect. So we used that for Julia Roberts—an oversized man's jacket hiding her little skirt and the boots up to here. Those boots, I had to have those boots! I had seen a pair in London, so we sent for them.

I researched strippers for The Last Boy Scout. Tony Scott, the director, had me in every strip joint in town. But I learned a lot. I'll put everything I've learned onto a character board, with colors.

Usually I come on the project six or eight weeks before shooting, depending on the film. Sometimes you sit and wait and you're on the payroll for months waiting for casting. Other times you'll have three weeks to pull something off. Twelve weeks is a luxury.

Tricks of the Trade

I might dress hundreds, even thousands, for a film like The Rocketeer or The Untouchables. We had a thousand people in Santa Rosa for the flying sequence in The Rocketeer. We had to dress all the people in the stadium and all the flight people. Many times we have workrooms that will run for twenty-four hours a day. I'll have twenty or thirty seamstresses, plus people who are constantly keeping the clothing clean.

Sometimes the costumes are farmed out to so many places, I can't even tell you. It could be shirts in one place, vests go to another place, suits go to somebody else. And maybe I'll make the shoes.

I take wool suits and dye them, just to break them down into a comfortable kind of a way because when you take things fresh off the rack, it's just terrible. You can't buy brand-new things and throw them in front of the camera. It just looks too crisp and scary. All you're noticing is the brand-new clothes people are wearing and it's a distraction.

Pretty Woman

When I did Pretty Woman I knew the Julia Roberts character would not think about fashion, but she had to be smart. This was about a girl who was a hooker, she was very gaudy and glitzy and had all this ridiculous amount of stuff on. How could she fit into this really understated, very wealthy, quiet man's life? I had her subdue the dress, pare it down. And it became very elegant. It showed that this was a woman smart enough to learn how to fit in. She realized how understated he was, she picked up on it immediately. In situations like that, less is more.

A lot of people remember her red dress. It started as a big ball gown because Garry Marshall wanted her to be a princess. But it was just too much, so I took it down and tried to do something else with it. I got the inspiration for the red dress from a period painting. It gave it that feeling of class.

We had to make Richard Gere's suits—all of them, because we couldn't find that simple, classy elegance. Everything we found was that Armani oversized suit look, but we needed a streamlined, classical character. I went with a French rather than an Italian look because we wanted him to have that kind of cool elegance, not too much fabric. The vests were deeper, to give him better shape in the shoulders. They looked wider, it gave him a really good line.

He went through torture for us. We had to fit him every day for weeks just to get the suits right. When you don't have a suit with texture, every little line shows. We did get the fabric from Italy though, because it had to lay just right.

Action Pictures

The problem with action films is that sometimes the character has to wear the same outfit for the entire film. We had to do this in the Die Hards, the Predators, Judgment Night. In Romancing the Stone, *Kathleen Turner had twenty-four outfits in different degrees of degradation. The same outfit made twenty-four different ways! We had to rip them into various shreds. You ask the big questions. What would happen to this outfit as she swings on ropes and vines in the jungle? How would her coat fall apart? How can we make her sexy and appealing when we started with this dowdy girl who's on the bus? Her suit starts to rip and then her jacket goes, the coat, the shoes.*

The most important thing everyone was concerned about was that Kathleen look sexy. "She has beautiful legs, we have to show her legs." I had that wrapped skirt made of raw silk so that as it shreds, it shreds in the most elegant, beautiful, muddy way.

Take-offs and Put-ons

The Breakfast Club *was another situation where you had to do more with less. No costume changes. These people are in a room all day! That's it. To keep up the visual interest, I had the characters remove pieces and layers of clothing. Emilio gets down to his tank shirt and Ally Sheedy has other clothing in her bag. We had to make all her clothing from scratch because we couldn't find any blacks that were interesting. She was a dark character who had to emerge as pretty so we gave her a pretty white camisole underneath that black. We also had to make that pouch purse she carries so she had something to keep all her treasures in.*

In The Untouchables *they carried weapons, so I had to accentuate suits and clothing with much more fabric than we would normally use. There were several sets of each costume, all with different fits. One costume might be fitted for the scene when the actor is carrying a gun. Another version of the same costume would be for a quiet scene where the actor is not actually carrying a gun, although you want to give the illusion of the gun. A third version is for when the actor is running. That suit would have a couple more inches of fabric in the right places because the shape still has to be maintained. It always has to look great, even when he's running or falling down.*

The Lines of Illusion: Make Them Look Good!

In costume design, you have to know how to make somebody look great. Many actors have real figure problems. Some actresses are very boxy and have a high waist, but you want them to have the illusion of having this wonderful figure. So instead of showing the figure, you slim her body, use a little extra fabric. There's a hint of something wonderful happening. You're not quite sure what it is, but it's there. You get that illusion. Line is illusion in many ways. It gives you that feeling of something that you want to get across on the screen.

For The Rocketeer *we had a very well-endowed actress and the director insisted that she wear white. I said, "White on camera—she's going to look terrible!" He said, "Not with the flesh and not with that baby face. It will all counterbalance. Each flaw will work against the other so it will be beautiful." Did it work? You tell me. White was a problem and so were those enormous breasts. We had to make up special bras just to keep her tucked in there.*

With men, you have a different set of problems. A lot of men have narrow shoulders but they're wider in the chest. Some actors, like Bruce Willis, are short in the leg and longer in the body. What I do with him is make a higher rise on his pants to reduce the amount of his trunk, give him a feeling of longer legs. For both of the Die Hards *and* Hudson Hawk *we made every ounce of clothing he wore because we needed to get his silhouette right.*

Designing for men is so challenging. With women you know that you can always make that transition, from plain to pretty or whatever. But with men it's so subtle and the taste thing with men is so off. But it's so much more rewarding because when it all comes together, it's very exciting.

Collaboration

*At the beginning, you get all your information from the director. You need a clear idea of what he sees. A director like Stephen Hopkins (*Predator 2*) is very visual—everything has to harmonize. It's like a symphony going on here. Whereas Garry Marshall focuses on the story—that's his thing. Garry might say something simple like "She's in a ballgown, she turns into a princess," and I take it from there. Of course, the minute the actor shows up, things are bound to change anyway.*

Then there is collaboration with the production designer. Surroundings are very important. In Pretty Woman *the interior of the hotel and the uniforms had to harmonize. Everything had to be just so. That just-so theme was carried through in the uniforms of the elevator operator, the man at the front desk, the manager, everybody. And all of that was juxtaposed with how Julia Roberts looked walking through the lobby.*

With the cinematographer, I have to know lenses and gels. Is he going to shoot in a special way? Are we going to use greens or blues? Only reds? Perhaps lots of warm whites or off-whites. Then we have to figure out how the lighting will alter the colors. It gets complicated.

For Judgment Night *the yellow sodium light softened everything and our bad guys started looking really soft. Not a good idea. So we had to change the lighting. But we found that red and blue played beautifully in the film, it was amazing.*

Sometimes with color, you begin by thinking warm and cool colors. But you must use a small palette of colors. You can't show off. There are times when you want to. But you can't. You're not doing this costume because you love it. You have to do what you feel is right for the movie. If it happens to take off as a fashion, that wasn't your intent. You just try to create this outfit for your character.

I see a lot of films now where the costume designers are trying to make a statement for themselves. Their concentration should be on the script and the character, not on the fashion. That's what I want from my team, from everyone. I can't afford to work with someone who has an attitude. We have to be a bunch of team players. It's about camaraderie.

Photographic Design

Haskell Wexler's work as director of photography on such diverse and memorable films as *American Graffiti, Blaze, Colors, Matewan, One Flew over the Cuckoo's Nest* and *The Thomas Crown Affair* has made him one of the most respected and sought-after cinematographers in Hollywood. He received Best Cinematography Oscars for his work on *Who's Afraid of Virginia Woolf?* and *Bound for Glory*. He was also the writer/director/cameraman for *Medium Cool*, a groundbreaking film set against the backdrop of the riot-torn 1968 Chicago Democratic convention that is still regarded as one of the best politically-charged films ever produced.

The one time "blacklisted" filmmaker now sits of the Board of Governors of the Academy of Motion Picture Arts and Sciences. While acknowledging the dramatic impact that new technologies have made on the role of cinematographer in recent years he continues to stress the "human" elements involved in creating a motion picture.

Many people think the director tells the actors what to do and the cameraman, the director of photography, takes the picture. This is true, but there is more to it. The transformation from script to screen happens through the funnel of the director of photography. Filmmaking is gathering together what's out there and filtering it through one device—the camera. Until that first frame is shot, it's only contracts, ideas, concepts, scripts and hopes.

My job is to help the director translate in an artful way the drama as expressed in the script and by the actors. This involves helping with the framing, staging, lighting and utilizing all the mechanical devices necessary to make the images tell the story.

The cinematographer heads up a team that executes the framing worked out with the director in rehearsal. He works with the camera operator, who physically operates the camera. The first assistant has many important responsibilities, some of which include focus pulling, changing lenses, setting the stop, dealing with diffusion and all filters, threading and making sure that the camera is working properly.

The loader, or second assistant, loads magazines, keeps camera reports and makes sure you don't mix up film stocks. He or she is the first to touch the film before images are on the emulsion.

The team the cinematographer heads up also includes the gaffer, who leads the electrical crew, and the grips, who handle the dolly or crane. The term grip often makes people outside our profession underestimate the creative collaboration that department has in the making of a good-looking film.

The look of a picture is only partially the province of the cinematographer. I won an award for Bound for Glory, but it was the plan that Art Director Michael Haller worked out with me that resulted in a beautiful subdued color look.

Preparation

There is no "right way" to prepare to shoot a film. I read the script first and decide if the ideas and emotions interest me and evoke images in my mind's eye. I talk with the director to get his general sense of the script and characters. This is an important time because a good collaboration between director and cinematographer will make a better film, not to mention happier people.

In the beginning there is test shooting for wardrobe and makeup. There may be screen tests so the director can see if the actor is appropriate for the part. I also shoot technical things in a controlled situation, to test for matches. You have to maintain the same quality of light and density throughout a scene. If you don't, the audience will notice something is a little off. You have a color chart and check the degrees of underexposure, overexposure, different film stocks, the matching of lenses. It gets complicated. The main thing is that when the film comes out, there can't be any mismatches.

Once the subject and location of the film are familiar, then the images come quickly to mind. Colors was about street gangs. It was shot in an area of L.A. that I seldom walk around in. So I spent time in that area with Dennis Hopper, the director. We just walked around and talked to people. I was seeing what caught my eye and whether those things were in concert with what Dennis saw. I don't try to just think of shots, I'm trying to think seriously about what the whole movie means.

The director and I are constantly discussing camera angles, color, lighting, blocking, movement of the camera. He knows what he wants. How it gets done is usually up to me. I might say, "We should see just a little bit of light on the candelabra over there because that's what [a character] will have to steal." You're looking for some way to dramatize or express what's important.

Since visual ideas are not easily translated from written script, we need frames of reference to communicate. Perhaps I might see films with the director, or we will look at pictures or paintings. I often use a video camera during rehearsals to present my suggestions on how a scene could be shot. Of course, a cinematographer has to offer ideas and accept rejection. The director is the captain of the ship. How much or how little he wants collaboration is ultimately his decision.

Moving Camera, Moving Pictures

We have devices now which can move even the biggest 65mm camera in ways never before possible.

The main factor in camera mobility is the freeing of the eye from the eyepiece. Crane arms previously had to support the weight of a camera and at least two people, now cameras can fly through the air on the end of a magnesium pole.

There are also helicopter mounts using video and gyroscopic stabilizers that allow for spectacular gyrosphere shots such as the end credit of the Paul Newman picture Blaze.

Lolita Davidovich comes out of the building where Paul Newman's character has died and the camera starts back. You see her on the steps, she gets into a car. Then the camera moves up the building, eventually you see the oil wells behind, then the Mississippi River. All one smooth take.

In order to bring the script to the screen, the cinematographer has to be aware of the up-to-date technological advances and how and when to use them. You also have to know good people in all departments with whom you can work creatively in friendship. Most importantly, one always has to remember that good photography cannot make a bad picture good. Choose projects with some humanity.

Photographic Design

Aussie native John Seale is another very sought after cinematographer. In fact, Director Lawrence Kasdan, who worked with him on *Dreamcatcher*, told one reporter "The problem with John Seale is that everybody who works with him wants to work with him forever so he's not available to everybody. It's a shame there is only one of him!"

Seale won an Academy Award for his work on *The English Patient* and was nominated for *Rain Man* and *Witness*, a film directed by fellow Aussie Peter Weir. He was asked to describe his highly regarded work with Weir in *Dead Poets Society*.

One of the first things I remember about Dead Poets Society *was the last week of preproduction. Peter set aside the time from eight in the morning until noon every day and the two of us would go through the script, talking endlessly, taking notes. We'd talk about how scenes would flow, how certain scenes might combine if there were two that were similar.*

Peter would scribble stick figures for storyboards, mulling them over. By then we knew every square inch of every location so we'd decide where the camera would actually go. But Peter's not cut-and-dried on this. He always works on a what-if system. What if the camera were over there instead of here?

He would be quite happy to change it if it enhanced his feelings for the scene. And of course I'd be ready to change with him, because as the cinematographer, that's my job.

Maybe all of this sounds like any conversation a director might have with his director of photography, but with Peter there is always something special. It's hard to describe. He carries these strong images in his mind, yet he's very open to collaboration.

You have your own ideas about where to put the camera and Peter is extremely interested in your ideas. He wants to hear them. I'll come up with an idea and he'll mull it and mull it, I swear he's got the entire movie going in his head. He'll run that little piece of idea backward and forward through his mind's Moviola and he'll come out with an answer. Maybe he'll use it, or maybe he'll say, "John, it's a powerful idea but I'm going to need that power later. We'll hold back for now and use it in a later scene."

That's why I think his pictures are so perfectly balanced in the performance—in the emotion, in the editing. Because he's always thinking about the whole movie. Before we had shot one frame he said, "I'm counting on the power of the editing room to make this film." And I think it did.

On the Set

When we started filming we began with some of the easier scenes so the boys would get to know each other before setting into the more dramatic scenes. We shot the soccer game on the first day. Then we did some work with the classroom scenes and then worked our way quietly to more dramatic scenes.

With the indoor scenes, you tend to get a bit of them here and there—you don't want to use them all up at the beginning. If you chew them all up too soon, you don't have them to fall back on when the bad weather comes.

We'd discuss the day's scenes in the morning on the way to work. Peter would always ride to work with the first assistant director, the camera operator, the continuity person and myself. We were his command vehicle.

We would be fresh and he would lay out the day's shoot. He would say something like, "Scene 53 is an 'A' scene and scene 72 is a 'B' scene." A "B" scene meant it might not be in the film after editing. He would know that the "B" scene could go if he had to shorten the film so he'd rather spend more time on the "A" scenes.

He'll still shoot the "B" scenes and shoot them very well, but he won't waste time on them. Peter's very unusual in that almost every shot he does helps build the story. Unlike most directors, he doesn't do master shots all the way through. He'll only do them up to the point that he intends to use them in editing, then he'll move on to his close-ups.

You can almost see where he'll cut—on the head turn, whatever. He'll know that ahead of time and so my composition is better because he knows where he wants to cut and he'll commit to it right there on the set. It saves a lot of time, and on the set, time is money.

Keep It Moving

About a week into filming, Peter said to me, "John, you're not a slow camera-man but can you go any faster?" He explained the problem and it was formida-ble. "I've got eight stories to tell, seven students, plus a teacher and a girlfriend. I need to have all of those stories to work with in the editing room." So we real-ly started moving. After shooting was over the production office happily told us that we had averaged twenty-one set-ups a day over the entire film!

The usual is about three to five, five to nine is moving right along, sixteen is regarded as pushing it a bit. In TV they might do that many, but not in features. So when it was all over I asked Peter, "Which story lines did you drop out?" And he just smiled and said, "I got them all in. All I had to do was trim them."

The Music Scene

Another unique thing about Peter is his use of music. He selects music for each scene, which gives us a rhythm and pace for that particular scene. It plays while the crew is lighting, rehearsing, getting all the equipment in the right position.

Sometimes he'll let it play until the last second before the actor speaks. Then he'll fade it out very quickly and leave the actor with this music in his head. Afterward the actors say what an amazing thing it is because the music kind of controls the speed of their movements and their reaction time.

It helps me as well because it will determine the speed at which I move the camera. I knew how fast to pan the camera, or tilt it or track it. Peter doesn't have to explain it with words, the beat of the music does it for him.

If you listen to the music he uses as you're doing a particular shot, you can pretty well work out where the cuts will be. So the music really gives you a feel-ing for how the film will be edited.

Seeing the Image

Peter's films are characterized by his use of images. With Dead Poets there were some memorable ones—like the birds. Not just the flocks swirling, but that scene of the owl on the night run to the cave. We trained an owl to fly from A to B, then when one of the boys stopped suddenly it was like the owl fluttered through this patch of time into the past. And there was that long run through the trees where the mist was hanging low—all these hooded figures. It was very powerful.

A lot of people remember the scene in the classroom where Todd (Ethan Hawke) comes up with his poem and Robin is spinning him round and round. We used a Steadicam to get it. The cameraman kept circling them, walking in an eight-foot diameter around Robin and Ethan.

We were both worried that this spinning background might be detrimental to the emotional connection between them. So we shot the same scene with a static camera. But when we saw the dailies it was obvious that the spinning shot worked perfectly and, of course, that's the one Peter used in the final version.

During the suicide scene, we used some subtle slow motion intercut with normal speed to give it a sort of floating feeling. This suspends time, manipulates time, it takes the film to a different level.

When the boy takes the crown of thorns off his head and puts it down, we're running the camera at 128 frames a second, which creates slow motion. But we also intercut with the normal speed of twenty-four frames per second. What it does is suspend him in that final mellifluous moment of his life.

Seeing the Light

The lighting on Dead Poets was as natural as we could make it, very realistic. The only time we would do something a bit different was when the boys went to the cave or were running through the mist at night. The school had to be lit much like in real life, so we started with what was there and enhanced it to a level that would allow us to film. Tom Schulman's words were enough. I didn't have to do much to enhance them.

I often feel that when the words are good and the actors are fairly humming on those words you could almost light up a movie with a flashlight. The cinematographer is there to enhance as much as possible but certainly not to override or overcontrol or start doing ridiculous commercial-type tricks that can detract from the real emotion. The classroom had seven little bulbs hanging down, I didn't mind that because that's reality. Same with the houses, they were just real houses the boys went to, where they had parties, so they had to be lit as real houses.

I found it very difficult to lay smoke into the classroom in order to get a sense of shifting sunlight. There was one scene where Robin and the math teacher were having a cup of tea and the math teacher was smoking a pipe. So I dropped a little bit of smoke in to give it a sort of ethereal look. The rest of it I just photographed as reality.

When the boy actually commits suicide, it's winter with snow outside, so that was done in cool moonlight with cool lighting. The available lighting came from the night outside.

In the father's bedroom when he awakens to the sound of something, the windows are cool, but it's not cool lighting inside. His bed lamp is warm lighting. Same with Neil's bedroom when he makes the fateful decision, his bed lamp was left as a warm lamp. It worked as a counterpoint against the emotion the boy was going through. Otherwise, you're using cold lighting to agree with the bleak feeling in his mind, which is really too much.

A Special Film
When we watch dailies, Peter will play the music he used on the scene. He says it helps him emotionally. I remember this one day I'm watching the rushes and the music is playing and I thought—that looks just right—and I turned to say something to the gaffer and he was crying. I couldn't believe it. I said, "You're a hard-bitten, twenty five years in the business, Los Angeles gaffer. You're not allowed to cry in dailies!" It was a wonderful moment.

Makeup Design
Makeup artist Peter Robb-King has worked on many of Hollywood's most famous faces. His credits include *The Jackal, Clear and Present Danger, The Fugitive, Patriot Games* and *Matrix Reloaded*. It was Robb-King who provided makeup for the humans who found themselves in Toontown in *Who Framed Roger Rabbit?* He was nominated for an Academy Award for his contributions to *Legend* and won the BAFTA, the British Academy Award, for his work on *The Last of the Mohicans*.

When I first read the script, I'm checking for what the concept is that was in the writer's mind, as well as the concept of the director. With any script, there's a huge range of possibilities. Until casting is complete, it's not always guaranteed that a character will stay the same race, religion, ethnic background, or even the same age.

So many times these days you don't get the actors until fairly late in preproduction. Without the actors you really are in the dark. It's very difficult to try out any kind of special makeup on a different person. A double or a stand-in won't work. You need the actor who's playing the part to make the final effect and show it to the director or the producer.

A lot of production companies would like you to start a day before shooting, but realistically it should take anywhere from a week on a contemporary piece, to a month on something more complicated. On something really complex, where you're going to be manufacturing prosthetics and other special equipment, it could take months.

Even on a "normal" project you need to start experimenting with the actor as soon as possible. At least a week before. In addition to hair and facial hair, there might be injuries, or old wounds or scars the script might call for. You want to set these up before you start.

Working with the Stars

When you're working with stars, you are mainly aware of a presence. Stars are really people whose audience appraisal of their work gives them the right to be a star. Normally they have gone through a lot to get to that position. There are very few overnight successes. They've learned a lot along the way and have fewer of the problems of somebody who is up-and-coming. The worst is someone who's trying to be a star when they're not. They can be tough.

In my experience, stars are the easiest people to work with. They've worked through the ranks. Yes, they realize their image is important, but they don't spend all their time worrying about it. They're very comfortable in their situation.

Much of my work with stars is enhancing what they have, bringing out the best in them. Which is basically all makeup can do. Sometimes you're trying to make them look correct for that particular story. But a lot of actors want to change their appearance, they don't like to appear the same every time. Occasionally you'll get the opposite, actors or actresses who are locked into a particular look. Usually this happens with the older performers who had a look years ago that they liked. It's like somebody gets married and twenty years later they're still wearing the same makeup. They'll insist on a particular range of makeup or a particular style of eye makeup or foundation. Nearly always, you're trying to improve things and bring in whatever you're trying to accomplish in the film. But you have to tread very carefully.

On the Set

We're often the first people there in the morning. Usually about six in the morning. The hairdressers come in at the same time and sometimes the costume people as well, if the actors need to be in costume before they get made up.

You get used to the early hours. Most makeup artists have a certain kind of personality. I think that the job involves a fair degree of psychology. You've got all these personalities to deal with, you've got to get them in makeup and on the set looking good and feeling good. If you create a bad atmosphere every morning, it's unlikely that you'd stay in the job for too long, even if your makeup skills were perfect.

In terms of time, for a man the minimum is ten minutes, the maximum, maybe thirty minutes. For a woman it can go from a half hour to an hour and a half. It depends on the script requirements and the look that you're creating. You can create a modern look but you may be putting false eyelashes on an actress, which takes longer than putting no lashes on. Or you may be doing a particular lip shade which may take longer than a standard lipstick. You may be doing more remedial work on one actor than another.

Some actors could sit in the chair all day, others want to be out in seconds. It's not that they don't like you, they just want to be out of the chair and on to something else. You can't control it. People assume that you always want to keep them there longer than you need to. It's not true. You would never be able to work in the industry if you kept people longer than you needed them.

But sometimes you can see it from their side. Some of the Legend characters took more than two hours to make up every morning. In Roger Rabbit Christopher Lloyd's character took two and a half hours. He had a lot of prosthetics. People may have thought that Lloyd looked like that in real life; luckily he doesn't!

We extended his face and made it look longer. There was a chin extension, nose and ear extensions, an Adam's apple. His head was shaved and some hair added when his hat wasn't on. All of this goes on while he is sitting in the makeup chair. He had that look every day and he certainly didn't have that look coming in off the street. It was a long, involved process, but he was great, he enjoyed playing that role.

You can add prosthetics to the cheeks, either from the inside or the outside. A small addition to the skin can make a huge difference to the look on the screen. The subtleties of makeup are never ending. And it's really all about the small differences. It's a subtle art. You can do something small and it can change someone's appearance quite radically.

Great makeup is a real asset to a production. It's not something the audience should be aware of. The best compliment for us is that our actors look good because they look perfect for the part.

The No-Makeup Makeup

Sometimes the director will want a no-makeup look, which can often take longer than a full makeup because you have to achieve a result on the screen that makes the audience think that they're looking at a person with no makeup. But you've also got to satisfy the actors that they'll look good on the screen.

It's complicated because the no-makeup look still demands makeup to correct whatever is happening with the actor that you don't want the audience to notice. He may come in in the morning and be flushed, have a rash or a zit. Realism may be great, but if somebody has a zit one day, they don't necessarily have it six weeks later when they're shooting the scene that will appear next in the movie. So if you use natural things, you're going to have to re-create them weeks later. You're always worried about continuity. People don't show up looking the same every morning and you have to present them to the camera looking the same as they did the day before.

In Case of Violence

There are many scripts where people have things happen to them that are, let's say, unpleasant. There are accidents with injuries, illnesses. People get hit or wounded. A lot of things can happen to the human body, so you're changing appearances all the time.

This is where research comes in. There's a lot of medical material available and illnesses and injuries have to be dealt with in a correct manner. We rarely re-create it totally to life, because the audience wouldn't want to see it. The real effects of gunshot wounds would be too devastating. I believe filmmakers would go further if the audience would accept it. But the reality is much worse than the audience might imagine. Generally, when we create a wound, we need to pull back.

For The Last of the Mohicans I needed to do research to learn what would happen to the body with a particular caliber bullet. Period firearms cause different types of wounds. The velocity of the bullet wasn't as fast, the wounds weren't as clean.

Special Challenges

Period films present many unique challenges. The Last of the Mohicans was an epic film made under difficult conditions. These days a makeup artist rarely has the opportunity to work on a project of this size and scope. We're talking about 1,500 actors on the screen in an eighteenth-century environment; the battle scenes, the sheer volume of work in re-creating a time and place that is long for-

gotten. There were fully tattooed bodies. The characters didn't wear as many clothes as we do today. So the whole body shape was important, muscles, everything. All of this in addition to the usual makeup problems that had to be solved if the script and story were to work.

Legend was difficult as well, but for different reasons. It was an amazing fairytale full of goblins and strange characters. The extensive makeup effects included foam rubber appliances and multi-piece prosthetics for almost everyone. It took five solid months dealing with those actors.

Aging a character is really one of the most difficult things we do. It's hard to know what someone is supposed to look like in the future. If we did we'd all be geniuses and that isn't the case. Too many films go to extremes in this regard. In the makeup world we know that it's a bit over the top. But the studios like obvious things, they prefer to see what they're paying for. The reality is often less. It's subtle, but it's there.

That's the thing about makeup in general. As I said, it's a subtle art. Actors think—why am I going through all this if it's just a little bit different? But that "little bit" is what we do and it can make all the difference.

Sound Design

Supervising sound editor Robert Grieve has contributed to the success of a number of classic films. His work can be heard in *Grand Canyon, Children of a Lesser God* and *Body Heat*. Often teamed with director Lawrence Kasdan, he worked on *Dreamcatcher* and with Kasdan's son on *Orange County*.

When I was very small, my parents thought I had a hearing problem. They took me to the doctor who had this machine where you put a headset on and they tune you in to these frequencies and ask, "Can you hear it now?" I said, "I can hear it now." And I remember the doctor saying, "You can't hear that," because it was higher than the usual frequency the human ear ordinarily hears. It was actually my ability to tune out my parents by selective hearing. This comes in very handy as a sound editor.

I know that the more you train your eye to see beautiful things, the more things like that catch your eye. I find that the more I listen to things, the more I strengthen all my senses. Training any one of the senses trains them all. An increased focus on sound heightens your sense of touch, taste, vision—every-

thing. If you want to heighten your senses, concentrate on one of them and the rest will follow.

As soon as I get the script, I start thinking about the sound of the film. There's a spotting session, where we literally "spot" the places where sound will come in during the film.

Some sounds have their source in the script—a car radio playing, or thunder as the character approaches Dracula's castle. Then there are sounds we add to enhance the mood suggested by the script. There will be music on the radio, but I will also add whistling wind and the sound of the car's tires. Sure, there's thunder as we approach Dracula's castle—But exactly what kind of thunderstorm is it going to be? Is it just beginning? How fierce is it? A lot of the mood will be determined by the sounds the audience hears.

In choosing sounds, I try to think of something that will add psychological flavor to the story without drawing too much attention to itself. It has to work on a subliminal level and enhance the mood that the director and the script determine.

We start with the natural sound that was captured during filming and we do what we can to control that as well. In the restaurant scenes from those old movies from the 1930s, there are often flowers in the middle of the table. The actor leans over when he talks because the microphone is hidden in the flowers.

We never want any extraneous sounds while shooting. If we do a restaurant scene, all the extras will be mouthing silent words so we can add whatever sound we want later. If the actors are in a car, usually the car is being towed so the natural sound doesn't have any car noise. This is done so there is no interference with the main dialogue; we add the sound of the motor later when we do the soundtrack.

We usually start on a job two or three weeks before the director's cut is finished. The first thing to be done is a quick, rudimentary preparation of the dialogue. Let's say a scene was filmed on a street and the actor was miked. You can hear car sounds in the background. Every time the editor cuts from one angle to another or one actor to another, you hear a "kkkk" sound. That's because the mike is in a slightly different position for each shot. So we have to smooth that out.

The other thing I like to do right away is to fill the scene out with background noises so that you get more of a sense of place. If you're in the woods, parking lot, et cetera, there will be specific sounds used.

Sometimes I might want to try something a bit offbeat, so we'll try that in the temp dub and run it for the director to get his ideas. Then we'll start perfecting the temp dub. Often this means going out and shooting some new sounds for the final cut.

The soundtrack looks exactly like film, it has sprocket holes and it travels back and forth with the film. When we start recording, we do a separate track for each sound you hear in the film. There can be as many as 150 tracks per reel. When it's mixed together we decide how loud each sound element should be and whether it should pan left or right, center, or surrounds....

Creative Sound

When I talk about getting creative I mean adding those little touches that help tell the story. In The Vanishing *Kiefer Sutherland's* character is approached by the man who kidnapped his girlfriend five years ago. He's never been able to find her, not one clue. This guy appears and he jingles her lost keys and says, "I'm the man you're looking for." Her key ring had this special little Bullwinkle toy on it, which Sutherland immediately recognizes.

The director was looking for something that could re-create a sound from when she was kidnapped. We didn't want to get corny or be obvious so we settled on a sea gull. You know how they sort of laugh and squawk when they are trying to steal food from one another? We put that in there along with the sound of the keys. And it worked perfectly to bring the audience back to the moment of her abduction.

Grand Canyon

In Grand Canyon we used a lot of helicopter sounds to give the feeling of being watched in the neighborhood. Of course, there were the baby cries and the sound of Mary McDonnell's character going through the bushes. That dream sequence gradually became a nightmare. In order to enhance that feeling we started putting beetles and bug noises and all sorts of buzzing sounds that kept getting louder.

You never know what will work. In one scene where Mary's character is running along she sees that bum in the alley. She's frightened. And then off in the distance you hear this ice cream truck playing its silly little song. The innocence and "normalcy" of the truck's sound contrasted nicely with the character's fear and tension.

There was also an earthquake sequence. We had a lot of fun with that. We wanted to make it as real possible, so we thought a lot about what happens when an actual earthquake hits. Just a moment before it hits you hear dogs baying off *in the distance. Then you hear all the car alarms going off at the same time and every dog in the neighborhood starts to bark.*

Body Heat

One of the things I remember about Body Heat *was that the wind was blowing a lot. The sound of wind is usually cold and yet the script called for humid heat. Even though it was filmed in Florida, it was about fifty degrees during the shoot. The thing everybody remembers is how the film makes it seem so hot, everybody is sweating. In reality it was freezing when they shot. And the wind was blowing all the time. So I'm thinking, how can we make the audience feel a warm summer breeze just by the sound? I started doing layers of crickets, then all the wind was recorded through palm fronds. It's sort of a clacky noise, a little thicker than wind through grass. These sounds are associated with palm trees and tropical warmth.*

Kathleen Turner's character had those wind chimes outside the house. I remembered the ones that I liked the best were my grandmother's. She had old tubular chimes with lots of interesting minor notes. Some of the chimes in the film were those old clay ones, but all of them sounded pretty horrible on the mike. We had to go out and rerecord them all. The studio interior sounded too "roomy." So we went out to the middle of the desert and found this old log cabin. It had this different kind of quiet. We recorded four hours of chimes and matched each sound with the right psychological moment in the film.

Children of a Lesser God

For Children of a Lesser God, *Director Randa Haines asked how we could intensify the feeling of the character being deaf. To achieve this I accented each sound just a little bit more than your ear would actually hear it. When William Hurt's character first drives up to the school, the truck passes by and we hear some leaves scratching along the ground. Then when he meets Sarah, there's the sound of her mop.*

In another scene there was rain on the window and you can actually hear the individual drops on the windowpane. To get that sound, we recorded the individual drops and then edited them one at a time. There was a general kind of a rain sound and then there were these very specific larger drips coming from the top of the windowsill. I wanted to hear each one. Sometimes, to enhance the mood, I work directly with the score. There's one scene where William Hurt's character is getting on a ferry to go to the school and there are sea gulls flying around the boat. We took their "caw," and changed the tone of it with a harmonizer so that it was tuned to the musical score that was playing in the background.

In the swimming pool scene I wanted to get a feeling of that sound you hear if you block your ears very hard and try to cut out all sound. You begin to hear a tone, a little like a seashell but purer than that. Then we shaped that tone, changed it gradually, because we didn't want it to be monotonous. Later in the film, Marlee Matlin's character yells out that first word. It was a big moment. We recorded her sound, but we wanted to make it uglier so we raised the level of the sound, just loud enough to make the audience jump in their seats.

At the very end of the film, the dance was going on in the background. Matlin was down at the dock and Hurt was at the top of the hill. We spent a long time balancing that sequence between music and silence. You could still hear the dance going on in the background, but we had to get out of it in such a way that you didn't miss it. Then suddenly you're alone and it's very quiet.

A lot of it has to do with pace and timing. I added the sound of the waves lapping against the shore and crickets singing in the night to help the mixer fade out the music without the audience ever hearing it go; it was just subtly replaced with the sounds of the night. You'd be surprised how much detail goes into even one little piece of film; it's much more than anyone could possibly imagine. .

Illusion Design

Ken Ralston is one of the most accomplished of the new breed of special effects wizards. For many years he was associated with Industrial Light and Magic located in Northern California. Ralston's four Academy Awards reflect his contributions to *Death Becomes Her*, *Who Framed Roger Rabbit?*, *Cocoon* and *Return of the Jedi*.

More recently he served as president of Sony Pictures Imageworks but stepped down to focus all of his efforts on the creative side for the company. If you liked the special effects in *Forrest Gump*, *Jumanji*, *Cast Away* and *Men in Black II*, you are already a Ken Ralston fan....

I probably have one of the few jobs in the business that is almost as involved as that of the director or producer. We work in preproduction, production and post-production, so we get to see every phase of the process. Our work is usually complicated, detailed and can take a long time. A large part of our job is creating effects that have never been done successfully before.

The World of Visual Effects

I grew up watching special effects, from King Kong *to all those old dinosaur and monster movies. Some were pretty poor, some were better.* King Kong *was state of the art for the 1930s and it was a knockout.* The Ten Commandments *had some powerful effects work. Everybody remembers the parting of the Red Sea. There is great work in science fiction films—*The Day the Earth Stood Still, Forbidden Planet, Metropolis, War of the Worlds, *et cetera.*

One of the reasons I'm even in this business is because of the work of Ray Harryhausen, who did effects for The Seventh Voyage of Sinbad, Mysterious Island *and* The Three Worlds of Gulliver. *Maybe they're not great movies, but they had some of the most ingenious effects works being done at that time.*

There are also some great films where you may not know that you're watching special effects. Citizen Kane *is loaded with effect shots, probably over a hundred. Almost every shot of Xanadu is an effect shot. They're either models or matte paintings. Sometimes they would use the bottom section of a big set and then do a matte painting for the entire upper ceiling area. So half is real and the other half is illusion.*

Another famous special effects sequence is the burning of Atlanta in Gone with the Wind. *I think what the studio did was burn the great wall down from their* King Kong *set, on the back lot and use that as part of the fire. Then they added miniature buildings, matte paintings, et cetera, to complete the shot. The first floors of some of the buildings were real, but the upper part, which was the incomplete set, was blacked out to camera and later, miniatures or paintings were inserted.*

The famous sunset shot of Tara is all special effects. Scarlett is in silhouette and the background is a matte painting. There are miniature trees in the foreground. It's another example of how, if we do our job well, you often don't even know those are special effects.

Creating Visual Effects

I begin by reading through the script and marking the scenes that look like potential visual effects. Then I meet with the director and the production team and go through the whole script to get a feel for how complex or how it will be.

At the simplest level, special effects include smoke, fire and explosions. More complex effects involve bluescreens, miniatures, paintings, optical enhancement, computer graphics, animation, et cetera. Often these scenes require the filming of two or more scenes which, when superimposed on one another and blended together so they appear as one shot, can create magic.

Sometimes, you work with models that are built to look like the set. The miniatures have to match the live sets perfectly, so when composited together, they look like it's all the same setting. In Back to the Future III we crashed a train. That was a big, quarter-scale, complicated miniature.

At ILM we also did a lot of manufacturing of creatures, body parts and unusual mechanical devices for operating aliens. Other times they are done with live actors and makeup, simple puppets and now, with the new technology, the help of computers.

Who Framed Roger Rabbit? combined cartoon characters with live-action characters. For two years I worked very closely with Richard Williams in England, who supervised most of the animation. I had to design a new system that could combine live action and animation, take what had been done before, and, using new technology, develop better techniques to add shadows, color shifts and blends.

There were so many details. I had to check the actor's eye lines to make sure they seemed to look directly at the cartoon character. The lighting on the cartoon characters had to look the same as the lighting on the live set. For Cocoon we did the effect of the sky opening and the spaceship coming down that was seen at the beginning and end of the film. You see clouds and a white beam come down through them and illuminate porpoises in the water.

The porpoises and spaceship were miniatures. The clouds were shot in a water tank using a latex mixture for the clouds. We also created the aliens for that film. The aliens are rather anorexic actresses in costumes. Then, in the optical printer, the device that combines all these elements, we created that wispy look and the smoky feeling. In this case, the aliens were never on the same set as the actors. So the actors on the set were always reacting to characters that were never there.

The same thing applies to Hook. The bluescreen technique has been around for years. All of Tinkerbell's flying scenes were filmed in front of a bluescreen. Julia Roberts was never on the set with the other actors. Afterward, the bluescreen "Tink" element was rephotographed to add all of her flying action and the wings were miniatures shot to match her every move.

Our job is to deliver whatever the director wants. In Back to the Future Robert Zemeckis took us to a location and said, "Here's a street and I want a Delorean flying through the sky." Steven Spielberg wanted that bicycle to fly *across the sky in E.T. First we shoot the street. Then we build a model of the bicycle or the Delorean. The model is set up in front of a bluescreen and shot. Then we create a black silhouette of the object called a black center—you may remember that you saw the bicycle in silhouette in E.T. Then the color positive of the Delorean is printed in that black silhouette area.*

So you're combining three different images—the set, the silhouette and the color object. In the final stage we use the optical printer to combine all these separate pieces of film into one image. However, using computer graphics has changed this procedure substantially.

Live Action Versus Special Effects

If you're doing live action on a set, you just roll the camera until the actors get it right. You might shoot miles of footage. But for special effects this is prohibitive because many effects are time consuming and can be costly.

Another problem is that effects necessitate a reversal of the usual filmmaking process. You need to know how everything is going to be cut in the editing room before you can do most effects. And it's very hard for directors and editors to make those decisions in preproduction. But they have to commit themselves because I can't change things dramatically in the first month or so because of technical limitations. We are locked into a deadline and there's no playing around with shots at that point.

To help the director we'll use animatics, which is a process of shooting the sequences on video using models. On Return of the Jedi we had sequences using funky space models shot on ticks [QuickTime's 1/60 of a second intervals] against a black background to give George Lucas something to edit with. And we made up some rough little models of what the speeder bike and storm troopers would look like.

We shot miles of video. Then George cut that together to give us an idea of exactly what the final sequence would look like. Shooting it in rough form tells me where everything will be in the shot—the size of things, the lighting, everything I need to know to make the shot work. It gives us the initial information of a scene so that we can plan the basic approach—scheduling, action, cameras needed, people, time and budget.

In Roger Rabbit we shot the five-minute sequence of Toontown on an ILM stage. We shot bluescreen with Bob Hoskins interacting with all the cartoon characters. The process took weeks and weeks. Then, as soon as we had a rough composite with the rough animation, we gave it to the director, who checked the tim-

ing and the position of the actor and his relationship to the cartoon characters and backgrounds in the scene. Then we sent it to the editors. The process repeated itself over and over again, always refining. Little by little everyone started to get a feel for what was happening dramatically. In the end I think it worked very well.

Death Becomes Her

With Death Becomes Her *we were fortunate to have had enough research and development time to test out some new theories. Everyone seems to remember the scene where Meryl Streep's head is twisted on backward. You could always do an effect like this in a schlocky way for certain films, but this had to be way beyond that.*

In the beginning I went out and bought a Barbie doll and turned its head around backward. This was a low-tech start, but it helped because it's a hard image to keep in your mind. In a way, creating some ten-headed creature from Mars would have been easier. So I sat there and looked at that and started to come up with a rough possible direction to go.

Then I went to the folks in the computer division and talked through my ideas. We did some tests with one of the women here at ILM on a little set that we built. At that time we ran through all the possible ways of doing the shot. We didn't know what would work best. We had her on the set doing dozens of different actions against a blue and a black screen. Then we started to narrow it down.

We studied the director's storyboard of the sequence. Then we went down to Los Angeles where the mansion interior was being constructed. We spent a day there and shot the whole twisted-head sequence on video with a stand-in. Bob Zemeckis, the director, edited the sequence as closely as he could to the final edit. That gave us an idea of what the shots were going to be like and gave us our blueprint for planning all the techniques, people, time and equipment necessary to pull it off.

There's always the budget to consider. Much of this type of work is so abstract that it's difficult to budget without actually starting to do it. You can talk about it for a year. You can pretend you know. But then that first day on the set, everything changes, it all goes out the window.

This was one of the rare times where many of the effects scenes were shot on video, while the film was still in preproduction. It helped because the scenes were so complicated and a bit frightening for all of us. We had to get a head start, no pun intended, to get a feeling for what we had to accomplish.

To create the look of the head on backward, the neck was created in a computer. That object doesn't exist—except in a computer. What is real is Meryl's body. But because of the way we had to distort the neck, we had to replace the chest and the neck with a computer piece which was blended in with her real head, shot on bluescreen.

It was pushing the effects envelope because shots were so long you could analyze our work very closely. Usually, with effects films, you have quick cuts or crazy explosions or bizarre alien things. Things that are happening are so wild that it's distracting and can make it hard to focus your attention on any one "trick." But here, the audience had plenty of time to scrutinize the effect. It had to be perfect.

First we shot her body and she did the whole scene as if she had her head on backward—which was an incredible acting job! Then we shot the area behind her head without her on the set. Then a month later she wore a blue leotard and we shot her head, bluescreen.

I then sat down with the rough cut of the sequence and plotted—frame, by frame, by frame—every position her head would be in. It was very labor-intensive. She sat in a chair and roughly duplicated each head position for every frame. And we also had to add the exact lighting to duplicate the lighting on the real set.

Then there was the ponytail factor. When we shot her close-up in front of the bluescreen, her real ponytail was cut off or hidden behind the blue outfit she was wearing. As we started to work out the head positions, we realized you'd have to see the ponytail. So we had her hairdresser send us one of the ponytail wigs. We had to take the ponytail and match it frame by frame as close as we could to what her head was doing in every frame. In the end it was one of the things that no one will ever know because it works so well.

I don't want to get technical, but you shoot film at twenty-four frames a second. If the scene is over three minutes long, you're looking at five thousand or so frames and you're doing everything frame by frame. It gets complicated. The work is so time-consuming and there's an intense amount of concentration on the smallest little detail. Eventually everyone went kind of bonkers. I know I did.

The project took about six months from start to finish and it's a good thing we started early because the final version of the scene was not done until the bitter end of postproduction. We needed every second of time.

The effects team for the whole movie was 250 people. That included our model shop, which built all the miniatures and our optical department. There was the computer graphics team, the editors at ILM, as well as the people who *worked with the film and production crew. Many others. We put everything we had into it.*

Cause and Effects
This job definitely requires a lot of discipline and concentration. It helps to have a strong background in art and filmmaking, the whole general process, because you touch on every aspect of it when you're working on a film. It helps to have a good knowledge of computer graphics, but to develop the computer literacy you need you have to actually be working in the field.

In a nutshell, the first 95 percent of what we do is manageable. But that last impossible 5 percent, that's the part that separates us from everyone else. That's the hard part. But it's that last little bit that allows us to pull off things that maybe haven't ever been done before. It takes the whole film to a different level. And maybe the audience never really thinks about it, but I think they appreciate it. That's good enough for me.

CLOSE-UP
THE PRODUCTION DESIGNER: WYNN THOMAS

Beginning the Process
As a designer, I try to provide a visual concept that provides a journey for us to go on as we travel throughout the movie. I begin my process by breaking the movies into three acts.

The first act of John Nash's life is a perfect world. This is the time period when Nash is at Princeton and he doesn't know that anything is wrong with him and we, the audience, don't know that anything is wrong with him. We see him as a kind of odd, bizarre individual, who's having a difficult time at the university, but in many ways it's an ideal time in his life.

For this section of the film, I tried to keep the sets fairly warm and comfortable—we see wood paneled rooms and the bar that they go to is really the classic hang-out that you envision students hanging out, so it's very late 1940s, very perfect and we feel comfortable in the environment.

In the second act of the film, he's starting to work for RAND and we're just beginning to get the feeling that something is wrong in

Nash's life—but we're not quite sure what it is. The image I used was shadows creeping up the wall. If you look at this portion of the film, all of the sudden there are dark shadows everywhere. From a cinematographer's point of view, there's an air of mystery in this portion of the film. We did this by using Venetian blinds so we control the amount of light that was coming into the room and sometimes we used a slash of light coming into the room.

From an image point of view, the shadows are beginning to grow; his mind is beginning to collapse, so the shadows are coming up and they're about to strangle him. And if you look at the picture very carefully, except for a couple of scenes, the color becomes very monochromatic.

When we go into Parcher's warehouse, which is a built set, there are no straight lines in it. If you look at the walls and look at the shape of the computers in that set, you'll notice that everything is circular. Later on, when we get to the mental hospital and Dr. Rosen's office, when they take him down that hallway, the hallway is also circular.

If you're looking down a straight hallway, you can see what's in front of you. When you're looking at a circular hallway, you don't know what's around the corner. We don't know where Nash is at that point, where he is in the mental breakdown, so this was a way to trying to make all the settings that were part of John Nash's mental breakdown similar. And therefore in a very subtle way, clueing the audience in to the fact something is very wrong here. What is beyond the corner?

If you look at the hospital, it's the same tonality of Parcher's office, almost all white and gray. When Nash wakes up in Rosen's

58-1

58 EXT STREET
POV SHADOW
MOVING DOWN
STREET

58-1

office, the office is wood paneled like Princeton, but it's a very dark wood paneled office. At this point in the film we don't know who Rosen is—we don't know if he's a spy or if he's a good guy or a bad guy—so I was trying to introduce the elements that were very similar to the first part of the film.

Then, when Nash comes out from Rosen's comfortable office into the hallway, we go on the same journey that Nash goes on, all of a sudden we realize he's in this nightmare of this psychiatric hospital. And he's pulled out into that circular hallway with no ending. Neither Nash, nor the audience, knows where he's going.

In the third act, he returns to Princeton and he and Alicia move into their home. Here, except for the yellow kitchen, I wanted to create a very bland existence. The wallpaper is sort of monochromatic and there's the bland porch scene. From an emotional point of view, we wanted to show he was in a no man's land in terms of his own development. So this concept takes us visually through what's happening with him.

Designing the Set/Studio and Location Shooting

We tried to design the set so the production design very subtly supported the mood of the story and corresponded with what is happening emotionally with Nash, instead of making it a lovely period film. It would have been so easy to fill the Princeton house—that he returned to after years in a psychiatric therapy ward—with lovely 50s motif and decorative items, but that's not where the story was emotionally. I'm much more interested in and showing visually where we are in terms of the emotional journey.

We only shot at Princeton for two weeks—one week at the beginning and another week at the end, so we primarily did exteriors at Princeton. Then I had to find a variety of locations in the New York City area to act as stand-ins for Princeton exteriors and I found several locations that had the appropriate feeling.

His dorm room was built in a studio and part of the dorm room exterior was also built in a studio so we could show seasons changing. We built his office and the outdoor garage where you see all the clippings on location and then we built the interior on a stage. This was a very difficult design challenge because it's about finding the right balance visually so that you were aware that the person was having a mental breakdown, but that Nash wasn't dangerous.

I had two scenic artists work on those collages on the wall of the garage—the use of string, the spider web images, lines connecting the patterns. They were very successful at getting into the head of John Nash.

The Collaborative Process

Ron is very open to suggestions. So you bring your ideas to the table and the Ron responds to that and often he'll embellish my ideas and take it one step further. So, I would tell Ron, "I think the first act is a perfect world" and he'd say, "Kind of like *Life* magazine." So he's taking my words and supplying his own words to understand the image. And then it bounces back to me and his image might make me think of other things.

When we worked on the garage interior, we did several test samples for Ron and Akiva. It was an evolving process which would start with myself doing my take and then Ron and Akiva adding to it. It became a total collaborative process between all of us, as we tried to find the proper balance of images and appropriate madness.

CLOSE-UP
DIRECTOR OF PHOTOGRAPHY: ROGER DEAKINS

It Begins with the Script

The script really drew me to this film; I thought it was a wonderful script and for me, the challenge of cinematography all starts with the story.

One of the crucial elements in the story is how much do you give away to the audience. The crucial question was: "How do you translate visually, in film terms, that this guy was living a life of illusion?" I believed that you do it by playing it down like they did in the *Sixth Sense*. In that film they didn't make it some big scary, high-tech visual interpretation, but they played it very naturalistically and low key.

Getting Started

I was hired about six weeks before we started filming. We storyboarded some sequences, like the fantasy sequence with the car chase where there was quite a bit of second unit work, but we never really shot the scene exactly like the storyboards. We were using them to sift through ideas. They got changed sometimes on the way to the location or by just talking about it. Sometimes they led to another idea that might go off in a different direction. Sometimes we'd look at the location and think,

"Wouldn't it be interesting to stage the scene in a such and such a way?" and more often than not on *Beautiful Mind*, the way the scenes were staged were driven as much by the actors as anything else.

Working Technically

On this film, I worked with a small gib arm which is a little remote head on the camera and that gives the camera a lot more freedom to move. Russell tended to like to have freedom to experiment and freedom of movement. With the gib arm, you don't have to have really hard, set marks, so moving the camera doesn't become a technical exercise. There's always a balance between the rehearsals where you work out the camera moves you want and allowing the actor freedom. This camera gives the actor more freedom of expression and I think that's important in a film like this.

We didn't discuss much about lighting, except for general conversations about the mood of the picture and the look of each particular block of the movie. Obviously *Beautiful Mind* has different periods and time so we discussed how to make distinctions between them. And we shot in winter, so we had less daylight.

We did discuss how to interpret the unreality of Nash's imagining. We talked about whether to make it stylized and graphic and surreal or more naturalistic. I was coming from the point of view that the more you play it down and the more you understate it visually, the more of a surprise it will be. The audience will think that everything is real and then they find out that Charles is not real and that a number of these characters exist only in Nash's mind.

Collaborating with Ron

Collaboration is different on every film. Ron is incredibly energetic, the hardest working person on the set. He's very concise in terms of what he wants the film to be, but I sometimes have a different take on things. Things get talked around, so it isn't one particular person's idea. *A Beautiful Mind* was a much more organic process. It's good for any director to have somebody with another idea coming from another perspective.

CLOSE-UP
MAKEUP: GREG CANNON

We did nine stages of make-up. Sometimes Nash had a one-day beard, sometimes a six-day beard. We tried to see subtle changes. We started with him looking as young as he could. We used a set of teeth to give him an over-bite. We used stipple on the eyes and tiny neckpieces and developed a silicone piece. I wanted to do overlapping silicone so we developed a soft, fleshy piece that wrinkles very naturally. We had to make one of these for every day of filming since, once it was used, it had to be thrown away. It's very mushy and stretches like real skin. It took about four hours to get Russell Crowe into this every day. At the end, it looks very real since everything is moving naturally. For the make-up in the last scene, I went much heavier with the eye bags at the end and we used a bald pate and a wig. But it looked very real. It's fun—you really feel you've accomplished something.

CLOSE-UP
SPECIAL EFFECTS: KEVIN MAC

We get involved very early. Once the script is finished, we talk through where we might want to do special effects. We talked about how Nash saw patterns, so some of those are special effect shots, such as the necktie shot at the beginning. We hadn't thought that you couldn't put a baby in a tub of water, so we had to put together the shot of the baby and a separate shot of the water and a separate shot of the refraction and then put all these pieces together.

We did special effects on numbers. I came up with this idea of having the text of the numbers come forward and whenever he had one of his epiphanies, we added a little sparkle to the shot. We shot the dating scene at the bar on bluescreen. You can see the tracking go in and out with the characters.

There's also a shot of the little girl (Marcy) running through pigeons—but they don't run away because she's not real. So we first shot the little girl running through the park and then shot the scene with computer generated pigeons and put these together.

We also did a shot of Nash in his dorm room working on his theory. This was a set piece and we added snow and then showed spring with a branch and a little butterfly and then combined them all together into a change of season shot.

For the Nobel Prize scene, we created a loop of extras clapping and put lights on top of the theatre. When you look at the scene, it looks like a large audience.

It's a great compliment when people aren't aware of the effect. The primary element is always visual storytelling.

LOW

BIRDS IN FOREGROUND AND B.G.

MARLEE RUNS THROUGH

PATH

MARLEE   ✓ CAMERA

HAS NO EFFECT

71-7

71-7 CONT

*Editing is the
last rewrite.*

—*Oliver Stone*

The Editor: A Way of Seeing

Depending upon whom you ask, film editors can best be described as rewriters, cooks, musicians or even painters.

Film editing is just like cooking spaghetti sauce, explains distinguished Film Editor Walter Murch in *The Conversations*. "You put some film on the stove with some heat under it and stir." Murch, who has worked with directors as diverse as George Lucas, Francis Ford Coppola and Orson Welles, continues. "You taste it occasionally and...gradually, organically, the volume of the film reduces to the appropriate level."

Editor Carol Littleton (*Body Heat, The Accidental Tourist, The Big Chill*) was Oscar-nominated for her work on *E.T. The Extra-Terrestrial* and won an Emmy for *Tuesdays with Morrie*. She sees a similarity between her job and that of a musician:

> *Dialogue, visuals, story all have rhythm. It's the editor's job to pick up on those rhythms that are internal in the scene and to make them play. Like the musician, you're going over the same material again and again, finding the nuances, making the slight changes, working on it until you feel you've extracted the best technical interpretation and emotional tone.*

Editors work with different hues of expression, meaning, camera angle, shading, camera movement, emphasis and perspective. Eventually all are blended into a final impression. "The editor is like an artist, working with light, color and composition," explains Joe Hutshing (*Almost Famous, Jerry Maguire*) who won editing Oscars for *Born on the Fourth of July* and *JFK*. "You might want a love scene to be warmer, so you pump more gold or red into the print. It's subtle, but it affects the reaction to a scene."

In Born on the Fourth of July there's a scene in the opening credit sequence where young Ronny hits a home run and it's just pumped with color. That was a process that we went through to enrich the color. It gives it a great feeling. Or it might be a memory and you want it to look like an old photograph, so you might remove much of the color and give it a sepia tone.

"It is like painting, but when you're editing, you have a limited palette," Hutshing explains. "You can only work with the shots you've got. But there's an infinite variety within that restricted palette. The goal is to create an intensely satisfying emotional experience. The difficulty is staying fresh to the material."

Cook? Musician? Painter? And then there is the writing analogy. Hutshing says the film editor must also act as a storyteller.

You have to have a good sense of story. You have to be excited by stories and know what will happen if you structure them in certain ways.

Does the audience see the bloody dagger before or after the door is opened? How will that affect the story? Maybe it should never be seen at all. How long do you hold on the shot? It's about rhythm, timing, pacing. And it all affects the story.

Carol Littleton agrees. "My job is to enhance the writing and to make sure that everything is clear in the final version. I decide what to include and how much focus to give it." Like most editors, she feels a special kinship with the writer. "I think that writing and editing are very closely related. Both jobs are more monastic than social." Like the writer, the editor labors alone in a room, a solitary world. Says Hutshing; "You're in the room twelve or fourteen hours every day, but if you're working on something that you really like, you don't really think about that."

From Script to Screen

Like most collaborators, Littleton starts with the script. It will be her responsibility to help bring the project from script to screen and there are always certain things to look for.

> *I use the script as my main criterion for whether or not I want to do the picture. I like to see a really good strong story with well-defined characters. I look for structure. I don't always get it. At the very least you have to see a possibility for restructuring in editing. There are so many variables over the course of a film being shot and edited that you really want a good script for your bible.*

Veteran editor Bill Reynolds "cut" seventy-two films in his remarkable career. Though he died in 1997, he will always be remembered for such classic films as *The Godfather*, *The Sting* and *The Sound of Music*. He often spoke of looking for "entertainment value" and those troublesome little warning signs.

> *When I read the script, I'm thinking, "Do I want to do this picture?" I try to visualize it and think, "Is this going to be a good picture and be good entertainment?" When reading it, I'm very much aware whether the characters are alive, strong, or funny. If you read a script and think "This is meant to be funny but it isn't," then you know you're in trouble!*

There are also scripts that represent such a challenge, the editors wonder if they can pull it off. Joe Hutshing admits to his own short attention span: "I'm bored easily." So what happened when he got all two hundred pages of *JFK*?

> *Oliver gave me a shooting script and it took me four days to read it. It was interesting but still so dense, almost unreadable. I got bored. You had to concentrate so much to get it. I knew it was going to be an incredibly tough editing job. I wondered if it could even be made watch-able, it was so incredibly complicated.*

On the other hand, there are those rare occasions when a great script can simplify the editor's job. Thom Noble (*Reign of Fire*, *The Mask of Zorro*,

Witness) encountered one when he was asked to work on "a different kind of road movie."

> *Normally, when you get a script and start talking with the director, you realize there's a whole bunch of stuff that you can lose—there's a lot of fat in most scripts. But* Thelma & Louise *was such a perfect script. You actually could read it and say, "There really isn't a word wasted in this entire script." And, of course, the women were just fantastic characters.*

Production: The Dailies

Once the editor has read the script and made the decision to come aboard, the first day on the job usually coincides with the first day of production. Carol Littleton has edited almost all of Lawrence Kasdan's films. Her experiences with him are somewhat unique.

> *Usually I start work on the first day of principal photography, but Larry allows me to be present during the rehearsals. At rehearsals, I'm looking to be a quiet auditor. It allows me to have a sense of the film; to experience it somewhat before it is actually shot.*
>
> *I also get a better idea of the problems that the actors encounter, as well as the delight they take in pulling it together and making their characters work. I take notes so that when the moment comes that I'm no longer fresh with the material, I can re-experience the emotional arc of the film. I'm able to use that when I'm cutting to help bring out the best in each scene and performance.*

It's interesting to note that Littleton's presence at rehearsals rarely extends to the set during shooting. "Usually I have too many other things to do. The set is about sitting around and waiting," she says with a laugh, "All I can think of is all that time that's going to waste."

Thom Noble agrees and stresses that he is on the set "as little as possible" and with good reason. "You see them setting up a shot and it takes a whole morning to do this one incredibly intricate tracking shot. The danger is that you might feel compelled to use it when you cut the sequence."

The raw footage comes in each day and the editor shows these "dailies" to the director. For Littleton, it's an opportunity to get inside the process.

"I'm hoping to be able to see in dailies the essential focus of the director's attention, what he was going through on each take. Sometimes it might be a practical consideration—such as perfecting a camera move. Or sometimes you see that each take is so different you're going to just choose what you like."

Bill Reynolds meticulously explained the steps the editor goes through as the actual cutting begins.

> As soon as you have a complete scene, whether it's the beginning, middle, or end of the movie, you can start putting it together as a scene. When you first look at the picture, you're looking for the story. The number one object is to keep the story moving, reveal the details of the story and get the best performances. You make the actors look as good as you possibly can, but most of all the objective is clarity.

Littleton reveals how she collaborates with Director Kasdan during this initial period. "Many times Larry doesn't say what he likes, more often he'll say what he doesn't like. I can see visually what works and what doesn't work because it's pretty obvious after you've looked at so much film."

Noble begins plotting how he is going to be able to integrate the best aspects of each take. "Every take will have a moment in it you want to keep. You might see that one take is lit more brilliantly, it looks great. So you think to yourself—I have to use this, somehow I've got to put this in." At the same time, he explains that the editor must resist the temptation to "overcut" in an attempt to get in every cherished moment.

> Sometimes a scene is perfectly performed in the master shot and you can let it sit there. At the same time there's a moment of a close-up of somebody that you've got to try to get in. Ideally you'd like to integrate it into the whole without there appearing to be a cut. In other words, you try to make it all appear as seamless as possible.

Assemblage: "The First Cut Is the Deepest"

Once the production has wrapped, the pressure shifts to the editor to produce an initial cut of the film. For Carol Littleton, there are a lot of personal choices.

The first cut is pretty much the editor's cut, assembling according to what the script says. You put everything in on the first cut; you see everything that was shot and everything that was considered. I try to choose the best from each scene. This is my interpretation: dialogue, mood, character, everything.

Of course I'm cutting during filming, but I'm cutting in the order in which it was shot, so it's a little bit disorienting. Throughout, I'm trying to cut the scenes as lean and to-the-point as possible. I'm not just assembling shots and stringing them together. I'm always trying my best to deal with performances and analyze the story.

In the first assembly Joe Hutshing tries to follow the script as closely as possible. "I try to be true to what was written and try to make it work, exactly as the script has it. Once that has been done then you can start making interpretations of it, refining it."

William Anderson has worked on a number of projects with Director Peter Weir and he stresses the independence the director gives him.

Peter basically leaves the first cut to me. He doesn't want to influence me or tell me how to put it together or even be in the cutting room. He'll come in after I've cut it and we'll start looking through and deleting scenes we don't need. Perhaps the scenes may be repetitive or they just don't work. Other than that I'm on my own.

Carol Littleton reveals that the first cut is often the time when the editor must be willing to let go of the script. At some point you realize, "The script was a wonderful guide and that's what was used for the shooting, but now we have to forget that and just deal with the film we have."

Even at the assembly stage, maybe *especially* at this stage, creative decisions are made by the editor that will largely determine if the movie will "play." Littleton tries to follow the director's lead, but many decisions must be made on her own.

With the first cut, I'm following the lines of the director's work visually. But which shot to use? The two-shot? Over the shoulder? Long shot? And for how long? The duration of the shot—if there's camera movement, obviously they want to be able to use that section. The director and the director of photography have decided the visual design, the lens sizes, the angles, the movement, the composition. The rest is up to me.

The parameters vary according to the director's instructions. Many directors prefer to use the same editor in project after project; a shorthand develops between them, an instinctive communication. Littleton has worked with Lawrence Kasdan so often that she anticipates his preferences. Since Kasdan usually writes his own scripts, she tends to return to them for guidance as she seeks out the emotional moments.

> *When you're reading the script, you know who the main character is in the scene and you know what the emphasis is. For instance, in* Grand Canyon *Danny Glover finds his nephew under the staircase. Who's more important—Otis, the kid who has seen some horrible thing in his life that has shocked him? Or is it his uncle?*
>
> *In this particular case, we had singles of both, wider shots too, but as it turned out, I used mostly the two-shot that was moving in. It ended up in very tight shots of Otis because the emphasis of the scene was on the kid's pain and this incredible realization in his life. That's where the emotional moment is.*

Joe Hutshing explains that there are also those times when the script can't be followed. "What works in a script doesn't always work cinematically. Maybe the location has fallen through, maybe the lighting is off, or an actor is sick; you have to make do with what you have."

> *It's a matter of redefining the purpose of the scene and making it work. I look at the film as a viewer. With* JFK, *since the subject matter was dry, although it's an exciting story, I was trying to keep from getting bored. It's important to keep the audience riveted on the story, so I watch it and try to keep it from getting slow. There was a lot of wonderful footage and a lot of stock footage and a lot of our work involved how we could creatively get to this point or that point and keep the story moving.*

Littleton begins by cutting out the repetition. "The biggest sin is to be redundant. The next biggest is to have things that are truly extraneous." Inevitably, it always comes back to what to leave in and what to cut. She tries to cut "things that really do not contribute to the through-line of the picture." At the same time she warns, "You can cut it down too far and leave out the emotions. You need to create the moments that allow the audience to come inside the story, to participate and be a part of the dramatic moment."

Thom Noble, who rose to prominence for his work on *Witness*, stresses that the best editing is usually invisible. "The effect that I always try for is that it looks as if it comes straight out of the camera that way, so you're not aware of all the cuts."

> *Of course, with some sequences it's important that you are aware of all the cuts. If it's an action sequence and it's all hectic, busy and exciting, then obviously the cuts matter. But if you're doing intricate dialogue sequences, people in a car or sitting at a table or having a dinner party, you've got to try to get every wonderful moment that the actor has given you and integrate it into the film.* Thelma & Louise *was like that. There were magical moments that Susan Sarandon would give and you just have to try to get them in. That's your job.*

And what a job it is! The editor must assemble the film in ten to fourteen days after the production wraps. So much film, so little time. Do directors appreciate this monumental feat? As a rule, no. Their minds are occupied with differences between script and screen, between what they thought they shot and what they actually have shot.

Leonard Nimoy made this painful discovery as he made the initial transition from actor to director.

> *I discovered when I directed my first picture that perhaps the low point in the making of a film is sitting through the first assembly of footage. It's disastrous. It's shapeless. It's formless. It's toneless. It's boring. It's long. It's wrong. It's not funny. It's not dramatic. It's just one long session of pain. When you've done it a couple of times, you're prepared for it, but when you come in as a novice expecting to see your movie, forget it!*

Carol Littleton agrees that after seeing the first cut, "There's the reality of what one might imagine shooting and the reality of what's actually on the film." She smiles. "Very often they're not the same. So it becomes truly collaborative at that point. Some directors just want to talk. Some are the monkey on your back and you can't get them out of the room."

The Director's Cut

During the next eight or ten weeks, the director and editor will work closely together to shape the film into its next incarnation: the director's cut. How close this version is to what is released will depend on the degree of the director's clout with the studio as well as other contractual obligations. Noble explains, "My first cut is really more than an assembly because every scene is cut as I would hope it would finally be. In the morning I show the director what I've done and we go straight through it. Then we'll have lunch and talk about it.

> Then we'll go back in the afternoon and start running it reel by reel. We're looking at every sequence. You've got ideas about what scenes should go, so when you come across those scenes you both agree to cut them. And then it's, "I think we'll come into this scene a little bit later and come into this one a little bit earlier." We know that some scenes are holding up the action of the picture, maybe they're not interesting or not good enough to stay in. So you'll lose them. Just in the first sweep through, you eliminate ten to fifteen minutes.

At this point Noble usually needs about a week to make the director's recommended deletions and additions.

> Then you run the picture again and you look at it and you realize that omitting certain things has really improved it. Then we look at each scene individually and see how we can pare it down. By the end of the second week you've got another five or six minutes out of the film; if you're happy with it and you feel that the film is going in the right direction, you'll try to put a soundtrack on it and get it out and preview it.

The preview process affords the audience its first opportunity to watch the movie. If you've ever attended a "sneak preview" that was early in the process, you probably noticed that some scenes didn't quite fit together, maybe there were sound problems or the music seemed a bit off. Yet even in these earliest screenings the director begins to gauge the audience's response. Are they restless at some point? Are there things that were supposed to be funny but failed to get a laugh? Noble continues:

> You assess the audience's reaction and you start paring the film down some more. Then you take it out and preview it again and see if your results (the audience approval scores) come up at all. In theory the studio has to stay away while the director's cut is being completed. Finally you show it to the studio, but first you add some music and temporary sound effects. That takes another couple of weeks. By now we've taken our eight weeks.

The crucial "studio run" will help determine the amount of publicity and advertising support the film will receive. And of course there will be the inevitable studio suggestions for change. Noble says this is where the director plays a pivotal role.

> Depending on the strength of the director, he either listens to them or not. Or he may listen and not act on any of the suggestions. Or he may say, "Let's do these things...." Then we'll show it to the studio again and they'll say, "We'd like to preview it in this shape." If it scores really well then we pat each other on the back and send it to the composer. On the other hand, if it's a disaster in preview, we may do all sorts of things in an attempt to please the public. Take that scene out or add that scene or restructure it in some way, make it more clear to the audience what the story line is.

JFK: The Ultimate Challenge

Looking back over film history it is difficult to imagine a project with more elements than *JFK*. There was footage from the networks, the famous Zapruder film, material from the Southwest Film Archives and from numerous other public and private sources.

Director Oliver Stone, renowned for his painstaking penchant for duplicating reality, had delivered the raw elements for a masterpiece. Somehow Editor Joe Hutshing had to make it come together to tell a long, difficult and controversial story.

I knew it was going to be incredibly tough. It was like looking at a schematic for a television set and then imagining actually watching the television. It was so incredibly complicated. There was so much information, really much more than there is in the final version. You overshoot intentionally to see what works and what doesn't work and then you pare it down and try to choose your best moments.

Was there ever a moment of his own when he felt overwhelmed by the task? Hutshing smiles a knowing smile that says there were probably more than a few.

Bill Brown, who was in charge of postproduction, thought of this great analogy of what it was like working on this film. He said, "Joe, did you ever see those pirate movies where they're out at sea with these sixty-foot waves and there's the ship but the sails are all down and no one is on deck and the wheel is just spinning?" I just thought that was the perfect analogy for this. It was so much beyond what anybody had done before. There was so much footage and so many ways to go with all of this stuff. It was a little bit scary. There were times I felt like I was drowning, that I was in way over my head.

In this case the life preserver turned out to be the energy of the film itself. Eventually Hutshing, working with three other editors, began to piece together a story that cried out to be told.

We had a lot of wonderful footage to work with. A lot of it was how we could creatively get to this point or that point and keep the story going. Each scene has to work on its own and then it has to work through the common thread of the structure of the film. Eventually you let the film find its own pace and you kind of work through it. Filmmaking is a very social activity for everyone except the editor. Editing is about taking a huge chunk and reducing it to something, making it coherent and pacing it correctly, making it smooth.

Hutshing pauses for a moment, trying to remember. "I think our first cut was about five hours long. The final version is three hours and eight minutes." In between there were a lot of crucial decisions to be made. In this particular case the "in between" became a classic example of the art and craft of editing film.

Visual Language: The Tools of the Trade

At every stage of the editing process, it is the editor's responsibility to help make the story clear to the audience. This is accomplished through the use of a visual language. Since the best editing often goes unnoticed by the audience, the editor's manipulation of images is vital but somewhat invisible. Hutshing traces the modest beginnings of this art.

> Originally in film, somebody would shoot somebody sneezing or a fire truck going by and people would pay to see that. Then editing started because they put two shots together. Then years later somebody invented the insert shot, so you'd have a wide shot of somebody looking at a watch and then you cut to the insert of the watch. At first people didn't understand that. Eventually they accepted that as part of the language of film.

Asked about the language of editing, Thom Noble is willing to summarize it in a single word. "Timing. Everything is timing. It's that intuitive sense of what the correct rhythm and pacing of any moment is."

Carol Littleton agrees. Her response is enthusiastic and takes on a kind of rhythm of its own.

> Timing is a big part of it; it has to do with musicality. The timing of a piece of music. The timing of a language, how it flows, how it goes from one moment to the next. The speech patterns of an actor have their own rhythm and musicality. It's timing in the musical sense, not in the sense of a punchline. It has to be a question of focus and intensity. The editor needs to have a rigorous discipline, to know why you're doing the picture; it's about sensitivity and selectivity.
>
> Sometimes editing has to be seamless. Other times things need to be revealed in a sort of jumpy way. You might go from a moving camera to a static camera and back to a moving camera. Maybe somebody is looking around a room. You need to see things from the actors' point of view. All of these things have their own musicality, rhythm, timing.

Littleton constantly seeks "the right combination of things" that will tell the story effectively. The quest is a never-ending one, but the tools of the trade remain the same.

You need to understand all the tools that you have at your disposal— image size, quickness of the cut, using camera moves, juggling the sequence of events around, staying with the linear sequence without interrupting the action, cross cutting.

These tools are learned in school or on the job; their effectiveness is honed by each project, their proper use discovered over a lifetime. In the end, they are all that the editor has to create the visual language that produces screen magic.

The Invisible Language

Since the visual language of editing is mostly invisible, is it possible to ascertain the editor's contribution when seeing the final product? This question surfaces each year at Oscar time as editors attempt to select their peers' best work. The rest of us must look to our favorite films, those we have seen again and again and think back to their most memorable scenes. It helps if you have the editor available to walk you through them!

Thom Noble was called in five weeks after *Witness* went into production. Director Peter Weir was unhappy with the way it was being edited and Noble had the opportunity to recut the opening sequence of the Amish farms as a kind of audition. As he began to look at the shots, he realized the film's extraordinary potential.

There is a sort of rhythm that the shots have and it kind of dictates how you have to do it. With the opening titles, that rhythm was dictated by the actual shots I selected. I used the ones with the long lenses, which made everything that much slower because you had to hold the shots a bit longer. This gave these first scenes a sort of dream quality.

Excited by what he had been able to accomplish, Noble screened the segment for Weir.

Peter and I were sitting on a rattan couch and we put up the first reel and I remember thinking, "This is actually a great reel. I've never cut a reel better than this opening." The dreamlike quality started with the Amish coming over the hill and everybody going into town and then the railway station and the little boy's journey with the balloon going by.

And I'm thinking I've really got this down and if he doesn't like it, I'm just going to slash my wrists right here! I was feeling very nervous and kept on looking at Peter, hoping he would look my way and sort of give me a thumbs-up sign or smile, but he was just looking intently at the screen. We got to the end of the reel and there was this long pause and I know that I was trying to stop shaking because the rattan was making all this noise and he said, "It's great, it's so European." That was the major breakthrough.

Another one came as he and Weir worked on the film's much-discussed "lost" scene. The experience demonstrates the nature of collaboration between editor and director.

The first editor had included, in the first thirty-five minutes, a scene of Book's sister, Elaine, and Rachel, where Rachel cleans Elaine's house. It's about six or seven minutes long. I recut that scene but almost imme-diately we decided we didn't need it. When you look at the picture as a whole, I'm not really that interested in the sister. The scene in the home was really the weakest scene in the entire movie, because it doesn't have anything to do with the real point of the film and Elaine is not a main character.

In the opening title sequence of *Grand Canyon*, Carol Littleton found a metaphor for the urban angst that the film explores so effectively.

Grand Canyon is an overall mosaic of life as we live it in L.A. At the beginning, you see the basketball game being played first on a backyard court and then the same game being played at the Forum. And you real-ize this whole sort of synergy of lives is being played, the same game, we're all playing this game. I saw it as a beautiful metaphor, going from the bodies in slow motion to the Forum full of fantastic athletes. And that same idea is reprised at the very end when Danny Glover and Kevin Kline play their friendly game at night in their backyard court.

The story really begins when Kevin Kline's car breaks down in a run-down neighborhood near the Forum. Littleton says, "You could call that whole sequence an action sequence, from the time that he turns off the boulevard on to these dark streets until the time that Danny Glover comes to rescue him and they're in the tow truck."

That was a sequence that was storyboarded and it had a certain logic. Certain things were going to happen before Danny got there and certain things were going to happen after Danny got there. Action sequences have an internal logic. You're thinking of pacing and rhythm, making it as exciting as possible.

In this scene, it had to do with how isolated you could make Kevin seem. I chose shots that show the threat, that show his anxiety, the most dramatic lighting. Where the gang of kids came up, there was a dolly move, the camera dropped down from where the kids were over to the top of the car to look in the window. It conveys a certain claustrophobia, a sense of being hemmed in. So you're going from a medium shot up to a tight shot during their dialogue.

Littleton's next decision was perhaps the most important one in the entire sequence.

The big decision involved how to reveal the gun. Are we going to reveal the gun casually, just a flash of the gun, or were we going to let the kid literally pull it back and show it, maybe reveal it over a line? But in the footage he actually didn't say a line there, so I had to move one of his other lines over it. That way the kid reveals the gun when he's saying his most threatening line.

The gun is especially crucial as the scene plays out. When Danny Glover arrives, the kid asks him if he respects him for who he is or simply because he has the gun. Glover's memorable reply: "Son, if you didn't have the gun, we wouldn't be having this conversation."

Though there are a number of memorable action sequences in *Thelma & Louise*, it is the dialogue in the car between Geena Davis and Susan Sarandon that carries the film. Thom Noble explains that editors have long struggled with ways to make these talking scenes more interesting.

> *In these situations I think the reaction shots are as important as the dialogue. If you just cut to whoever is talking, then back when the other person says something, well, that's a hopeless way of cutting a dialogue scene. The reaction is often much more interesting than what the person is saying. It's a lot more than just looking at the material and saying, "This is a great reaction shot." I have to find the ideal moment to come off the speaker's dialogue to get the other person's reaction. Sometimes you might overlay the dialogue. Action sequences you can do most easily, but to actually get somebody's dialogue perfect, that's tough.*

With *Thelma*, Noble had an unexpected luxury. Director Ridley Scott had come up with a way to run all three cameras at once, so the soundtrack was always in sync, no matter which shot Noble ended up using.

> *Every scene in the car would have a camera on Geena, a camera on Susan and a camera on the two of them. So you actually had one common soundtrack all the way through. The overlaps that are usually a nightmare were no problem because they could "interrupt" each other seamlessly. I'd work it through in my mind, all the various places and the moments. You learn to go with the flow. The performances are so good in that film, they kind of just run away with it. Let the camera run, be on Susan at that point and be on Geena at the next point and just let it play. There was always the opportunity to play a reaction shot rather than hurry it along.*

Themes and Things

Sometimes the genre or subject matter of the film will help determine the appropriate editing style. Carol Littleton notes that Lawrence Kasdan's *Body Heat*, his directorial debut, was really a homage to film noir.

It's a certain genre with certain strict rules. Not only the visual style but the storytelling has to fit within the genre. In that film, you had to have the entrapment of the man and the unraveling of their plot to kill her husband. They had to be interlaced so there was a sense of the eroticism and the mystery. You had to know what to reveal, how much and when to reveal it.

My role was as a sort of built-in censor to make the film erotic rather than pornographic. Larry shot a lot of footage that was rather explicit and it was up to us in the editing room to determine how far to go and how much could be tolerated by the audience. I think Larry wanted to make the film as erotic as possible, and there's always that question, how much do you show and how much to withhold? I think that suggestion is far more erotic than being totally explicit. The time that these characters are apart is just as erotic as when they're together.

From the erotic to the esoteric, themes seem to define most memorable films. "For me, Oliver Stones's classic movies have a theme you can say in one word," explains Joe Hutshing. "*Wall Street* was about greed. *Born on the Fourth of July* about sacrifice. With *Talk Radio* it was hate. Conflict was *JFK*, conflict between people and the government, between truth and fiction. With *The Doors*," he says with a laugh, "it's got to be *excess*." He points out how editing is influenced by genre and theme.

With The Doors *we used a lot of dissolves because it was this hallucinogenic, drug-induced life-style. For* Wall Street *Oliver used a lot of camera movement to give a predatory feeling, like sharks. You can cut anywhere with a moving camera. There has to be a reason for the cut, but we found that a moving camera was so much fun to cut back and forth with. On the other hand, with* JFK *we used hard cuts and transitions that stood out, things that were in your face. Somebody would be watching television, watching Oswald being processed at the police station— and then you'd see the close-up of the TV—and then all of a sudden there would be a mirror where somebody would walk in and it would go full screen with stereo. It was like you were there.*

Finally, there are those scenes that the editor must "save" if the film is going to work at all. These often result from problems encountered during filming or decisions made in postproduction. With *JFK*, Hutshing was asked to combine two scenes where Mr. X (Donald Sutherland) reveals crucial information to investigator Jim Garrison (Kevin Costner).

In the script there were two separate scenes. First, in the middle of the movie, he goes to see this guy, X. Then at the end of the film, after the trial, he goes to see him again. And X says things like, "You were right about that." The problem was there were too many endings! When Oliver decided on another ending, we had to take the second X scene and combine it with the first one.

The combining of two similar scenes in similar locations should have been relatively easy, but there was one major obstacle.

The problem was in the second X scene they were dressed entirely differently. In the first scene he's in a blue suit, the second scene a brown suit. I couldn't use any of the dialogue. So I took all the information that was in the second scene and shifted it into the first one. That's why you see a lot of stuff played off of Costner, over the shoulder—because we were putting totally different words in Sutherland's mouth. Then we added stock footage, like the plane flying over, to add some variety to the long scene. I tried to go back to Sutherland when I could, but it's heavily weighted on Costner listening. It had to be!

Hutshing is quick to point out that the scope of *JFK* required a unique collaboration between the editors, since there were four of them assigned to the project. "It's a little unnerving for older editors to have to work with a lot of editors on a project, but I'm used to it," he says.

Indeed, the use of multiple editors has become something of an Oliver Stone trademark. Hutshing doesn't mind. "I enjoy the collaboration and I also like to see what other editors can do. I make a pass on a scene and give it to somebody else. I can get bored with scenes—so if you're switching around with another editor, for me, it's actually a lot of fun."

Increasingly, the image of the editor working "alone in the dark" is being replaced with the reality of multiple editors. Hutshing attributes this to postproduction time pressures. "I think the studios want to see a return on their money faster, so a way of shortening the time is to put multiple editors on each project."

If actors do their best work when inspired by one another, why not editors? It provides another example of how the art of filmmaking is increasingly collaborative in nature.

Beyond the Cutting Room Floor: Collaboration with the Actor

Is there anyone who has a more comprehensive view of the actor's film performance than the editor? Every take is viewed, then seen again and again as the editor makes creative decisions. With this in mind, it's interesting to ask editors about their view of the acting process and how it relates to their own work on the film. Hutshing stresses continuity, a familiar editor refrain.

> *Everyone has a way of approaching it, but someone like Martin Sheen is the same in every take and every take is excellent. He gives the same readings every time; you can transfer the words from one take into another because he gives them at the same pace. He's an editor's dream. Tom Cruise tends to know his character well and keeps it a certain way each time. Other actors experiment more. Robert Redford does things differently each time. And maybe the actions don't always match, but I enjoy the fact that Redford gives you the option of all these different takes. He'll give you a lot of choices about which way you can go.*

William Anderson reveals that working with Robin Williams on *Dead Poets Society* was an especially interesting challenge:

> *Of course, Robin Williams is a unique performer. Peter told me about the three different performances for each scene and he trusted me to just go with whatever I felt was right. On the one hand there's Robin being Robin, ad libbing. which can be over the top. Then there's Robin close to the script and then there is Robin somewhere in the middle. I just followed my instincts and found a balance between all three. There was a scene that I didn't use initially when Robin was in the class, doing his John Wayne impersonation. Peter decided that we should try it at a*

screening. The scene played well, so we kept it. Other than that, Peter mainly went with what I selected in my first cut.

Even the looping sessions, where actors have their dialogue re-recorded to match the picture, can demonstrate certain unique performance abilities. Hutshing explains that most actors can loop only a few words or a sentence at a time. "Donald Sutherland is a very studied actor and he would come in and do his looping in whole paragraphs, pages at a time. He'd watch himself once or twice on the screen, then do it perfectly."

Continuity is also a major consideration for Carol Littleton. "I want the actor to be decisive about the character at all times, to give a truthful performance."

> *But often it's ragged. Maybe they picked up the glass with the right hand and then in the next take they pick it up with the left hand. It's better if the actor can remember continuity and still give a truthful performance. If they don't remember their continuity, the editor's choices are greatly diminished.*

For Littleton, "Being technically accurate can be as important as being emotionally accurate. I get crazy over this." Actors tend to think of the editor as the enemy, someone who is likely to leave their best performance—or their entire performance—on the cutting room floor.

> *The actor has to realize that we are not sitting here passing judgment on what we like and dislike. We are their best friends, trying to do the best for them. But we can't present their best work if it's compromised by technical incompetence. We are a very respectful lot, we editors. But if we're not able to cut it, we'll have to compromise and it will be at their expense.*

Bill Reynolds often pointed out that editors are often asked to compensate for an actor's performance problems. "You can save a bad performance by placing a part of his dialogue on his back or on the cut-aways to other actors. You might place the dialogue offstage or have somebody else react to what is being said offstage."

Since editors see every mistake and are often frustrated with the actor's work, it's always interesting when they are impressed by a performance. Carol Littleton admits to a personal favorite:

Mary McDonnell is incredibly alive and real in the moment. You really feel it when you see her dailies; you really know the takes when her skin is tingling and the takes where she was either confused or trying something that didn't work. It's a palpable difference between the takes that are truly successful and the ones that don't really make it. Because she's experimenting, she's allowing herself to find something that works for her within the character. And as long as the director is patient and she feels comfortable and free and secure, she'll thread herself right through all the minefields. Not many actors can do that. It's part talent and part hard work. And when she hits it, it's pure with incredible emotion. And it's so exciting to see that. She can be very still, very concentrated and completely in the moment.

Collaboration with the Director

Editors and directors tend to form long-term relationships and work together on many projects. Each knows what to expect from the other. Each has certain needs that must be fulfilled if the collaboration is to be successful. For Bill Reynolds it was always about flexibility.

What the editor really wants from the director is coverage—enough material to work with because the director is producing the material from which a movie is going to be made. If you have coverage, you have flexibility. There are always unforeseen problems; maybe some scenes are overwritten and say more than they need to say. If you've got good coverage you can still create a perfectly smooth flowing scene that serves its purpose. Of course, it will be much shorter than it started out to be.

Carol Littleton seeks an understanding of the material she is given to work with—and that can come from only one place.

From the director, I look for continuity—particularly continuity of performance. The actor has a very big job. He's the custodian of his own character and he has to know how to feel now, how he was supposed to feel before this scene and how he will feel coming out of this scene.

The director's skills are honed in recognizing a good performance and knowing how to move from take one through take two, three, four, et cetera. He needs to elaborate on a specific idea and to refine it through each take. I'm looking for the subtleties of the take to see what the director was actually attempting. You'd be amazed how many directors do not know how to judge performances while they're being shot. They shoot a lot of stuff and say, "We got it in there someplace!"

But where? That's when things become difficult. "I'm stuck with this endless footage," she says. "And I'm doing the director's work or the actor's work. Why did they do twenty of this? What were they trying to accomplish? And I haven't got a clue."

Joe Hutshing's experiences with Oliver Stone speak to the need to generate excitement in the audience.

Oliver is open to suggestions and encourages collaboration constantly. The worst thing he would say to me was, "Joe, that's so conventional!" That's one thing he really hates. I learned that early on, not to give him anything conventional. In a scene where he had more conventional coverage, he would have me junk it up. He'd say, "It's too clean, make it dirtier, make it seedier."

Hutshing's experiences on *Born on the Fourth of July* proved very instructive in this regard.

In Born, when Tom Cruise first gets to Mexico, he goes to this outdoor cantina and they're all drinking shots of mescal and smoking cigarettes and playing poker and there're hookers around. That scene was shot with various angles and had clearly shown the poker game and everything the guys were saying. Tom was coming in, a little bit shy, trying to get to know the guys. He didn't speak the language. He was confused. I kept cutting the scene and bringing it to Oliver and he kept saying, "This is so boring, I can't even watch it."

Finally I was desperate. I said, "What am I supposed to do?" He says, "Just cut it in half!" I said, "Yeah, but it won't make any sense."

He just told me to try it. So I just kept making the scene more and more shredded, jarring, discordant, chaotic and that's exactly what he was trying to get out of it. The cuts were to make sure the scene didn't flow because if it did, it wouldn't duplicate the emotion you were after with respect to the character.

Again and again, it tends to come back to the working relationship between director and editor. Says Anderson about Weir:

Working with Peter is always special. We discuss changes and then he leaves me to it. He has a great respect for people's creativity and for people who work hard and get the job done.

At the end of the day editors and directors are trying to accomplish the same thing. Their collaborative success comes from a deep understanding of one another—almost an empathy. Hutshing pauses for a moment. "You know, Oliver [Stone] could have been a great editor. He's extremely visual and has a very good story sense." Coming from an editor, this is the highest tribute any director can receive.

The Audience: The Final Collaborator

Editors often say that they are the "first audience" to see a film. The audience remains uppermost in mind as they go about their task of trying to tell the story in the clearest, most cohesive and visual manner. Perhaps the single greatest concern among today's editors is that they are required to accomplish this at an increasingly rapid rate.

Is there really ever enough time? Hutshing would have liked to have had more on *JFK*. "There were a lot of things I was really unhappy with when the movie came out, but I just didn't have time to redo them. Little things." In this case there were some interesting studio politics at work as well.

The problem was we kept showing it to the studio and they would say things like "You can't show that much of Kennedy's brains on the table," [during the autopsy] so we would change that. After a couple of screenings, it was clear that we were starting to take out more and more of the "offensive" stuff. Oliver is sensitive to people's wants, but he starts get-

ting worried that he is sanitizing his own movie. So he told us it was up to us, do we want to work seven days a week and get it out earlier and have a rougher movie or take longer on it and have a more sanitized version. There was no question for us, we said, "Let's get this out now; let's do it." And maybe it was a little rougher for that, but it was a stronger statement that way.

Embodied in this story is the spirit that accompanies Hollywood's most successful editors as they come to work each day, bringing their unique vision to the cutting room.

Like all of film's collaborative artists, they will probably fail as often as they succeed. Nevertheless, armed with nothing but a sense of story and a few tools of the trade, they speak the visual language of film. When they do succeed, their work touches us and moves us in ways we can't even begin to describe. Editors may be invisible, but what they do leaves an indelible impression on the lives of the rest of us—the audience "out there in the dark."

"Some directors say all editors care about is if the cut works," concludes Joe Hutshing. "And that's not true at all. We have to worry about everything. You worry because you love film and because it's important to visualize how something will be. It's a way of seeing."

CLOSE-UP
THE EDITORS: MIKE HILL AND DAN HANLEY

MIKE HILL: We came into the process the first day of production. We started a week early just to get everything set up and then as soon as they start shooting and as soon as there are complete scenes, we start working on it.

DAN HANLEY: Mike and I have worked together on all of Ron's pictures, starting twenty years ago on *Night Shift*. We were originally supposed to be assistant editors on that picture, but the editor had a stroke and we were moved up instantly into editing. Ron liked having two editors and he liked both of us, so we've been with him ever since.

MIKE: As a team, we have our separate editing set-ups and rooms. We do our own scenes, which we randomly pick. It's nice to have another editor there to back you up and if the scene is difficult, it's good to have another editor take a look at it.

DAN: There's an advantage with two editors. There's more input, different POVS, and we can really work the scene a little bit longer on our first cut. When I first started editing, everything I did I thought was the most precious thing in the world, but it's part of the process to collaborate. And, if one of us is stuck, it's so simple as open the door and say, "I'm kind of jammed up there," and, "What do you think of that?" The major challenge for me as an editor and the toughest part of my job, is the first cut, because you're trying to figure out the internal rhythm of the scene and trying to figure out what the director is looking for and you're trying to figure out the best performance. You're looking for that general rhythm of the scene.

MIKE: We usually do one edit and then make suggestions on each other's cut and when we've assembled all of our scenes into the actual film, Ron then comes in and starts working with us on the scenes. For the first cut, we have complete freedom to do what we want.

DAN: Then we start working with each other and with Ron. Early on, I dreaded that part, perhaps it was the ownership thing, but now I love that part.

MIKE: The collaboration works because there is no ego problem. We trust each other completely, and we've known each other so long, that it works very well. During shooting, when we watch the dailies, Ron will point out his favorite takes. He might say, "Good take," four different times on the same shot and then we go ahead and structure the scenes the way that feels best to us. When he's done shooting, we go through it scene by scene with him and take all his notes and do whatever changes he wants and go from there.

DAN: Because of working with Ron, we've had the good fortune to work on so many different kinds of movies and not get pigeon-holed into a certain genre as editors. We've worked on such diverse films as *Apollo 13*, *Parenthood*, *Night Shift* and *Ransom*. Ron sets the rhythm of the director and he has a certain point of view and a certain tone, but he gives us a lot of free rein to also come at it with our own point of view.

MIKE: As editors, we take our style from the material. I pretty much consider my editing philosophy to be that an editor shouldn't have a personal style, but he should adapt his style to the material that the director delivers to him and what the actor gives him. Those dictate how the movie is edited. If you want to impose a style, you might do that later—in the final stages—if you feel you need to change the pacing or rhythms or if you want to slow the scene down or speed it up. But when you're initially cutting, you're going with what you're given. And the way the actors do the performance and the way the director shoots it will really dictate the style of the film.

DAN: I think style depends on the sensibility of the director, whatever his style may be. Sometimes it's a process of learning and that sensibility might change with different movies. You're creating a flow to the entire film. Sometimes a certain scene works great, but it interrupts the flow of the movie for some reason, so you have to work the scenes together. There's a scene we shot where Nash is at the hospital talking with Rosen. It's a scene where Nash gets a glimpse of schizophrenia because he sees a schizophrenic patient in the background. But this scene was one of the first to go, because it was selling the point a little more than we needed to right then. If you keep hitting the point that Nash is schizophrenic too hard and too soon, well, then that whole conspiracy idea doesn't work.

MIKE: As editors, we're also trying to follow the rhythms of the actors. Russell did a lot of different variations of the scene, giving us a lot of options as to the degree of the bizarre behavior. He would give us some takes where he was acting pretty normal and then he would step it up to slightly weird and then he'd go really weird. We tended to go with the middle most of the time. The first half of the movie we would tend more to the normal and when the whole thing was revealed, we could go a little more with the weird, more quirky takes. Ed [Harris] is so solid from take to take, that he doesn't really vary them that much. Jennifer also pretty much gives a similar one. So Russell was the only one who wasn't totally consistent, but that was on purpose.

DAN: We talked early on about certain things that Ron wanted to convey with the delusional characters. They were always introduced from the point-of-view of John Nash and we were very conscious of always introducing that character with a sound first. When Ron had researched schizophrenia, he learned that it was often auditory, so we wanted to use that. Ed Harris was introduced with the sound of a door and a footstep. There was a cough off-screen when

Charlie entered. I asked Ron, "How are we going to do this, Ron, where it doesn't feel like it's kind of cheating? How are we going to keep protecting the audience?" He decided we should play it real once the characters are introduced.

MIKE: *A Beautiful Mind* was not as difficult as some other films we've done with Ron, such as *Apollo 13* or *Willow*, both of which had a lot of special effects and computer work. *A Beautiful Mind* was pretty much a straight drama, which I prefer anyway. It was written so the audience would be surprised about halfway through, so we wanted to make sure we didn't give anything away in getting to that point. We had to make sure that there weren't too many clues that he might be delusional. But since it was written so well and shot so well and directed so well, we really just had to go with the material. Not to say it was easy, since none of them are easy, but it went together very nicely.

DAN: It goes together well partly because Ron is one of the most collaborative, creative people I've ever worked with. He has a point of view and it's a strong point of view, but he wants our creative input. He is not only comfortable and confident, but he's able to articulate his point of view. I think Ron sees that in a script or something he's going to make, there has to be something that he can get his hooks into creatively. He looks for something you can relate to. There's a positive humanity in every one of Ron's movies.

ON NASH
TURNING TOWARD
THE WINDOW
PARCHER (OS)
PROFESSOR NASH

39-3 CONT

NASH POV
PARCHER INTRODUCES
HIMSELF
PARCHER "WILLIAM PARCHER

PUSH IN

39-4

> *My job is to take over where the director left off and to tell those things that you can't tell in pictures or in words and to do it elegantly.*
>
> **—Hans Zimmer**

The Composer: Invisible Bridges

It's an unlikely resume. He grew up in Germany with no formal musical training. ("I couldn't get a job there," he explains.) Then he went on to become a pop music "one-hit wonder" in the early 1980s. In fact, his group The Buggles found brief fame when their "Video Killed the Radio Star" became the first video ever played on MTV.

As he faded out of the pop scene, he began to get work scoring films. A unique ability to combine electronic and acoustic sounds honed during his pop years served him well. Twenty years and seventy-five films later, he has won every musical award imaginable.

So if you have ever seen *Gladiator, Black Hawk Down, Rain Man, Thelma & Louise, The Thin Red Line*, or *The Lion King*—for which he won an Academy Award—then you have heard the music of Hans Zimmer.

In person, Zimmer's smile speaks volumes. In his spacious music studio, he is surrounded by odd instruments of every conceivable description, not to mention a mind-boggling array of synthesizers and computers capable of producing virtually any sound. What's the toughest part of being one of the most successful film composers in Hollywood?

> *You're the first person the director can't really talk to about what's going to happen. He doesn't know about it. He can speak about the scripts, the actors; he can look through the lens of the camera. But when it comes to the music, suddenly he loses control.*

Watching Zimmer work, it's easy to understand what he means. To enter the world of the film composer is to enter a techno-environment that seems a world apart from that of any of the other collaborators. To alleviate this problem, Zimmer begins by getting to know his directors as well as possible.

I try to hang out with the director, find out what makes him tick. With Ridley Scott in Thelma & Louise *for example, we spent forever just going out to dinner, talking about friends, talking about other books we read and somehow talking around the gritty subject of the movie.*

Generally the last artist to work on the film, the composer begins when everyone else is finished, when the director hands over a "final" version of the film. Final, that is, except for the music. Going last has its hazards. The collision of art and commerce that is the Hollywood studio production process accelerates as the project nears completion. If ever there was very little time, it's now. With multiple millions of dollars at stake, the pressure to deliver a final print is intense.

"About 99 percent of the time, we're brought in too late and we're always doing eight weeks' work in three weeks' time." Veteran composer David Raksin smiles. "You have to have a certain versatility and a kind of idiotic innocence to be a movie composer."

Raksin, forever remembered as the man who created the haunting theme for Otto Preminger's classic murder mystery *Laura,* has worked with many of Hollywood's best directors. A body of work spanning nearly eighty decades has taught him a fundamental truth about film composing. Says the man widely regarded as "the best film composer never to win an Oscar," "We're manipulators. It's about affecting the audience subliminally. The manipulation involves the music, which helps tell the story."

Bill Conti has a knack for knowing how to make the music tell the story. Seen each year conducting the orchestra on Academy Awards night, it is easy to forget that he is the man whose music for *Rocky* catapulted him to the top of his profession and into the loftiest tax brackets as well. When the movie scored a knockout at the box office, that "low-budget job" turned out to be a film composer's once-in-a-lifetime opportunity.

The result is a sprawling home, complete with medieval paintings and tapestries from the far corners of Europe. "This is the house that *Rocky* built," he says with a laugh, though it is hard to imagine Sylvester Stallone's alter ego amid such splendor. When it comes to the music, Conti explains:

> It comes from inside. It's unique, original and interpretive. Above all, it's entertainment. We're looking to entertain. You have to use artistic means to do something that is really not artistic, in the classical sense. Mozart didn't write just to entertain. He wrote as art and it entertains. We're not confused about why we're doing this—we're entertainers.

Zimmer once told the *Christian Science Monitor* that his son put it all into perspective for him. When he mentioned Mozart the boy looked up at him and asked, "What movie did he write for, Daddy?"

To Read or Not to Read?

Every other collaborator begins by reading the script. Yet by the time the film reaches the composer, it can, quite literally, be a different story. Some composers read the script beforehand to familiarize themselves with the story. Others prefer to preview the film before meeting with the director.

For David Raksin, the key is the contrast *between* what's in the script and what's on the screen.

> There's a great difference between the script and the movie. I usually read the script, but not always. Directors are often under the impression that they've said certain things or done certain things that are simply not there. You're a lot more useful to them if you come in without having accepted any of that. I want to be inspired by what they have on the screen, not by what they think they have on the screen.

The late Henry Mancini's name will forever be synonymous with memorable film scores. He created the music for *The Pink Panther* movies and of course it was he who wrote *Moon River*. "The main reason to read the script is to find the source material that needs to be written before filming begins," he once explained. "But when I read the script ahead of time, I forget it, because there is many a slip between the page and the screen.

Maurice Jarre won Oscars for scoring *Lawrence of Arabia, Doctor Zhivago* and *A Passage To India. Gorillas in the Mist* and *Ghost* also bear his distinctive stamp. "During shooting, I go to the location to see how the director is working. What is his aim, what does he want to say with his theme?"

Bill Conti agrees that it can be advantageous for the process to begin while the film is still in production. "Sometimes the director sends me dailies on videotape, just to familiarize me with what's going on. I deal with the vision of the director, even though the writer has begun the process."

Hans Zimmer agrees, "Your responsibility is to the movie and it has to be the director's movie, not the writer's." At the same time he laments, "One of the tragedies of making movies is that there is such little regard for the written word. What a film should do is to tell you a story. Music can really help that process, but unless you're careful, it can also undermine it."

The Temp Track

Before the composer begins working, the director or music editor will create a temp track. This consists of music that seems to fit the film and provides hints at possible directions for the final film score. For Barry Levinson it became a vital part of the collaborative process in *Rain Man*, the Academy Award-winning story of an autistic patient (Dustin Hoffman) and his con-artist brother (Tom Cruise) who hit the road together.

Levinson's path to the final soundtrack provides a glimpse into the collaborative process and the vital role of the temp track as well.

> *When I do a temp track, I work with several different music editors. I'll have discussions about what I'm thinking. Then the music editor will give me many suggestions. I may wind up with six hundred songs and I may be looking for two. A lot of things kick off ideas.*
>
> *In Rain Man I had to figure out how to do a score without strings because I thought that strings would be too sentimental. And I wanted to eliminate guitars because you always associate guitars with road movies.*
>
> *I was sent some pieces from Johnny Clegg called "Scatterlings of Africa." I loved them and said they would be great to play in the movie when the car is driving to Palm Springs and the windmills are there. I*

told Hans Zimmer, "That's the sound of the film—the music is very rhythmic." It fit because in one of my discussions with people involved in autism, they mentioned that autistic people respond to rhythms.

So before I shot the movie I knew I would use "Scatterlings" and "Dry Bones" for the end. I played the movie with the temp track for Hans. He would bring in something, we'd try it, then go take a look at the movie and keep molding it and changing it until it became a sort of cohesive piece.

Often music from the temp track seems so right the director will keep it. In *Platoon*, Oliver Stone had chosen Samuel Barber's "Adagio for Strings" for the temp track and its impact, when combined with the footage of the burning village, was perfect. "Someone had suggested the 'Adagio' to me and although Georges Delerue scored the film, much of the temp track was used and combined with Delerue's music."

Alex North's experience with *2001: A Space Odyssey* provides another example. North did an original score, but Stanley Kubrick threw it out and kept the now-famous temp track that included Johann Strauss's "Blue Danube" and Richard Strauss's tone poems.

Finally, some composers prefer that there not be a temp track at all because there are simply too many associations possible with *any* music that's used. When David Raksin was asked to compose the music for *Laura*, they were going to put "Sophisticated Lady" on the temp track. "I could see, with them using 'Sophisticated Lady,' that they were going to use the old cliché with the saxophone or muted trumpet. Not too much of a theme, in my opinion." Instead Raksin responded by composing the main theme song in a weekend so the director would never hear the scene with the "wrong" music.

The Spotting Session

In theory at least, the composer's actual work begins with a "spotting session" where she or he will sit down with the director (and sometimes the producer) and watch the film to determine where the music will go. Like most composers, Bill Conti prefers to preview the film. "I'll watch the film before the spotting session. The more you look at the movie, the more thoughts start to take shape about what you want to do."

As the spotting session begins, the role of the music director is crucial: the composer tends to discuss the "big ideas" of the picture with the director, but it is up to the music editor to take notes and to listen to what is being said. He's the one who is watching the footage counter and noting each cue.

Composer Shirley Walker (*Willard, Final Destination*) reveals that these notes can become important later on, in case there is a dispute regarding what was agreed upon.

> *The notes are a protection for all of us so they're sent to the director and the producer. Then as we're discussing these things and someone says, "I thought that was going to be a murderous rage-filled moment," we can look at the spotting notes and see that the consensus had been that it would be a tender moment. Of course, we might mutually decide to rethink this.*

Once the spotting session is over, the composer begins searching more intently for the musical options within the film. Since each film is different, the need to recognize the essence of the story and follow through on it is at the heart of the process. Walker begins by identifying what she calls a "core concept."

> *If I don't have a core concept of the story and the characters, then I'm just spewing out a bunch of notes. The core concept is always something about the story and the storytelling. Once I get that core concept in place, then I start letting it turn into music. It's like having a skeleton first and then the music is the flesh and the muscle. I'll sit and create numerous different emotional contexts. I like to play those into a tape and just listen to it again over a period of a few days, get that material cycling around by itself. Then I take it into the director and say, "Here's what I'm going to base the score on."*

"I may spend several days trying to get material that I think is right," Henry Mancini explained. "Once you have that set, once you know your material, it's like you're going to build a house. Style comes into it, attitudes, tempo."

The analogy surfaces yet again as David Raksin describes the inherent structures of film composition.

> *There is always an architecture. There is a certain structure and you have to find out what the scene is about and what position it occupies in the whole film. When I get the scene breakdown, I circle with red everything that is really important, things I can't overlook.*

Like writers, directors and other film collaborators, Raksin will seek out the emotional moments in the story and attempt to find a way to portray them honestly. Often this does not come without an internal creative struggle.

> *You have to figure out the emotions and the flow of the scene. You hope you can write chronologically so you have a sense of it as it develops. I'll be working on a long scene and I'll say to myself, "It doesn't sound like this is going to work." but I'll just keep writing.*
>
> *For* Laura, *that weekend I must have written forty or fifty themes and not written a bunch of others that I thought of but which weren't good enough to write down. Finally on Sunday night, as a result of all of this, I came up with the real thing. When I played it for Otto Preminger, he realized it was something special.*

The Theme's the Thing

Many composers think in terms of composing specific themes for the main characters that can be played in many different styles. Sometimes the theme might be scary, played with bassoons, or romantic, played with violins. As the film goes on the themes might be put into minor keys or given different harmonies.

Hans Zimmer tries to keep the process as flexible as possible.

> *I often have themes for what the characters are going through. But I never stick with my themes. My themes are always changing.* Rain Man *is actually the craziest theme of them all. Because you never really hear a theme. You'd only hear it if you took every piece of music in the movie and bundled them all together, then you would get a complete tune.*

Here is where the music becomes more than a mere emotional blueprint for the movie; now it actually serves to illuminate and underscore the story.

> *The whole idea is that Raymond (the autistic brother) goes on and on and you never get the whole picture. So the tune begins with the first note on the first reel and it's never complete until the last note of the end titles—so it's this huge arc but it's always interrupted by mayhem.*

Some of the most memorable movie themes originated with other characters or even other projects in mind. Henry Mancini actually developed *The Pink Panther* theme before the panther was ever conceived.

> *"The Pink Panther" was actually written as a theme for David Niven, the jewel thief. He was a roguish character, very light on his feet and I just happened to come up with the opening of "da dant, da dah" before the sax comes in. Then Blake Edwards, the director, wanted an animated main title and the theme was perfect with the sax and flutes. It keeps winding through the picture, constantly changing.*

And there are composers who prefer not to write for specific characters. Thomas Newman is best known for his work on *American Beauty* and *The Green Mile*. He is also the composer behind the theme for TV's *Six Feet Under*. In an interview on National Public Radio he explains that unless you are doing some sort of "opera" where good and evil are spelled out clearly, there is little need for a character theme. "I do not write themes for characters," he explains, "I write music under which a character lives."

Hans Zimmer explains that, like other creative people, composers start to get ideas, then live with them. Under incredible time pressures, they are stretched to their creative limits. The process is more about feeling than thinking. Each project tends to occupy the mind night and day.

> *I digest it, sleep it, dream it. Try to see what it smells like, what the scent of it is. Searching for themes is like hunting animals. You hunt, you hone it down, I have to get all of my rationalizing out of the way first. It's got nothing to do with thinking.*

Music and Pictures: Together at Last!

With the main themes established, it's time to review each scene and decide how the music will be used. Often this involves working closely with the director to make sure that the music not only complements what's on the screen but also provides a requisite tension or underlying emotional context that contributes to the story as a whole.

How much can the music convey? How much *should* it convey? There are a number of schools of thought about this. Shirley Walker might be classified as a minimalist. "I don't like music in your face. I come from the school of film composing where underscoring is truly underscoring. In *Memoirs of an Invisible Man*, the music is more of an invisible presence than a manipulative force."

Newman agrees and explains that it is really a "generational thing" because movie music in the '30s and '40s tended to be melodramatic and "large in scope." Today's composers tend to be more subdued. "I tend to be spare, I freeze moments a lot."

> In the Bedroom *had a very small score. It was clear that a lot of music would make that a tedious movie. It would be commenting all the time and perhaps saying things that would make the dramatic intention less ambiguous, and ambiguity can be compelling....*

Interestingly, films that are best remembered for their music are not always those that contain the most of it. Henry Mancini once revealed that the scores for *Breakfast at Tiffany's* (which included "Moon River") and *The Days of Wine and Roses* each contained about forty musical minutes. Still, the two projects netted him three Academy Awards.

Maurice Jarre had a similar experience when he and Peter Weir worked together on *Dead Poets Society.*

> *The first thing Peter said was, "I don't think we need a lot of music, probably not more than thirty minutes." He already knew the film would be better if it wasn't overloaded with music. You don't want the music to get in the way. Often you have to explain this to a director, but Peter knows.*

Still, the power of music in a scene is undeniable. Bill Conti's scoring of love scenes has always contained a special quality. "There are so many ways to work the emotions. The film says 'they're going to get up and kiss' but the music can say 'we don't want them to do that, the kiss is not right and they know it.' What's amazing is that the music alone can do that."

David Raksin reveals what he feels is the single most difficult task for film composers. "Music can't save a picture, but it can help hold a picture together. It can tell the audience on a subliminal level what is happening."

Shirley Walker agrees and explains the limitations. "Music can't save a bad film. We jokingly refer to these situations as 'dressing the corpse.' If it's dead, it's dead and all we can do is dress it up and give it a pretty surrounding. But a good film can just be put over the top by a great score."

Rocky certainly serves as a classic example. Bill Conti faced a real challenge scoring the famous montage scene near the end—where the underdog fighter prepares for the big championship match.

> *Director John D. Avildson had about five miles of film with Sylvester Stallone doing one-arm push-ups, running, jumping. We worked our way up in thirty-second increments till we had about three minutes of montage. Our objective here in the tenth reel is to make the people think, right before the fight, that this guy has a chance, although in our exposition and development of the film story this guy doesn't have a prayer. So somehow we have to say "This guy might have a shot at it." Obviously it worked.*

Another more subtle challenge came as Hans Zimmer worked with the producers and director of *Driving Miss Daisy*. The simple, leisurely paced period film went on to Oscar glory. Most critics felt the score was a big part of the reason why. Zimmer explains how it happened.

> *The score that director Bruce Beresford wanted for it is very different from the score I actually wrote. I have a feeling that Bruce wanted a far more classical score. We're dealing with old people, there has to be some dignity involved. Bruce is a huge opera buff; if I had pulled out a couple of tunes from some opera, he would have been deliriously happy. But co-producer Lili Zanuck got me thinking when she said, "The problem with old people is the way we see them as tired and sitting on the sideline*

somewhere. We young people make them into this. But they have a lot of energy, they have a lot of zest." And Miss Daisy (Jessica Tandy) is definitely feisty.

As with so many composing dilemmas, Zimmer finally found that one creative breakthrough, the moment of clarity that brings together all the elements and sets the tone for the entire film score and for the film itself.

I was looking for a rhythm and I looked at the way Miss Daisy walked— those feisty little steps as she walked to the Piggly Wiggly. The way her face was, the way her feet moved, the way it was lit. That was it! When I saw her walking, I heard the tune.

I thought of the clarinet as the solo instrument for Miss Daisy. I wanted to have this one, crystal-clear line that goes all the way through. Just the way her stubbornness goes all the way through the film.

I specifically stayed away from that soothing pretty music with lots of strings. There are no strings in the whole thing. The whole score is electronic and I think it helped carry what was really a very slow but wonderful movie.

Creative breakthroughs can come at any time but don't always lead directly to the perfect film score. With *Rain Man*, Zimmer encountered a very different predicament.

I'm sitting there and I start to write this tune and I start to get a little buzz and I say, "Wow, this is happening." So the producer, Mark Johnson, walks by and hears it and says, "This is a great tune," and he tells Barry about it. The only problem was by this point I'm listening to it and I'm having my doubts. "This isn't right, but Mark thinks it's wonderful and says we have to have it everywhere in the movie." So Barry Levinson, the director, comes and says, "Okay, let's hear it." Finally by the fourth bar, he doesn't have to say anything. Maybe it was a great tune, but it had nothing to do with his movie.

The creative relationship between the director and composer is at the heart of the composing process and like all other collaborations, it doesn't always go smoothly. Zimmer recalls a fundamental misunderstanding that led to near disaster on *Backdraft*:

> *I nearly got fired off the movie because I kept writing the wrong thing. I wrote the fires like an action film, having forgotten our conversation about bringing them to life. Ron Howard, the director, realized these fires could have a personality, that they could have a spirit of their own.*
>
> *When he heard the music for the first fire, he was totally freaked out because it was all wrong. I changed thirteen bars and suddenly it was all perfect, because once you press the right emotional button, everything else falls into place. It's like building houses, it's all wrong until the roof is on, or actually until the windows are there and it has its character.*

Zimmer's German background has occasionally led to misunderstandings on his American projects, like the time Penny Marshall had to explain baseball to him for *A League of Their Own*. At the same time, he recalls occasions when he feels his background has worked for him.

> *You have to remember I know nothing about America other than what I see in the movies. If you think about what Barry Levinson did in* Rain Man *by getting an Australian cameraman and a German composer to be the eyes and ears of America—it worked because we look at America and think, "Wow, how wonderful, look at this place!"*
>
> *You've seen it all, we haven't; we're still awed by it. So by giving it a slightly different twist, America might see the wonder of its own place again. With* Thelma & Louise *it's the same thing because Ridley Scott, an Englishman and a great visualist, is having a good look at America.*

The Score and More: Interesting Choices

Once the major creative decisions are made, it's time for the composer to get down to the business of writing the score. The length of the score for each film varies. There may be as little as fifteen or twenty minutes of music in a two-hour film, or as many as a hundred minutes. The average is about fifty to sixty minutes.

The memorable score of *Driving Miss Daisy* contains less than thirty minutes of music and took Hans Zimmer about two weeks to write. The amount of music required generally determines how long the composer will be on the picture, but there are exceptions. More ambitious projects take more time. Zimmer worked on *Toys* for about a year, though he also completed *A League of Their Own* and *The Power of One* during that period.

Henry Mancini tended to compose very quickly. "I average about three to five minutes a day. That's as fast as you can go and still be good. Most pictures take two or three weeks, it depends on how panicked they are."

As final deadlines draw near, the composer's choice of instruments becomes a significant part of the creative decision-making process. Each instrument is chosen with the story and the characters in mind. Thomas Newman describes it as an artistic process.

> *If you're doing a movie like* American Beauty *you probably don't want to use a lot of brass instruments. You could say, "Well, brass gives me this kind of feeling," and this kind of feeling is not the kind of feeling I find in* American Beauty. *It's stripping out all that doesn't work and kind of discovering your palette and then going from there.*

The director and other collaborators may play pivotal roles. With *American Beauty* Newman explains that director Sam Mendes wanted "very much to deal with percussion instruments. So I think he pointed me in that direction."

> *And then I went in with a group of players I have worked with for a long time and started bandying different ideas around. And a percussionist I worked with picked up a set of tablas and started rhythmicizing to these ideas. And oftentimes I think that some of my best music just evolves because I try to allow other players just to get into a space and do things that interest them.*

Most successful composers are not afraid to experiment with nontraditional and unorthodox instruments, as long as they fit the mood of the picture. In 1962 Henry Mancini used an Autoharp in *Experiment in Terror*, "It was being used in hootenanny groups at that time. You hit a note and it sounds like it's an echo chamber. It worked great because of the echo." The African locations in *Hatari!* led him to use African thumb pianos, giant pea pod gourds and shell gourds.

Maurice Jarre recalls matching instruments to scenes and characters in *Dead Poets Society*.

> *I used the bagpipe for the beginning procession and then a solo bagpipe, very dramatic, right after Neil's suicide. It was so dramatic, so touching, because it was the only sound and because we hadn't had any music for a long time. That makes it special. For the character of Knox Overstreet we used a Celtic harp with metal strings. There are two kinds of Celtic harps; one has regular strings, but I used the one with metal strings because it has more reverberation. It's more poetic. At the beginning, when Knox rides the bicycle, it's like the wind. It's almost like the instrument is coming from the wind.*

Bill Conti is also noted for his use of unusual instruments. "I have a history of finding that unique little instrument, a funny little sound, a whistle. We all want to compose a distinctive story. Instrument choices are one way to be unique."

Shirley Walker explains that often the composer works closely with an orchestrator who will assist in finding just the right sounds.

> *On projects where I was the orchestrator the composer might say, "I want the brass to have the melody until the kiss and then during the embrace the violins should soar and take over and carry the emotion." And I'll execute that. Other times I might go back and say, "I like your idea of using the strings here but what about the possibility of French horns in this line?" It warms up the sound. And when it works, the composer is giving you permission to make a contribution on that level.*

Throughout the process the composer always deals with one fundamental dilemma. This is precisely why movie work is so different from that of a recording artist. "You only get to hear our stuff once," Conti explains, "so we've got to catch your ear. If it works once, that's all we care about."

Take It from the Top

It's late afternoon on the Disney lot in Burbank. Bill Conti stands on a sound stage in front of a huge orchestra. It could be opening night at the symphony except that everyone is dressed casually and there is no audience except for a dozen sound technicians and crew members. It is the final day of recording for the three-hour film project Conti has been working on for nearly a year. Again and again the scene is projected on a large screen so the musicians can match their performances with each visual cue.

During the seven-hour session the same piece of music will be played over and over again as separate soundtracks are recorded for the guitars, brass, percussion and finally for the full orchestra.

Conti gives the musicians a break and explains that tonight's final session will be devoted to the music that will play over the end credits. "Of course no one will ever hear it!" He laughs. It is ironic that so much time and money is devoted to music that will play to a mostly empty theater.

There is time for one more question. How does he know how many musicians are required?

> I hear what the film should have, there are blocks that come into your mind. A symphony orchestra—eighty-six, ninety-six, a hundred. A chamber orchestra, Mozart, thirty-five. A wind ensemble, rock 'n' roll. I'll have something in mind and I'll say it's going to be around fifty or sixty players, because the things that I'm hearing in my mind can't be done unless there are fifty or sixty players. If they say, "It should be like a '40s movie," boom, eighty-six comes right to mind, eighty-six players will do this because they didn't do this with less than that in the 1940s. That's what it takes to be effective.

To the untrained observer the recording process goes so smoothly that it's hard to believe there is little or no rehearsal time. Yet none of these musicians has ever seen a note of the music until they all come in for the session. Shirley Walker explains.

> Here in Los Angeles we have musicians who are third-generation film music performers. And remember, film music is a very different type of performance than symphonic.
>
> People get the two mixed up because they're both orchestra. But it takes a hell of a player to play film music and most orchestra musicians are very timid. Some producers might want the London Symphony, but Los Angeles musicians are the best.

Collaboration and the Composer

As each piece of music is recorded, it will be played for the director. Some directors also make it a point to attend recording sessions so they can get a feel for what's going on. Nevertheless, it is a rare producer or director who has any technical musical knowledge. Conti says as a result, the collaboration process that ensues is not always pretty.

> *The director is the master sergeant who makes decisions at all levels. But could he possibly be qualified at all levels? No, he can't be. I have to play a piece of music for him and he has to respond. The guy who equivocates is the guy who really hurts everybody. If he says, "I don't know. Could you try it more like this?" now, that's more difficult. I want him to know his own feelings enough to say, "I like this. I hate this." I might go to the piano, "You mean like this?" But you don't want them to start talking notes or instruments.*

Newman recalls that *American Beauty* director Sam Mendes definitely had his own ideas, but in the end it was about collaboration.

> *There are things he would like, things that he would like more than other things. He was very egalitarian in a way. I mean, he knew what he wanted and he certainly wasn't afraid to express what he didn't like. At the same time I think Sam is really an excellent collaborator. I think he knows how to bring good things out of people. It was give and take—like anything.*

Maurice Jarre has worked with director Peter Weir on *Witness* and *Dead Poets Society*.

> *For me especially, it's always interesting to work with Peter because he's very musical, he has a tremendous sense of music culture, which makes communication very easy. He knows classical, avant-garde music, new age, electronic opera, ethnic music—everything. And that's so rare for a director. He knows exactly what kind of sound he wants and where the music is supposed to be. He knows if he wants an orchestral or electronic score. Best of all, he knows what the music is supposed to do. Other*

directors might say, "Let's try this with oboe or trumpet," or they might want to keep improvising, but Peter always knows what he wants.

You can't arrive at the recording studio and experiment with a different way of orchestration. Even at the spotting session, Peter is prepared to tell the composer what he wants. At the same time, he's very open to ideas, always willing to try something new. It's a very rare form of musical collaboration.

Emotion in Motion

Since the movie is often nearly complete by the time it reaches the composers, they are really the first audience members to preview a film. The difference is that it is also their job to provide the last coat of paint—the invisible musical bridges that pull the audience into the experience.

We all remember our favorite film moments. The best composers seek them out for us in advance and provide the music that helps lead us to them. They also take us all the way back to those "footprints in the dark," the glowing remnants of the original vision that began when the writer typed FADE IN.

To accomplish this, composers must get in touch with their own emotions. Often these are linked to specific instruments. Thomas Newman was asked about the "feelings" he explored when he scored *The Shawshank Redemption*, a movie set in prison.

> *Maybe you'll start with a piano, the idea that you want something but you don't want it to be overly emoting and it has a colder feeling to it—you start associating, I guess, instruments with certain kinds of emotional states in the movie.*

Bill Conti reveals that the emotional process is not without peril.

> *Unfortunately, to write sad music, you have to feel sad. I'm feeling the feelings that I'm supposed to feel because I'm writing the music that makes me feel them. A project that is depressing depresses me when I'm doing it. I'm numb. I'm in that place.*

That I use intellect to write music is without question. But I have to drag the music up from someplace. No one knows where it comes from. It's a physical, emotional thing.

Suddenly a smile returns to his face. "Of course, the day I wrote the *Rocky* theme, I felt like I wanted to go punch someone in the face!"

When all is said and done, we have to translate emotions into a particular style, using melody, instruments and textures. We're counting on the fact that we all share our emotions because of our humanity. I'm hoping that when I write the music that makes me cry, you'll cry. Our stock in trade is to scare you, make you excited, laugh, feel alone, feel alive. We're musicians. That's what we do.

CLOSE-UP
THE COMPOSER: JAMES HORNER

Beginning the Process

I don't read the script because I come into the process in postproduction, beyond the script level. What's on the page can be brilliant, but the director sets the mood of the film so I begin by looking at the film. Usually when I look at the film I haven't talked to the director about music. I'm looking at it as a virgin, so when I see a film, it's an immediate process. I have an emotional and auditory reaction and that's what I discuss with the director.

By the first viewing, I'm already beginning to hear the sound. It's an emotional reaction. Since I'm a composer, as opposed to a sculptor, director, painter or cinematographer, I have to figure out how to capture the moods and emotions in my particular craft, putting them into notes, as opposed to putting it into paint or cameras or lenses or shots.

At the beginning, I'm just thinking about style and instruments, never melodies. It's very painterly. I think of broad stroke colors. What is the best way to paint this particular emotion? Should I use a boy soprano, a flute, an electric guitar? I try to find the color that matches what I'm feeling.

Sometimes by the second screening, there's a temp track that's been added by the director or a music editor. I like to deal with temporary music since it's a good starting point for discussion. I can respond to it by telling the director, "That works really beautifully, I know exactly what you're looking for," or I can say, "You think that works great but it's horrible, horrible. I beg you not to make me do that!"

I compose at a desk. I don't use a computer or a piano. I find that if I compose at the piano, that my fingers start to work in a predictable comfortable pattern, so it's easier for me to write it at a table and then sometimes check it at the piano.

I find I can hear it in my head really clearly and it's just much easier to write on a piece of paper. In my head, it's perfect, but when I play it on the piano, it can change because of how the fingers work.

Instruments and Melodies

At the beginning, when I think of the music it's very abstract. I'm not thinking of melodies, but of what instrumental color will convey the emotion I'm feeling.

If there needs to be melodic writing, usually that's a little bit further along. If I get the instrument right, I can do the melody very fast—whether it's a pretty melody, or spooky, or dark—it's pretty easy for me. What's harder is to find exactly the right instrumental color.

It was my intention in *A Beautiful Mind* to have the sound fluid, so you didn't always know if it was music or sound. I find that I solve fewer and fewer problems with an orchestra. Emotionally, I'm just used up with an orchestra because it's an overused color. A large orchestra and certain instruments sound a certain way. If I tell you I have a beautiful tune that's going to be played on an oboe, it doesn't really matter what the tune is, because your mind has already conjured up what an oboe sounds like.

I had this abstract idea that music and the whole art of mathematics, when you get above a certain stage, is not just literally numbers and solutions, it's more like looking through a kaleidoscope. I saw changes occurring, like fast-moving weather systems. I had this image since Nash's character was shifting constantly.

The kaleidoscope image seemed to work since, when you look through a kaleidoscope and you slowly turn it, the patterns change in this ever-changing complexity. For the opening, I wanted it to be like a mathematician's mind, like a kaleidoscope. To turn this into music, I used five pianos and had each of the pianos playing a different pattern and the whole thing sounds like this texture with piano and voice. The texture keeps gently changing underneath, like turning the kaleidoscope.

I used very little orchestra, except after the mental institution scene. I felt that after that scene, the film needed to be grounded more traditionally in order to really sell some of the ideas that I was trying to get across. I couldn't stay as abstract or as vaporous so I locked it in with more conventional colors and a more conventional approach.

Ron and Brian were very afraid when I said I wanted to use Charlotte Church. When I said "voice," they thought of 15th century motets and then they thought of *Gladiator* but I said, "No, trust me, this will be an absolutely different world."

Charlotte was never featured. It was never designed that way. It was designed so that she was one of the pianos, so to speak. It was a lovely color to have and I chose her because of the color of her voice and because she has this unique quality—she's neither child nor adult. I didn't want an opera diva, or a boy soprano. I wanted something that was sort of amorphous. I was looking for a very particular color that only Charlotte Church could fulfill. Her voice brings a sort of magic and other-worldliness to this film. It floats around.

The Collaborative Process

There's always a lot of give and take in the process, because it is not my movie. Ultimately, I'm working for somebody, so even though I may want to make it high art, I owe the director to make it as much to his liking as I can. But I also want to put in as much of my own feelings about it as I can. So the whole process is shifting and there's never a fixed "This is it, take it or leave it!"

It's even abstract when I talk to Ron. By the time I'm committing it to paper, I will have played the main construct for Ron on the piano. I don't believe in mocking it up all on synthesizers, using fake guitars and fake violins. So I talk through the arc of the music with Ron. I always talk about the arc, I think that's imperative and I think Ron understands that.

There is always some fluctuation but I don't play too much of the music for Ron or get too literal with music until I'm at a point where

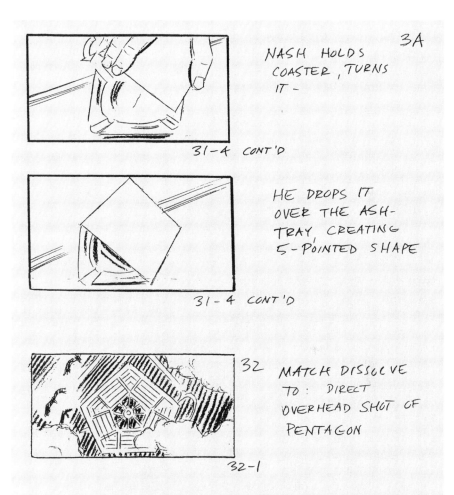

NASH HOLDS
COASTER, TURNS
IT –

3A

31-4 CONT'D

HE DROPS IT
OVER THE ASH-
TRAY, CREATING
5-POINTED SHAPE

31-4 CONT'D

32 MATCH DISSOLVE
TO: DIRECT
OVERHEAD SHOT OF
PENTAGON

32-1

I can support everything and manipulate it in my mind—so he can throw anything up against me and I can rebut it. If I'm in a position where I don't have the solution then I'm too early in the process to be playing music for him. I want to wait until I have it all in my head, not literally, but abstractly, so I can give him an idea of where I want to go with it.

Ron mentioned the idea of motets and he said to me, "Why don't you listen to this, I thought this was sort of nifty." I said to Ron, "When you see the world of motet, I'm not sure that's what you want," so I played him three or four motets and it wasn't what he wanted. It was the idea of what he wanted, but the structure and the sound were not what he wanted. It may have seemed fine when we talked about it in the abstract, but when he actually heard it and put it against the movie, he knew there was no way that could work. And my job is to translate that desire into something that does work. The only vestige of motet in the whole score is Charlotte and that's far from motet.

Ron and I talked about the pivotal scene in the film, when Nash realizes he has a problem. When he realizes he can't really distinguish between what's real and what's not and the world changes for him. It's a really important part of the film. The scene shows this realization when Nash runs out in the rain and plants his hands on the car and he tells Alicia, "Marcy never grows old." That's an absolutely hinging point in the movie and that's where the orchestra comes in from there to the end.

Before that, you're in this netherworld; you don't know what's real. Nash doesn't know what's real, the wife doesn't know what's real, but at this point, through sheer logic, he understands. It's very important to lock that in without hitting the audience over the head.

When I first saw the film, Ron had that scene cut quite short and I said, "As a new viewer and as the composer, I need more time." It was crucial to me, and musically it's crucial to the audience, so they re-cut these scenes.

After we've agreed, then I move on to orchestrating it and playing it for Ron and Brian. We've worked together so many times; there are certain understandings and trust. They're able to understand the abstract language of music and we agreed we wanted it to feel both otherworldly and real.

There are other directors who treat each scene as a be-all and end-all. That's very dangerous because each scene may sound perfect, but when you stitch it all together it's a hodge-podge. I think about how the film will start—the first sound the audience hears after the logo of the movie company—and the very last sound the audience will be left with right before the lights goes up.

The Last Collaborator

The journey from script to screen can be seen as its own epic adventure, a quest as cerebral as *A Beautiful Mind*, as political as *JFK*, as whimsical as *American Beauty* and as inspirational as *Dead Poets Society*.

In the first act, the writers, directors and producers, armed with only a script, must test the courage of their conviction that these hundred or so pages can be magically transformed into a wonderful movie.

In the second act, they go forward to assemble an army of collaborators who will share their vision and contribute their talents to the cause. The army labors day and night and when the battle is over, all that remains are a few images captured forever on frail strips of celluloid.

As with all third acts, pressure mounts as the adventure nears its conclusion. Millions of dollars are at stake. Will the film be delivered on time? Will the spark of the original vision make the final cut? Everyone hopes so. Everyone has done his or her best.

As the climax draws near, it is time for the final collaborator, whose last-minute appearance will determine if there is to be a happy ending. That "last collaborator" is the audience. The fate of each and every film rests squarely on their shoulders.

As we have seen, in order to gauge audience response, filmmakers and studios hold previews of soon-to-be released films and obtain quantitative feedback via response cards. Filmmakers are sharply divided on the utility of previews. Many feel the more important aspects of the filmmaker/audience relationship involve social responsibility. In their view it is about qualitative concerns, not quantitative responses.

Quantitative Response: The Preview Factor

In legitimate theater, the tradition of holding preview performances in order to fine-tune new works and actors' performances in them has long been widely accepted. In motion pictures, there is a tendency to view the process with a certain trepidation.

Hollywood lore is full of stories about how a studio, buoyed by data from preview performances, butchered a great film by changing the ending or injecting more sex or action into the final version.

Editor Bill Reynolds once said, "Previews are helpful because you can find out what audiences like or dislike, what they understand or don't understand."

> *Often they will think something is funny that isn't supposed to be funny. Of course, if it's dramatic and they're sitting on the edge of their seats holding their breath, you get a sense that it's working. Even previews cards can be helpful, if there's a certain consensus. But that was the old style of previews. Today the emphasis is on analyzing how to sell the film.*

Editor Carol Littleton agrees, while noting that the crucial distinctions between the production and marketing previews have been lost.

> *Production previews have always been useful in helping us make the best possible film. We need to know what the audience is getting and not getting. Marketing previews are another matter. The emphasis on numbers is an attempt to quantify a film and I've seen wonderful movies destroyed by this process. The studio will insist that you cut the film for the lowest common denominator.*

Often the studio will use focus groups to try to get a sense of how the audience will feel. For Littleton the problem is that, "One loudmouth can take the discussion and pervert it, so you're cutting the movie for that one jerk."

It's very frustrating to see the original vision of a film successfully exe-cuted all the way through production, only to be lost when marketing previews are used to determine the final cut. The magical moments that make a film unique are often lost. One reason why so many movies are unsuccessful today is that they've gone through this process six or seven times. What you end up with is a movie that will offend no one and move no one. The studio bought the original vision, but now instead of figuring out how to market that movie they want to turn it into a differ-ent film—something that they think will be easier to sell. Movie making is about intuition and alchemy, it can never be a science.

Producer Kathleen Kennedy says that she finds the preview process valuable to a certain point. "The trick is knowing when to shut it off and go with your gut."

The point is that, as a rule, the movie is what it is. Unless you are will-ing to go back and spend a lot of money re-shooting scenes and taking the movie apart, you're not going to be able to do anything to change the picture that's really significant.

Kennedy adds that stories pitting the studio against the director are often the result of filmmaker frustration about power plays. While these sit-uations still exist, she contends that they are increasingly rare.

Most studio executives are not really going to go in and take the movie away from the director. The result would be that those people would never come back and work with them again. It's a small town.

Kennedy does feel that the situation is getting better. "The atmosphere today is more collaborative. I don't see the studio as an adversary; I see them more as partners. There are some very intelligent people working at the studios and they have contributions to make that can be very helpful."

Qualitative Response: Social Responsibility

Predicting the responses of "the last collaborator" can be a very tricky process. In their attempts to bring classic films from script to screen,

Hollywood's most successful and distinguished filmmakers walk a fine line between keeping the audience in mind and pursuing their own unique vision. While their methods of accomplishing this may be diverse, the common theme uniting their efforts is a tremendous respect and affection for the audience. There is also a willingness to accept responsibility for what is created for those people "out there in the dark."

Remember, it was screenwriter Akiva Goldsman who had enjoyed tremendous commercial success but nonetheless yearned to write something that was very particular to his own experience, "otherwise I will have squandered this enormous opportunity," he explained. That yearning became *A Beautiful Mind*.

And it was writer Tom Schulman who said, "If you write about things you feel deeply, you're bound to touch people."

Producer Richard Zanuck noted that "You can't just make an ordinary picture—you have to make an *extraordinary* picture. Find a subject that is exceptional and people are going to be attracted to it because it is unique."

Director Ron Howard talked about "the force within us to be better people. We have it within our power to actually phase out certain behaviors, such as violence, and create viable alternatives." The work of Howard and other socially committed directors explores these themes in a dramatic context that entertains and informs the audience.

The most highly regarded actors and actresses are aware of the power of the medium and are committed to harnessing that power to move our society forward. Mary McDonnell feels a "tremendous responsibility to find the female roles that I want to see out in the world. I don't want my work to feed into the old clichés about women that we have been struggling for decades to eradicate."

> *I certainly don't want to put those clichés up on the screen for millions of young women to get attached to. That doesn't mean every woman I play is a heroine. But the dilemmas of the women I do play must be those that I can support. They must be truthful and provide the audience with an opportunity to see how women can make a difference in our world.*

In an interview at his home, surrounded by friends and family, Edward James Olmos shared a plea for an awareness of the awesome power of the medium and the responsibilities that go along with it.

Film is the most powerful medium ever created by humankind. It will affect the subconscious mind like no other medium can. No live performance, television show, or book can quite match up to the power of the audio-visual event projected on a big screen. It's literally larger than life.

The artist must take responsibility for the work that's up there, period. "Who did that? I did." When I speak to young people I tell them to educate themselves and then get into this medium. It's open. You can learn it all. But you always have to remember that intent is content, so examine your own intent. If your goal is to be rich and famous, do something else. Greed and economics too often drive our industry. That's why Hollywood makes so few films that truly make a difference. You've got to take the long view, think about how your work will be assessed hundreds of years from now, because it will still be there.

These concerns run through the work of all of Hollywood's best collaborators, from famous actors to those behind the scenes. From costume and production design to cinematography and special effects, each collaborator feels a certain responsibility to the audience.

Every classic film is the net result of the work of all who helped bring it to life. Sometimes the most difficult decisions are made by those who sacrifice their own needs for the greater good. This was the case when editor Joe Hutshing and his team were asked by Oliver Stone to work around the clock to make sure that their collective vision of *JFK* could emerge successfully. "Maybe it was a little rougher for that, but it was a stronger statement that way," he explained.

In assessing his own contribution to the filmmaking process, composer Bill Conti said, "We're counting on the fact that we all share our emotions because of our humanity."

It is precisely this oneness with humanity that surfaces again and again with respect to the audience's role as the last collaborator. Oliver Stone always considers the larger lessons he has learned during the ups and downs of his own filmmaking career.

In this business it's easy to be consumed and surrounded by it all and to be cut off from experience. You must never forget that the umbilical cord is to real life, real people. In this way you become more human, more humanistic through the work. Of course it's about collaboration with your cast and crew, but you also have to be collaborative with mankind. You have to be out there in the street sharing everyday experiences as an artist with other people. It is only by doing this that you are able to reflect the fears, concerns, desires and joys of the human experience.

Finally, Peter Weir always has the audience in the back of his mind.

You have to remember that the audience is sitting in their seats dreaming and if you can connect with their unconscious, you really have a powerful connection between viewer and screen. The true test of it is when you come out of a picture and you can't remember whether it was day or night when you came in. "Where did I put the car?" That is the ultimate. Lost in the world of the film.

And so the epic adventure that is the journey from script to screen begins with the word and finally spreads outward to theaters around the world. There, in the dim light, you can see the tears and laughter of humanity reflected on the faces of the last collaborators.

Sources

AAP Newsfeed
Peter Mitchell, "US: Seale's Cool Head Ideal for Frozen Filming," March 17, 2003.

The Boston Herald
Stephen Schaefer, "Movies; Composer Captures Film's *Spirit*," May 27, 2002.

BPI Entertainment News Wire
Glenn Abel, "Classy Horror Films," September 25, 2002.

Business Wire
Press Release; "*Dreamcatcher*," January 17, 2003.

CBS News Transcripts: The Early Show
Laurie Hibberd, "Director and Producer Sam Mendes Discusses His Latest Film, *Road to Perdition*, and His Career," July 12, 2002.

Chicago Sun-Times
Maria Garcia, "Director Shelton Currently in His *Blue* Period," March 7, 2003.
Angela Dawson, "Zucker Gets Back in the *Rat Race*," August 17, 2001.

Christian Science Monitor (Boston, MA)
Gloria Goodale, "The Music Man of *Gladiator, Pearl Harbor*," July 6, 2001.

City News Service
"Interview; Haskell Wexler," February 14, 2003.

CNBC News Transcripts, Show: Business Center
Ron Insana, May 24, 2002.

CNN
Larry King Weekend (Transcript), March 17, 2002.
Bill Hemmer, CNN Live Event (Transcript), February 12, 2002.

CTB Television News
Sandie Rinaldo, "Norman Jewison, in His Own Words," October 5, 2002.

The Daily News of Los Angeles
Glenn Whipp, "From *Boyz* to *Boy*," June 29, 2001.

Glenn Whipp, "Ron Howard: *A Beautiful Mind*," March 17, 2002, Valley Edition.

Bob Strauss, "Something Extraordinary, *A Beautiful Mind*'s Jennifer Connelly Finds the Formula for Success," March 21, 2002, Valley Edition.

Evan Henerson, "Sweet *Dreamcatcher*," March 21, 2003.

The Daily Telegraph (London)
David Gritten, "Life After *American Beauty* Leads to the Grave; David Gritten Talks to Screenwriter Alan Ball About How Quality Programmes Can Still Be Made," May 19, 2001.

The Denver Post
Kyle MacMillan, "Conti Gives TV, Film Music Its Due," March 10, 2002.

Hamilton Spectator (Ontario, Canada),
Murray Tong, "The Art of Film Editing Comes Alive," September 14, 2002.

The Herald (Glasgow)
Rebecca Mcquillan, "Back to the Killing Fields; Three Years After Quitting Film-Making, David Puttnam Is Returning to Cambodia," January 6, 2003.

The Hollywood Reporter
Brett Sporich, "Two-Disc *Cast* Shoves off with Blistering Sales," June 21, 2001.

Sheigh Crabtree, "CG Seen as No Threat to Actors," August 15, 2001.

Borys Kit, "Scriptors Honor Writers Behind *Beautiful Mind*," March 18, 2002.

Angela Phipps Towle, "Tube Ties; Grazer Pioneered Imagine's Successful TV Division," March 6, 2003.

Stephen Galloway, "Idea Man; Producer Brian Grazer Has Forged a Successful Career by Recognizing the Importance of Ideas," March 6, 2003.

Los Angeles Times
Kenneth Turan, "Sundance Film Festival; A Tragedy—and Unique Love Story; Handled With Skill and Care," January 22, 2003.

David Wollock, "Metropolis/Chat Room; They Shoot, He Scores," January 26, 2003.

Dennis McLellan, "Obituaries," February 8, 2003.

Motion Picture Newsletter
Michael Polakow, "Interview; William H. Reynolds," September/October 1997.

The Nation (Thailand)
Maurice Jarré, "Bangkok International Film Festival: Master Composer Is Just 'Lucky,'" January 18, 2003.

National Public Radio
Lisa Simeone, "Thomas Newman Talks About Composing Music for Film and Television," August 12, 2001.

NBC
NBC News (Transcript) "Actress Jennifer Connelly Discusses Her Role in *A Beautiful Mind*," January 3, 2002.

Matt Lauer, "Ron Howard and Jennifer Connelly Discuss *A Beautiful Mind*," (Transcript), February 12, 2002.

New Statesman
"Unheard Masterpiece," May 21, 2001.

Newsweek
David Ansen, Jeff Giles, "Art & Entertainment: Break on Through to the Oscar Side," January 21, 2002.

The New York Times
David Schiff, "Music; Taking Movie Music Seriously, Like It or Not," April 22, 2001.

Anthony Tommasini, "Music Review; Hollywood Denizens, Like Stravinsky," April 24, 2001.

Bernard Holland, "Critic's Notebook; Hothouse Romantic Brooding Under the California Sun," November 1, 2001.

Rick Lyman, "Watching Movies With/Barry Levinson; Telling Complex Stories Simply," April 26, 2002.

Dave Kehr, "Film Review; *A Beautiful Mind*," July 19, 2002.

Pittsburgh Post-Gazette (Pennsylvania)
Andrew Druckenbrod, "No Movies Music Man; Film Composer Bill Conti Carries a Big Stick as Oscars Conductor," March 5, 2003.

Playback
Mark Dillon, "ASC Celebrates Jewison's Ongoing Collaborations," February 17, 2003.

PR Newswire
Press Release; "ASCAP Honors Top Film and Televison Composers and Songwriters at 17th Annual Awards Gala; Alan Silvestri to Receive the Henry Mancini Award for Lifetime Achievement; Van Alexander to Receive the ASCAP Foundation Lifetime Achievement Award," April 8, 2002.

Press Release; "Buddy Baker, Prolific Disney Composer of 200 Scores for Films, Television Shows and Theme Park Attractions, Dies at Age 84," July 29, 2002.

Press Release; "Universal Pictures to Unveil *The Hulk* in TV spot on Sunday, January 26," January 25, 2003, European Edition.

Press Release; "ASCAP Honors Top Film & Television Composers and Songwriters at 18th Annual Awards Celebration; Hans Zimmer to Receive Henry Mancini Award For Lifetime Achievement," April 10, 2003.

Press Release; "Universal Pictures Announces Incredible Promotional Program for Its Highly-Anticipated Summer Release *The Hulk*," PR Newswire, February 5, 2003.

Press Enterprise (Riverside, CA)
Carla Wheeler, "Four Film Careers in Spotlight; Honored: Composer Hans Zimmer Says Working on His Latest Movie, *Black Hawk Down*, Was a Deadline Challenge.", January 11, 2002.

Radio Times
Radio 4 ,"This Week's Choice; The Life of Henry Mancini," February 01, 2003.

The Record
Bettijane Levine, "A Book Signing, A Big Moment," March 31, 2002.

The Santa Fe New Mexican
Teri Thomson Randall, "Hollywood's Last Taboo," February 21, 2003.

Sunday Times (London)
Paul Donovan, "Pick of the Day," February 2, 2003.

Sunday Tribune (Ireland)
Ciaran Carty, "The Zimmer Frame; Film Interview," June 30, 2002.

The Toronto Sun
Louis B. Hobson, "Beautiful Roles: To Jennifer Connelly—Praise Is Great, But Being a Mom and Working with Russell Crowe Are Real Prizes," Jan. 9, 2002.

United Press International
Karen Butler, "Russell Crowe—Interview of the Week," Janury 11, 2002.

Vanity Fair
Michael Shanyerson, "The Intriguing Miss Connelly," September, 2002.

Variety
Army Archerd, "Just for Variety," June 22, 2001.

Marc Graser, "Tech Wizards Eye New Directions," January 14, 2002.

Sharon Knolle, "Steadicam Inventor's Lasting Contribution," February 15, 2002.

Jon Burlingame, "Pic Composers Tune up for Tube," June 17, 2002.

David Bloom, "Imageworks Buoys Execs," July 19, 2002.

Jon Burlingame, "Buddy Baker," August 5, 2002.

The Weekend Australian
Juliet Herd, "The Mendes Touch—How Britain's Golden Boy Brought You *Oliver!* and *American Beauty*—Play It Again, Sam," May 18, 2002.

A Beautiful Mind—EPK, Universal Pictures, 2002 (various excerpts).

FOR THE SCREENWRITER

HOW NOT TO WRITE A SCREENPLAY
101 Common Mistakes Most Screenwriters Make
by Denny Martin Flinn

Having read tons of screenplays as an executive, Denny Martin Flinn has come to understand that while all good screenplays are unique, all bad screenplays are the same. Flinn's book will teach the reader how to avoid the pitfalls of bad screenwriting, and arrive at one's own destination intact. Every example used is gleaned from a legitimate screenplay. Flinn's advice is a no-nonsense analysis of the latest techniques for crafting first-rate screenplays that sell.
$16.95, ISBN 1580650155

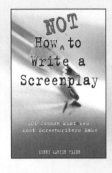

THE SCREENPLAY WORKBOOK:
The Writing Before the Writing
by Jeremy Robinson and Tom Mungovan

Every time a screenwriter sits down to write a screenplay, he has to grapple with the daunting question of, "Where do I start?" The preparation time, or the writing *before* the writing, can be intimidating. *The Screenplay Workbook* is an instructional manual combined with proprietary worksheets, charts and fill-in lists designed to give screenwriters a better way to focus on the task of writing a screenplay. All of the organization is done, the right questions are asked, the important subjects are covered.
$18.95, ISBN 1580650538

ELEMENTS OF STYLE FOR SCREENWRITERS
The Essential Manual for Writers of Screenplays
by Paul Argentini

Paul Argentini presents an essential reference masterpiece in the art of clear and concise principles of screenplay formatting, structure and style for screenwriters. Argentini explains how to design and format manuscripts to impress any film school professor, story editor, agent, producer or studio executive. A to Z listing of format terms and examples. Includes a special section on stage play formatting.
$11.95, ISBN 1580650031

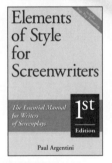

POWER SCREENWRITING
The 12 Stages of Story Development
by Michael Chase Walker

Michael Chase Walker offers a clear and straightforward framework upon which to build story plots. Standing on the broad shoulders of Joseph Campbell, Christopher Vogler, and others who have demonstrated how mythology is used, Walker brings passion, insight and clarity to a whole new range of story traditions never before examined. Walker offers a wide variety of alternative principles and techniques that are more flexible, adaptable and relevant for the modern storyteller. This book gives insight into the art of storytelling as a way to give depth and texture to any screenplay.
$19.95, ISBN 1580650414

FOR THE SCREENWRITER

THE COMPLETE WRITER'S GUIDE TO HEROES & HEROINES
Sixteen Master Archetypes
by Tami D. Cowden, Caro LaFever, Sue Viders

By following the guidelines of the archetypes presented in this comprehensive reference work, writers can create extraordinarily memorable characters and elevate their writing to a higher level. The authors give examples of well-known heroes and heroines from television and film so the reader can picture the archetype in his or her mind. The core archetype tells the writer how heroes or heroines think and feel, what drives them and how they reach their goals.
$17.95, ISBN 1580650244

WRITING SHORT FILMS
Structure and Content for Screenwriters
by Linda J. Cowgill

Contrasting and comparing the differences and similarities between feature films and short films, screenwriting professor Linda Cowgill offers readers the essential tools necessary to make their writing crisp, sharp and compelling. Emphasizing characters, structure, dialogue and story, Cowgill dispels the "magic formula" concept that screenplays can be constructed by anyone with a word processor and a script formatting program.
$19.95, ISBN 0943728800

SECRETS OF SCREENPLAY STRUCTURE
How to Recognize and Emulate the Structural Frameworks of Great Films
by Linda J. Cowgill

Linda Cowgill articulates the concepts of successful screenplay structure in a clear language, based on the study and analysis of great films from the thirties to present day. *Secrets of Screenplay Structure* helps writers understand how and why great films work, and how great form and function can combine to bring a story alive.
$16.95, ISBN 158065004X

THIS BUSINESS OF SCREENWRITING
How to Protect Yourself as a Screenwriter
by Ron Suppa

Practical tips for the writer, with advice on crafting marketable treatments, pitches, spec screenplays and adaptations. Plus important information on how to protect your work, get representation, make deals and more! Calling on his years of experience as both a buyer and seller of screenplays, Suppa conveys a taste of the real world of professional screenwriting to help writers survive and thrive in the sometimes messy collision of art and business.
$19.95, ISBN 1580650163

FOR THE ACTOR

HOW NOT TO AUDITION
Avoiding the Common Mistakes Most Actors Make
by Ellie Kanner and Denny Martin Flinn

This book is mandatory reading for any actor smart enough to realize that it all starts with the audition and can easily end there as well. All great actors are unique. All bad actors are the same—they can't get through the audition to nail the job. While Kanner and Flinn can't guarantee actors a gig, they absolutely can make sure aspiring actors don't blow their auditions. Written with an edgy sense of humor, this book will steer the reader through open-calls, pre-reads, callbacks, and second callbacks.
$19.95, ISBN 158065049X

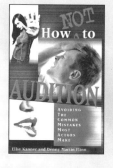

HOW TO AGENT YOUR AGENT
by Nancy Rainford

Nancy Rainford takes the reader behind the scenes to reveal the techniques, politics and unspoken rules of agenting. Agents and managers are the gatekeepers and power brokers to getting work in Hollywood. With an easy style, Rainford candidly delivers fresh insight into the mechanics and motivation of agents and managers at work. Get the tools you need to protect yourself, build a career, and train your agent to work for YOU. Filled with industry anecdotes, uncensored descriptions and accounts of show-biz players, Rainford gives you the advice and know-how you will wish you'd learned years ago.
$17.95, ISBN 1580650422

THE ACTOR'S ENCYCLOPEDIA OF CASTING DIRECTORS
Interviews with Over 100 Casting Directors on How to Get the Job
by Karen Kondazian with Eddie Shapiro, foreword by Richard Dreyfuss

Kondazian has compiled insider information and intimate profiles from talking to premier casting directors in film, television, theatre and commercials from Los Angeles to New York. Casting directors speak on the record to reflect and convey expert advice about how to get in the door and how to prepare effectively for readings. Find out from casting directors what's hot and what's not.
$19.95, ISBN 1580650139

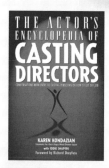

HOW TO GET THE PART... WITHOUT FALLING APART!
Featuring the Haber Phrase Technique® for Actors
by Margie Haber with Barbara Babchick, foreword by Heather Locklear

Acting coach to the stars Margie Haber has created a revolutionary phrase technique to get actors through readings without stumbling over the script. The book helps actors break through the psychological roadblocks to auditioning with a 10-step method for breaking down the scene. Actors learn to prepare thoroughly, whether they have twenty minutes or two weeks. Includes celebrity photos and audition stories.
$17.95, ISBN 1580650147

FOR THE FILMMAKER

THE IFILM DIGITAL VIDEO FILMMAKER'S HANDBOOK
by Maxie D. Collier

Maxie Collier's book covers the creative and technical aspects of digital shooting and is designed to provide detailed, practical information on DV filmmaking. Collier delves into the mechanics and craft of creating personal films and introduces the reader to the essential terminology, concepts, equipment and services required to produce a quality DV feature film. Includes DVD.
$24.95, ISBN 1580650317

THE INDIE PRODUCER'S HANDBOOK
Creative Producing from A to Z
by Myrl A. Schreibman

Myrl Schreibman has written a straightforward, insightful and articulate account of what it takes to make a successful feature film. Filled with engaging and useful anecdotes, Schreibman provides a superlative introduction and overview to all the key elements of producing feature films. Useful to film students and filmmakers as a theoretical and practical guide to understanding the filmmaking process.
$21.95, ISBN 1580650376

FILM PRODUCTION
The Complete *UNCENSORED* Guide to Independent Filmmaking
by Greg Merritt

Merritt cuts through the fluff and provides the reader with real-world facts about producing and selling a low-budget motion picture. Topics covered include: pre-production, principal photography, post-production, distribution, script structure and dialogue, raising money, limited partnerships, scheduling and budgeting, cast and crew, production equipment, scoring, publicity, festivals, foreign distribution, video and more.
$24.95, ISBN 0943728991

THE ULTIMATE FILM FESTIVAL SURVIVAL GUIDE, 2ND EDITION
by Chris Gore

Learn the secrets of successfully marketing and selling your film at over 600 film festivals worldwide. Author Chris Gore reveals how to get a film accepted and what to do after acceptance, from putting together a press kit to putting on a great party to actually closing a deal. Gore includes an expanded directory section, new interviews as well as a new chapter that details a case study of the most successful independent film to date, *The Blair Witch Project*.
$19.95, ISBN 1580650325

To order, call 323.308.3558 • www.hcdonline.com